THESE PEOPLE KNOW DON BARON

Read what people in the know say about
the man and his book,

Canada's Great GRAIN Robbery

"Don Baron has written a powerful indictment of the economic ignorance and ideological folly that has crippled the progress of Canada's breadbasket."
David Frum,
Financial Post & Sun Newspapers columnist, author and
Senior Fellow, Manhattan Institute, Washington, D.C.

"This tells the fascinating history behind the grain marketing battle that is engulfing the Prairies today. And the lessons are clear. When we use big government to solve our problems, it is not the rich and powerful who are hurt but rather the freedom and livelihood of ordinary people. We must especially be wary of the world of socialism wearing the sheep's clothing of Christianity."
Stephen Harper,
Vice-President, The National Citizens' Coalition

"An all-too-accurate history of the myths and false prophesies that have haunted the West and its farmers since the beginning - a story of political meddling that has locked farmers into inefficiencies and excessive costs. This is must reading for every westerner and every Canadian politician."
Buck Spencer,
President, Western Barley Growers Assoc.

"A fascinating well-documented account of why Canadian wheat is considered 15 percent protein and 85 percent politics. A great read!"
Charlie Mayer
Former MP and Canada Wheat Board Minister.

"Earthquakes are caused by lack of movement. An earthquake is about to happen in the grain industry - and this story leaves no doubt why."
George Fletcher,
Former President, Western Wheat Growers Assoc.

"An enlightening expose on the plight of prairie farmers - and why politicians should ACT NOW! to restore Canada to its rightful place as the world's breadbasket."

Larry D. Hurd,
Calgary lawyer, author of *Master Procrastination NOW!*

"The best account of the grain farmers' struggles yet. It offers unknown insights and stories, shows why people have found it so difficult to understand why we must move to freedom. It's must reading for anyone with an interest in grain - or in Canada."

Art Walde,
Kindersley, director, Western Barley Growers Assoc.

"I loved the story. It offers insights that have been unavailable, tells the true story of the freedom struggle in Western Canada."

Karen Morrison,
Alberta farm-wife, columnist and author of *Keep Your Stubble Up.*

"An epic account of how and why the state-control police stifled prairie farmers and their productivity these past 60 years and how farmers are finally freeing themselves from their chains."

John Clark,
retired editor and publisher, Grainews.

"Punchy and pungent, Don Baron's latest work truly represents the anger and the anguish felt in the Prairies, points a way to future justice. This is must reading for every westerner. If Ottawa's political and bureaucratic elite would read it too, we might get this country moving again."

Paul Jackson,
Associate Editor and political columnist, Calgary Sun, Co-author, *Battleground.*

"A fantastic story - a classic! It puts into a clear perspective little-known events that shaped the industry and the country. All of us who were trying to deal with forces racking the industry two or three decades ago lacked these insights and thus an understanding of the real issues."

Bob Hart,
Regina, retired Head, Plant Products Division, Canada Department of Agriculture.

"Don Baron offers a blueprint that will help farm leaders and politicians lead Prairie growers out of the wilderness."
John Schmidt,
long-time reporter and columnist in the West and Ontario, author of the Western Stock Growers history, *An Experiment That Worked.*

"It shines a fresh light onto today's challenge, shows how Ed Partridge and Tom Crerar and other UGG founders faced the unfair power of the railroad/grain companies monopoly. My grandfather was there. These men won their freedom. But today we face a new monopoly - a government one - and look at the price we are paying. Fifty years ago Saskatchewan was Canada's third province in population. It had over 20 MP's - and political power. Its population has hardly increased since. Its a scam and this book tells the story. We must be the new torch-bearers for freedom."
Jim Pallister
Farmers for Justice leader, and Portage la Prairie, Manitoba, grower.

"A rattling good history of Western Wheat from the beginning to the present, complete with details about its passionate heros and perceived villains. Buy a copy and read it over and over. It is also a great reference of names, dates and issues without which the whole thing sinks into a vague flawed mish-mash. The printed word is the master medium. Without good clear prose good people are prey to tyrants, spell-binders, rascals and fools who use sophistry to further their ends. One mild criticism - you pussy-foot around the real issue. I looked for a clear unequivocal statement, "The Wheat Board Monopoly is Absurd."
Alf Bryan
columnist, author of I May Be Wrong But.... Tugaske, Sask.

"A remarkable history. I was not aware of some events Don Baron documents, and he includes many things that should be said. Some people will dispute parts of it, but the fact is many industry decisions have been made for the wrong reasons. And many events he describes are forgotten, so people don't realize what the industry has gone through."
W.B. Parrish
Parrish and Heimbecker Ltd.

"This book is long overdue. I needed it months ago as we stock growers tried to address the Wheat Board problem. It tells why we are in our present troubles, shows how we can move ahead. Its a great read."

Norman Ward
President, Western Stock Growers Assoc.

"An incredible effort to piece together the jigsaw of our Prairie roots. Don Baron offers a new and unique insight into our past - an untold chapter in our history. This is a must-read textbook for growers and would-be politicians."

Joe Ralko
President, Marketing and Communications Inc., former editor, award-winning radio correspondent, and photojournalist with Winnipeg Free Press.

"Mac Runciman's vivid recollections offer essential insights to understanding Prairie agriculture and UGG's long struggle to win the growers' freedom."

Roy W. Piper
Sask. Vice President, UGG.

"It reads like a spy mystery. Intrigue, good guys, bad guys, double-dealing, suspense and murder - the murder of the rights of the individual. He tells of UGG's years of struggle against big government, encouraging individual initiative and an understanding of market forces. And the growers' uprising to form wheat and barley and rapeseed groups to throw off political oppression. He explains one puzzling anomaly. Alberta and Saskatchewan, with similar climate, resources and people, yet diametrically opposed outlooks on politics, business and industry! Saskatchewan became home of the Social Gospel where big brother Government was to do everything for us. "Profit" was a dirty word, the co-op movement was twisted into a system of repression, and individual rights were trod upon in the name of the common good. Must reading for anyone interested in Canada's economy."

David Marshall
author of Me and George, the Canadian army's liberation of Holland from Nazi Germany.

"Don Baron's usual candour and clarity shine through - his story reflects the views of more and more farmers who finally see they were duped when they accepted monopoly Wheat Board control as part of their anti-Nazi war effort. They have been held captive - victimized by the only War Measures Act provisions to remain government policy half a century later. Don's careful analysis won't be welcomed by everyone - it's an article of faith to many that our wheat is the best and buyers will beat a path to our door so long as our marketing is manipulated to bring social change. But Don's research reveals a shocking story of how Ottawa ignored changes in world grain marketing to the detriment of farmers. Through his career, Don has never hesitated to attack sacred cows. This time he properly argues against the entrenched wisdom of a bureaucracy determined to prolong a doomed marketing policy."

Fred Cleverly
Winnipeg Free Press columnist

"Informative. Revealing. Exposing. And possibly Explosive. This is a good book....there is no escaping the arrogant condescending bearing of Canada's grain marketing junta. One day, a Wheat Board official was being taken to task for an obvious...discrepancy in the price of durum. He was losing the argument and...in exasperation...demanded, "When are you people going to wake up and realize that from the minute the seed is in the ground, "That Wheat Belongs to Us!" Meaning the Wheat Board. In the flick of an eyelash, he was confiscating billions of dollars of private property to manifest his unlimited power. The Wheat Board is beyond salvation, the author of its own destruction."

Lyle Walker
rancher, columnist

"Congratulations to Don Baron on the thorough research and its logical compilation"

M.W. Dorosh
President/Publisher, Agriweek

"Mac Runciman recognized the true value of livestock to Canada's prairie economy and he worked hard to free up the system so more could be raised. To understand how the industry was hurt, you must read this book."

Boyd Anderson
rancher, former Pres., Western Stock Growers Assoc.,
Author, *Grass Roots*, and *Beyond the Range*

v

"Even in the heat of harvest, with time so precious, I couldn't put this book down. At last, the real story is told!"
Gordon Brooks
Belle Plaine, Sask.

"History is incomplete without this detailed accounting from one who was there. Agree or not - it's a must read."
Larry Schneider
President, Prairie Implement Mfrs. Assoc., former
Member of Parliament, former Mayor of Regina
"Don Baron explains how Canadians blessed with a continent's resources but damned with an obsession for security and control, could turn a golden opportunity in grain into a frustrating political swamp. This is an indictment of our obsession with security and our failure to value individual freedom. The story comes alive with its account of the politics, the promoters and the demagogues. Thankfully it offers hope for a return to enterprise where the only promise is the freedom to pursue opportunity, not the guarantee of success."
Lou Shizas, *The Money Manager, ckmx AM 1060*
Financial Advisor, Journalist, Broadcaster. Calgary

"If you've ever wondered why Canada's grain handling system is in constant crisis, why the world's most productive farmers are saddled with an outmoded transportation network, why some producers risk going to jail to sell their wheat in the United States, Don Baron's book is a must read. Its insights are thought-provoking - and controversial! An unabashed free enterpriser, Baron traces many of its current problems to the Social Gospel's influence on the early co-operative movement. This book will infuriate left-wingers like National Farmers Union members and others who believe free markets and the profit motive have no place in agriculture. But it will delight those who applaud recent changes such as the Crow Benefit pay-out, construction of large inland grain terminals, Saskatchewan Wheat Pool's public share issue and ADM's acquisition of 45 per cent of UGG. Don raises doubts about the co-operative movement's altruism - especially the wheat pools - in its costly and ultimately futile attempt to circumvent the open market during the 1920's. The Pools' ideological hostility towards open markets helped lay the groundwork for the costly and inefficient grain handling system that plagues Prairie producers today."
Bruce Johnstone
Financial Editor, The Leader-Post

"Don's book is what good journalism should be. His history of UGG and the development of the western grain industry is deeply researched. His prose is rich in detail and brings to life the many personalities that shaped the business of prairie grain. Every grower, grain exec. and industry observer should have this book on his office or library shelf."

Kevin Archibald
First Vice President, Western Can. Wheat Growers Assoc.

"Fascinating! Its the only explanation I have found as to why we have been endlessly bogged down in grain marketing, unable to address the issue directly. The Social Gospel resonated with the belief of early growers that farming is a religious calling - that feeding the people is fundamental. And it appealed to many of those who had this quest for power and formed the co-ops and Pools (and particularly after the Pools went bankrupt.) The co-ops and the pools believed they were on a holy crusade. Universities weren't allowed to teach marketing in earlier days, and government workers couldn't discuss it with farmers. This story explains it all."

Jack Gorr
long-time leader in Barley and Wheat Grower groups,
and government extension worker

"This book should be mandatory reading for all elected officials - its the single most educational and pointed account of grain farmers' struggle to rid themselves of socialism's shackles. Don Baron combines history and education to offer a road map of how the food industry can regain freedom and produce more wealth - of how to build a better Canada through the free market. This can show politicians the follies of 'a false Social Gospel' so Socialism will finally give way to freedom and wealth."

Craig B. Chandler
National President, Progressive Group for Independent Business

"Everyone who wants to stay in agriculture and the grain industry must read this amazing Social Gospel story. I could never put my finger on the underlying reason why change was so difficult to bring about over the years. I kept asking, "What am I missing?" But here is the link. I knew of many events Don describes but I have never seen them catalogued in this way."

Don Dobson
13 years a UGG Director, 8 years as Manitoba VP

"Don Baron's unofficial history of UGG explains why many farmers have long rejected the prairie mythology that has grown up around single desk wheat sales and should help shape an understanding of the industry in the debate that looms ahead."

Murray Lyons
Star- Phoenix writer

"I always felt something was missing in the history of grain marketing that I was able to read. This book tells the untold part of the story. It is the missing link"

Leon Benoit
Alberta Reform Member of Parliament and farmer

"I found the book very interesting in gathering together a lot of things which otherwise might have been lost. I dare to say that I thought the presentation had a bit of a partisan twinge to it!"

Hon. Otto Lang, Former M.P.
President & C.E.O. Centra Gas

"Fascinating, inciteful and an easy read. What every farmer and city slicker should read in order to understand this vital sector of our economy."

Brian Lee, Author of Satisfaction Guaranteed
Founder of Custom Learning Systems

"My family had two farms. They went broke both times. After reading Don's book, I now know why."

Merv Dorsey
author of *There's a Horse in the Cellar*

WHAT DOES A POLITICAL SCIENTIST/COLUMNIST SAY OF THIS STORY?

As a professor of Political Science at the University of Calgary, Barry Cooper's job is to understand the politics of the west and the country and to continually keep abreast of developments. He says of *Canada's Great GRAIN Robbery*:

"This is more than a good yarn, it is rich in telling detail, and while it doesn't have a happy ending yet, if enough prairie farmers read it, it will."

Don Baron never loses sight of his theme - an old one on how...

The best laid schemes o' mice an' men Gang aft a-gley
And leave us nought but grief and pain
For Promised joy

The origins of farmer cooperation lay in the experiences of pioneer life. The early farmers' success in meeting undoubted hardships led visionary leaders to project their dreams onto a rosy future once the final evils were eliminated. Thus were born the agrarian utopias of the early twentieth century.

Like all utopias, they were out of touch with the realities of human nature; like all utopias, they inevitably damaged those men and women they were designed to benefit. And once the damage was done, rather than re-examine their own foolish assumptions, the utopians looked around for others to blame.

Once that happened, debate and reasoned disagreement about what to do grew increasingly difficult. The irrationality of the utopians has poisoned the entire political process because the genuine interests of farmers - about which reasonable people may disagree - have become shrouded in myth and distorted by moralism.

Of all the early farmers' organizations, only UGG has been able to resist the deceptions and self-deceptions of agrarian utopianism. One reason for this, no doubt, is that the organization and the membership kept in touch with the realities of the market. It is easy to attack the virtues of markets, for markets are merely efficient. They are not the noblest of human inventions.

When agrarian utopians attack markets in the name of human nobility and high aspirations, they seem always to lose sight of what markets do best. And by losing sight of the bottom line, they lose touch with an important reality. Then they blame reality for not conforming to their utopian dreams.

This vicious spiral of utopian dreaming explains why prairie farmers supported the Crow rates for so long, and why they distrusted the Winnipeg Grain Exchange, and why so many still support the CWB. But one can oppose or ignore reality for only so long. Eventually the dream ends. Even the NDP must eventually balance its books. (Barry Cooper is also a Globe and Mail columnist)

Canadian Cataloguing in Publication Data

Baron, Don, 1927-

Canada's Great GRAIN Robbery

Includes bibliographical references
ISBN 1-55056-545-1

1. Grain trade - Prairie Provinces
2. Agriculture and state -
Canada I - Title
HD9044.C23P7 1998   338.1'8712   C97-910959-0

Cover Photo of the author, Don Baron, outstanding in the field by Michael Intevisano
Mirror Image Photography

Cover Design by
Leo C. Peters, The Creativity Coach

Don Baron Communications
14 Wood Crescent,
Regina, Sask.
S4S 6J7
ph./fax 1-306-586-4578

Printed and bound in Canada by
Friesen Corp.

This book is dedicated to
my four year old grandson
Scott Andrew Baron,
and to others of this
new generation, whose
ancestors have been part
of this freedom struggle,
and who benefit so richly
from the values passed
on by those unyielding
pioneers and those who followed.

ACKNOWLEDGEMENTS

It would be impossible to list all the many people whose help made this book possible. But I must mention Mac Runciman, President of UGG for 20 years, who led the struggle in that time for the farmers' freedom. Mac was ultimately my boss when I was Country Guide editor and with his strength of character, he never wavered in his support when so much of what we reported was considered by many to be politically incorrect. In recent months, Mac worked tirelessly with me on this book, remembering events of those days and putting them into his clear perspective. In a major sense, this is the Mac Runciman story, an in-depth look into the fierce and unceasing politics of the West and Canada itself. Current UGG President Ted Allen provided access to many company records and thus further insights into the political and economic struggles of the grain industry.

Paul Earl's landmark PhD thesis threw a blazing insight on a major event in Canada's history which strongly shaped (or misshaped) the country. All Canadians should be grateful to him. His findings are embedded in this story. I also thank the many farmers and farm leaders (and particularly Clarence Taylor with his brimming library and his keen memory of so many events) who were unstinting with their time and with their recollections of happenings that I did not witness personally.

In bringing this story to print, Leo Peters, The Creativity Coach, provided his artistic and marketing know-how (no, his brilliance!) in shaping the book and moving it to market. Sally Banks brought her writing and editing skills and her sheer unremitting zeal to be certain this story is well told. And not last, my wife Rene, who was patient and cheerful and kept serving up better meals than anyone deserved, as I spent long hours in libraries, and with my computer, in what otherwise would have been family time.

And I must mention those who were good enough to read a "Preview Copy" and send along testimonials which appear at the book's front.

I accept full responsibility for any weaknesses in this story.

CONTENTS

Prologue

PROLOGUE

TRAPPED LIKE THE WILD HOGS OF HORSESHOE BEND!

Years ago there lived a herd of wild hogs in a great horseshoe bend down a river deep in the southern United States. Where those hogs came from no one knew. But they survived floods, fires, freezes, droughts and hunters. They were so wild the greatest compliment a man could pay to a dog was to say it had fought the hogs in Horseshoe Bend and returned alive. Occasionally a pig was killed either by dogs or a gun - and became a conversation piece for years.

One day, a lean-faced man came by the country store on the river road and asked the whereabouts of these wild hogs. He drove a one-horse wagon, had an axe, some blankets and a lantern, a pile of corn and a single-barrelled shotgun. He was a slender, slow-moving man who chewed his tobacco deliberately and spat very seldom.

Several months later he came back to the store and asked for help to bring those wild pigs out of the swamp. He said he had them all in a pen.

Bewildered farmers, dubious hunters and storekeepers all gathered in the heart of Horseshoe Bend to view the captive hogs.

"It's all very simple," said the patient lean-faced man. "First, I put out some corn for them. For three weeks they wouldn't eat it. Then some of the young ones grabbed a cob and ran off into the bush. Soon, they were all eating corn. Then I commenced building a pen around the corn, just a little higher every day. When I noticed they had stopped grubbing for acorns and roots and were all waiting for me to bring the corn, I built the trap door.

"Naturally they raised quite a ruckus when they seen they was   trapped. But I can pen any animal on the face of the earth if I can just get him to depend on me for a handout."

Author unknown

Canada's huge grain industry was in crisis in the late 1960s when President Mac Runciman of a farmers' grain company began telling this story of "The Wild Hogs" in talks at prairie farm meetings.

His message was simple - but of awesome importance to growers and the entire country. Prairie grain had been Canada's engine of growth from the beginning. Now, however, it was caught in the grip of politics. The market-place was often forgotten and the customer seemingly little more than an afterthought. In the business of growing and marketing grain, the priceless ingredient of success was not market information, it was political power. The predictable results were all too apparent.

"Bureaucratic red tape is strangling the cash flow needed to make the industry viable," Runciman kept repeating, "smothering its initiative, preventing it from responding to world markets." Like those Wild Hogs of Horseshoe Bend, growers and their huge industry were trapped.

During his 20-year presidency of United Grain Growers Limited (UGG), Runciman became an unyielding leader in the fierce and often bitter struggle to free up the grain industry, and Canada itself, from the political chains shackling them. He and those around him were joined by other industry leaders and increasingly by farmers who formed their own industry groups to try to make their voices heard. Their views are finally beginning to prevail. But this begs the question, why has this battle for freedom been so fierce and prolonged?

The Untold Story - Nearly a Century of Mismanagement

Although Mac Runciman kept repeating his story of the Wild Hogs of Horseshoe Bend during the 1970's, he found resistance to change by an entrenched political establishment almost insurmountable. He finally exploded, labelling the vital grain handling system "a failure." Soon, with progress still stymied, he offered an even harsher appraisal. "Our rail system is little changed from the horse hauling days of the 1930s. Storage and handling charges have been closely regulated since 1912....Much of our elevator system is over 40 years old...and is hopelessly expensive to operate, needs upgrading."

His devastating conclusion: "The system is 20 years behind that of the US."

What had gone wrong? The truth was hardly known then, but new studies and events have revealed the surprising truth. Misguided "Social Gospel" politics had delivered Canada's vital grain industry into the hands of the politicians rather than the marketplace. Growers and industry leaders were forced to devote too much of their effort to politics rather than serving their customers.

The government-imposed Crow rail rates prevented the railways from recovering their hauling costs, so they quit buying new grain cars, forcing government and the Canadian Wheat Board (CWB) to grab taxpayers' and growers' money to buy them. Meanwhile grain-moving costs had soared to dollars a bushel on some obsolete rail lines, but regulations prohibited their abandonment. The devastating result was that grain companies often had to store grain rather than move it to market.

This massive system breakdown often left Vancouver's English Bay wall-to-wall with ships awaiting grain, forcing despairing buyers to look elsewhere. Growers unable to move grain through the jammed system, and lacking money, returned to the days of barter, hauling their grain to dealers to trade for tractors, combines, trucks and supplies. An embarrassed Prime Minister Pierre Trudeau urged a shift away from this costly political marketing system, suggesting open-market pricing for domestic feed grains.

But politics reigned supreme. The great prairie breadbasket remained in a stranglehold, with growers and industry unable to fully use it to create wealth and jobs for Canada let alone to help fight the world's war on hunger.

Desperate for new sales and revenues, growers and the trade focused on an obscure new crop, rapeseed, that could be sold outside the Wheat Board's monopoly grip, urging plant scientists to tailor it to the mushrooming world market for oilseeds. And in a brilliant success story, they built it into a "Cinderella crop" (now called canola.) But the vital wheat crop along with feed grains remained under monopoly control.

In retrospect, the truth shines through. These events were simply the tip of the iceberg - fragments reflecting nearly a century of socialist thinking that repressed and brought mismanagement of the great prairie resource area.

Consider this. Saskatchewan is perhaps Canada's most resource-rich province. Yet the death-grip of regulations blocked a resounding move there to cattle, hog, turkey and chicken production, and to processing and manufacturing grain, meat and other products. Needed investment stayed away. The devastating result is that Saskatchewan's population - which was nearly one million 60 years ago - remains at one million today.

This sad story had its beginning with the pioneers

who first settled Canada's great North-West. When those homesteaders broke the virgin sod and built their farms, homes and communities, and shipped their grain to market, they found themselves victims of a railroad/grain company monopoly. They rose up in anger and formed their own grain company (which was to become United Grain Growers Ltd.) to free themselves from it.

But their success was betrayed when another monopoly - a government one - emerged. The resulting red tape trapped growers (much like those Wild Hogs of Horseshoe Bend) and blocked development.

That Holy Crusade Against Freedom

What led to that betrayal? Here the story gets strange indeed. Walter Rauschenbusch and other Protestant pastors in the United States in the early 1900's were certain they had stumbled upon a new universal truth. "Abolish capitalism!" they cried, labelling it and the open market the cause of human misery. Their preaching became known as the Social Gospel. It was scorned in the US, but when they began arriving in Canada, they were welcomed by Canadian pastors who soon joined in their crusade. When Canadian Salem Bland cried out, "The distinctive task of the age is the abolition of capitalism," he was applauded wildly. At a boisterous 1918 Winnipeg meeting, church and labour and socialist leaders stood and cheered the Bolshevik Revolution.

These pastors, and those who joined them, were oblivious to one vital truth - competition and the free market are the very basis of personal freedom and wealth-production. Canadian historian W.L. Morton has since labelled that Social Gospel a "false doctrine." But the social gospellers carried their holy crusade to the centre of Canada's politics in an all-out assault on capitalism and the free market. Yes, Canada's grain industry has been mired in politics almost from the beginning.

The rhetoric surrounding these events has been so fierce that few Canadians have grasped the real issues. This book tells the dark story of how mistakes made in those early years went to Canada's heart at untold cost.

A New Canadian Martyr

As this book goes to press, the name Andy McMechan is being written into Canada's history. Andy is the prairie farmer who made news when he was caught red-handed, apparently riding roughshod over Canadian law. Instead of delivering the grain grown on his Manitoba farm to the monopoly government Wheat Board, taking his initial payment and then waiting for his final cheque to arrive (a cheque which he considered inadequate), he had trucked his grain to waiting buyers in North Dakota. There he pocketed the money and returned home to buy groceries, pay his bills and repair his machinery so he could keep farming and educate his family. For this brazen act, he was arrested, handcuffed and marched off to jail.

During his five-months' incarceration, he kept asking, "What law did I break?"

He got no satisfactory answer. But he must have committed some serious crime and justly earned that sentence. Surely growing and selling grain is a business enterprise - not an exercise in politics! Or is it? Canada's justice system would never jail an innocent man over some partisan political issue, would it?

McMechan's stay behind bars set off a curious chain of events:

• Friends and neighbours came with their combines to take off his 1996 crop, and brought hammers to fix his cattle pens. Many of them joined with other growers to create a new farm organization, Farmers for Justice, to fight for his freedom.

• The high-profile National Citizens' Coalition smelled injustice and began raising funds across Canada to help get Andy out of jail and to break the industry's shackles.

• CBC's *W5* did a television feature on McMechan and Farmers For Justice which blazoned his name in prime time across the country (although it seemed to miss the central issue of the story.)

• Wheat Board Minister Ralph Goodale's name began appearing in the media almost daily, attacked in letters to the editor and in tv and radio interviews, for his stubborn fight to preserve the Wheat Board's monopoly and to continue to deny Andy and other growers the freedom to sell their own grain.

While McMechan languished in jail, one of his sons had to stay home from university, while a daughter's university tuition fees were paid by neighbours. McMechan lost much of his farm machinery because of lost income, and when he finally walked free, he faced massive fines which he couldn't pay.

Yes, this was a family tragedy. But surely, since Andy had broken some law, he had to pay the price. Now, his name could drop out of the news. But the public seemed curious about his fate and the media responded.

Did this story speak to a larger issue, to a sickness at the very root of Canada's political structure? In recent months, one thing has become crystal clear. Andy's stay behind bars marked a momentous turning point for the huge grain industry and for Canada itself.

When Wheat Board Minister Goodale finally allowed barley growers to vote in early 1997 on how their grain would be sold, he refused to offer what so many wanted - the choice to sell either through the Board or on the open market. He insisted the Wheat Board's monopoly be continued, or all barley would go on the open market. Denied a choice, an astounding 37 percent voted for the open market, even if it meant ending the Board which many growers consider almost sacred. Such a response would have been unthinkable only months earlier.

But this didn't end the issue. Grower groups kept reminding Goodale, "We do just fine selling our canola and flaxseed and other grains ourselves. Why won't you give us the freedom to sell our barley?"

The result was inescapable. Andy McMechan the "criminal" was emerging as a sort of folk hero, perhaps a martyr. *His martyrdom can now be seen as one more symptom of the flaw identified by Runciman that lies deep in Canada's soul.*

Other events were helping to propel the issue to the forefront and catching public attention. The Alberta Barley Commission and the Western Barley Growers' Association along with 21 growers, had brought an action against the Wheat Board charging their right to earn a living and their freedom of association was undermined by being forced to sell wheat and barley through the Board. Judge Justice Francis Muldoon dismissed the action, ruled it was up to the politicians, not the courts to open grain marketing to an unfettered free market. But this only added to the turmoil. Alberta farm columnist John Schmidt said the judge had ruled in favour of a myth when he said the CWB achieves its legislated objectives of orderly marketing.

"What is orderly marketing?" asked Schmidt. Muldoon had failed to explain it nor did anyone else supporting the Board. Schmidt referred to Dr. Paul Earl's little-known PhD thesis (reported in this book beginning in Chapter 1) which he called a "blockbuster" that explains it all. Many early western farm leaders had been certain "orderly marketing" (getting rid of the Grain Exchange, the open market and private grain companies in favour of a government monopoly board) would put millions of dollars more into growers' pockets. But this idea had failed and was discredited.

Western Barley Growers President Buck Spencer accused the judge of prejudice in favour of monopoly Wheat Board marketing. Spencer said the judge went out of his way to sympathize with witnesses like National Farmers' Union President Nettie Wiebe, because she ran a family farm (although the growers challenging the Board were also family farmers,) and that she had a PhD so was educated and thus surely superior. Yet Spencer said growers get better returns for the crops they sell outside the Board than for the barley and wheat they must deliver to the Board.

Spencer said Muldoon agreed that the CWB Act denies equality before the law because it only applies to farmers in the designated area and he agreed "we showed him we could do better without the CWB, and that shows we are disadvantaged." In fact, claimed Spencer, Muldoon admitted the Wheat Board's burdensome buyback costs, unfair storage and handling costs, loss of local value adding, adding dockage at terminals and charging farmers for unnecessary cleaning are perhaps unfair. But Muldoon had advised growers to elect a party that supports their cause if they want change.

Responded Spencer, "I guess we need to establish a Natural Grain Sales Party!" He left no doubt - the growers would take the issue to the Appeal Court.

While this dispute was claiming news headlines, several dozen Farmers for Justice members, who had been charged at a border demonstration in April, 1996, were still waiting their day in court. And many cases of civil disobedience by farmers who took grain across the U.S. border without a Wheat Board permit, were on.

To maintain the pressure, Farmers for Justice now called for a demonstration imaginatively dubbed the "Andy 500" in honour of McMechan, to bring hundreds of growers and others to the North Dakota border on July 15, some to haul grain to the U.S. without a Wheat Board permit to again challenge the system. This was set aside at the last minute, to be replaced with a spirited rally in Regina of 500 growers.

Ripping Off The Shackles - A New Industry Emerging

While Andy McMechan's martyrdom helped focus attention on this sickness at Canada's heart, it also turned the spotlight on a momentous happening. After so many decades, *the political shackles are finally being ripped off the massive industry. Breathtaking change is returning lost freedoms and responsibilities to growers and grain companies and the railroads.*

Months earlier, the stultifying Crow rate which subsidized and perpetuated the inefficient grain-moving system and blocked a massive advance to cattle and hog and poultry feeding and to food processing in the prairies, was finally ended.

Meanwhile, Saskatchewan Wheat Pool - which had been the prairie's largest grain handler for decades and had always fought hard for monopoly government selling and other social gospel methods - stunned the industry, joining with Cargill Ltd., (one of the world class grain companies which had long been reviled by social gospellers) to build a huge export terminal in Vancouver.

SaskPool was also shifting into a massive diversification/expansion/marketing program. It planned to build a $175 million port facility at Delta, B.C. (to open in 2000) in order to move more grain to the mushrooming Asian market. Astonishingly it also aimed to build an $85 million import-export facility called EuroPort, in Gdansk, Poland, as a window into Europe. And it began handling more non-Wheat Board grains, getting crushing and handling operations in Mexico, moving strongly into cattle feeding and hog production and processing in the prairies, and taking shares in breweries, feed mills, fertilizer plants and the Robin's Donuts chain. In a final shock to its members, it went public and began selling shares on the open market.

United Grain Growers, which had always opposed monopoly government control and fought for market freedom, sold shares to the public in 1995-96 to raise capital for needed expansion and upgrading. It fended off a hostile takeover bid from Manitoba and Alberta Wheat Pools in early 1997. And then it made another stunning move.

Illinois-based agribusiness giant Archer Daniels Midland Co. (ADM), which bills itself, 'Supermarket to the World,' is a huge commodities trader through its 50 world-wide trading offices, is said to have the largest flour-milling business in Canada, as well as connections in the world marketplace. Now UGG joined forces with this world leader, bringing ADM's processing and commodity trading expertise to UGG. The deal united the two companies in a "shared vision," gave ADM up to 45 percent ownership and UGG $50 million of needed capital. ADM promised not to raise its stake in UGG above 45% for the next 10 years

Said optimistic UGG President Ted Allen, "We see the...pipeline, which gets grain from farmers to end users increasingly integrated...and the Canadian industry becoming less regulated and more dynamic."

Even though much of the Wheat Board's monopoly remains as this book goes to press, one thing is clear - the growers' demands for freedom can no longer be denied. Other grain giants are moving relentlessly to help power the long-delayed explosion of growth. The Canadian arm of grain and food giant ConAgra Inc. of Omaha announced in 1996 its first venture into Saskatchewan - it would build three massive grain terminals, perhaps "the most efficient grain-handling terminals on the Prairies."

The consequences of these events are beginning to emerge. A new and vastly-changed grain and food industry is taking shape. But long-cherished political beliefs are inevitably being crushed so the public debate will be loud and continuing. Uncertainty and political conflict will be intense.

As in the beginning, Canada's political focus will turn again to its great North-West.

1

THE CHURCH INTRUDES INTO POLITICS - UNWITTING PAWNS

Crisis Time

Alarm bells should have rung out in Parliament and throughout the West and in news head lines and on editorial pages across Canada in 1973 when a report on the country's grain handling/transportation system was made public. Had the country been alert, those findings by an industry-wide committee would have shaken it to its foundations.

The prairies had been Canada's engine of growth in earlier years as tough settlers broke that virgin land and transformed the vast area into a giant breadbasket. The wheat they grew moved in a trickle, then a stream and then a river into world markets.

Winnipeg exploded into a booming and boisterous frontier city. More wheat was passing direct from farmers through the Grain Exchange there by 1910 than even through the half-century-old Chicago Grain Exchange. That prairie boom town was said to have 19 millionaires, only two fewer than Toronto. It was seen by buyers in Europe as the world's greatest primary wheat market.

A sea-to-sea Canada was being built, with the prairies its engine of growth, and promising to bring more wealth than even Prime Minister John A. Macdonald had imagined. Now, in the 1970's it should have been leading the way in the world's growing challenge - how to feed the exploding populations. In that war on hunger, the prairies could have put Canada on world centre stage.

But that 1973 report described an industry in shackles, unable to respond to beckoning markets. Grain had been at the centre of Canada's political wars from the beginning. Now the worst fears of many farmers and farm leaders had become a reality. Their industry had become a massive bureaucracy. Growers and the country itself were suffering a catastrophe.

That report came from a committee set up by the new industry-wide Canada Grains Council to examine problems plaguing grain. Its authors had found, "a pattern of policy and operation decisions...which bespoke a continuing mistrust of markets to allocate resources and which proceeded with inexorable logic to add one policy instrument upon another until...grain farmers were left with an unresponsive and decaying transportation and handling system."

It was a ringing indictment of the system on which every prairie farmer, and the country itself, depended. If ever a report demanded response, this was it.

But politicians and the media largely ignored it, complacent with a monopoly system that was failing. That system denied growers the freedom to use their initiative and energy to market their crops or seek new crops to sell in an expanding and changing marketplace, and it denied grain companies the freedom to fully use their expertise to the industry's benefit.

Return To The Days of Barter

Three years before that report was released, another event occurred that would change the destiny of Canada's breadbasket. Wally Nelson was a hard-nosed no-nonsense overachiever, a mechanic-turned farmer who cropped the deep black soil at Avonlea south of Regina. He was also building the province's biggest John Deere dealership and a General Motors one as well. But his focus was on grain. He couldn't sell the big crops he harvested nor could his neighbours sell theirs.

"We had tens of thousands of bushels of wheat piled up on our farms," he recalled later. "Our cash flow had stopped. Things had come to a halt."

The days of barter had returned - customers who wanted to buy cars and trucks and farm machinery were offering grain as payment. It was crisis time in the West - and that meant a crisis in Parliament and in Canada's political life. "Our farm organizations and the government kept saying, 'There isn't a market,'" said Nelson. "But newspapers kept telling how a Japanese sale was lost or some other sale missed."

He and a few neighbours began meeting weekly through the fall of 1969 trying to find out why their good wheat wasn't moving to market. When they invited local politicians and farm group leaders to a meeting in January, 1970, and couldn't get answers, nine of those farmers headed for Winnipeg.

"We talked to grain salesmen and international export agencies, visited the Grain Exchange trading floor, the Wheat Board and anyone who could tell us how our grain was sold," said Nelson. "One two-hour appointment lasted two days and two nights.

"The truth began to dawn. We growers had gone for years with no idea of how our grain was marketed." Their industry was dominated by politics - and crippled by it.

The growers dug deep into their own pockets and headed for Ottawa to ask more questions. They got a sympathetic hearing but were dismayed to find the system was set up "to bring about social reform, not to sell wheat," said Nelson. "We were using our selling program to give every producer a 'fair' share of the market no matter what kind of wheat he produced. Everyone confirmed how bad the situation was. We couldn't find anyone to dispute these findings."

Farmer Bob Ferguson exclaimed in amazement, "We've been too busy trying to be efficient growers to worry about what happens after our wheat leaves the farm."

Growers were increasing their harvests year by year, but now they couldn't deliver the grain to market. The system was breaking down - the grain pileup was the most visible sign of the crisis.

Nelson and his little band began to sense an even greater issue. World leaders proclaimed the most critical challenge on the world's stage was how to feed the mushrooming populations. Prairie farmers had a huge potential to grow more grain. They could have led the way in that war on hunger, and in doing so, they would have created more wealth and jobs right at home, and put Canada front and centre on the world market.

Anger, even rage, was now their mood. Beefy Vern Wildfong who farmed eight-and-a-half sections at Craik was one of Nelson's little group - a jovial and gregarious man whose smile had been overtaken by the grain pileup and the lack of cash flow. He kept repeating a simple message to anyone who would listen. "We farmers are bleeding....We are just about bled to the last drop. We are ready for reform now."

Recalled Nelson, "This was our wheat. We had to take action - to find a way to get it back into the market."

Their challenge was the politics of grain - they had to find a way to exert their own political influence. And now there was no denying them. They called meetings across Saskatchewan. When they invited 80 farmers, 300 showed up. Halls overflowed. Nelson growled out their findings and urged, "We farmers must begin to take an interest in how our wheat is sold. We need to provide leadership to get back on track."

They chose a name from the southern prairies where the highest quality red wheat was grown, and on April 3, 1970, chartered the Palliser Triangle Wheat Growers' Association, "to effectively promote policies relating to high protein wheat."

They were beginning an explosive journey to try to understand their politics-mired and crisis-ridden industry - to learn how it could have gotten into such a state and how to bring their viewpoint into play to save it.

The Social Gospel's Attack on Capitalism

Paul Earl was a young and energetic employee of the farmer-owned grain company, United Grain Growers Limited (UGG), when he was tapped on the shoulder and named to the committee which studied the grain industry and made its devastating 1973 report. As it turned out, that shoulder tap was a fateful one. The report's findings were largely ignored for 17 years. But when Earl began studies for his Doctor of Philosophy degree at the University of Manitoba in 1990, he returned to them and chose for his thesis, "RHETORIC, REALITY AND RIGHTEOUSNESS - The Ideological Debate Between the Farm Organizations and the Grain Trade."

His research documented a stunning phenomenon - the leading role played by Protestant church pastors in the public debate that shaped the industry and the country.

Earl found that as those early homesteaders were transforming the prairies, momentous events were taking place south of the 49th parallel. Pastors caught up in the social upheavals of industrialism were preaching sermons and writing books attacking poverty and the resulting suffering. They called it evidence of capitalism's failure to fulfil a promise of universal prosperity.

They blamed the world's ills on "the capitalist system" and offered a blindingly simple remedy. "Abolish capitalism and the open market."

Their preaching became known as a "Social Gospel," grew into a furious attack on *laissez faire* and liberal economic theory and finally became an all-out assault on capitalism. Some of those pastors crossed the border into Western Canada.

"The most eloquent proponent of the Social Gospel..." wrote Earl, was Walter Rauschenbusch, an American who seemed convinced he had made a blinding discovery of a new universal truth. Rauschenbusch blamed the most severe of the world's ills on the capitalist system and on human corruption.

He proclaimed, "Competitive commerce exalts selfishness to the dignity of a moral principle...pits men against one another in a gladiatorial game in which there is no mercy...{and} has poured vast wealth into the lap of a limited number." He charged that this "parasitic wealth...create(s) a vicious luxury which then acts as a centre of infection for all other classes."

These American social gospellers were joined by Canadian pastors including Salem Bland, "a Methodist minister, author, lecturer at Wesley College in Winnipeg and a firebrand speaker at grain growers conventions" from 1905 to 1918. Bland argued passionately that modern capitalism based on private property rights in industry and motivated by a competitive individualism was "the primary impediment to the full realization of democracy and brotherhood." He preached to all who would listen. "The distinctive task of the age," he said, "is the abolition of capitalism."

Earl found that Saskatchewan Methodist preacher H.D. Ranns was just as certain of their cause. "No two organizations mean more to prairie life than the church of Christ and the Grain Growers' movement," said Ranns. "Each needs the other and neither can fulfil its due destiny without the assistance of the other."

Farmers were then founding their co-operatives as a way to reshape society and Earl found them "the preeminent reform group in Western Canada." The social gospellers spared no effort to take their message to them. Rauschenbusch sold over 50,000 copies of his 1907 book, *Christianity and the Social Crisis.* The three provincial grain growers' associations seized on this message, began holding "Grain Growers' Sundays" in 1916 and 1917.

American-born Henry Wise Wood, a prominent Alberta and Western farm leader, was also caught up in the Social Gospel movement. He extolled the concept in the pioneering farm paper, *Grain Growers' Guide.* Addressing a United Farmers of Alberta Sunday Service, he targeted "the small group of financiers who practically ruled the destinies of Canada," called it absurd for a nation "governed by Mammon" to boast of her Christian civilization. He said such a civilization could only be attained by "tearing down our social fabric and rebuilding on a foundation not of selfishness but of mutual love taught by Christ."

Paul Earl dug deeply into these events and found himself focusing on the startling story of what one historian called "the development of a social purpose in the Protestant churches." By 1913, this Social Gospel had gained such a hold on Canadian thinking that religious student William Magney wrote, "It was assumed by all that God had called the church in Canada to the high task of nation-building based upon Christian principles of liberty, brotherhood and justice."

In Earl's view, this intrusion of religion into a mounting attack on capitalism by cooperatives gave the attack "authority" in the eyes of many. He came to a stunning conclusion. It would be difficult to overestimate the Social Gospel's impact in shaping the prairie grain system and the country itself. For while farm people drew their ideas from British and American cooperativism, they drew their *inspiration* from Protestant religious thought - and specifically from that *social gospel.*

Yes, grain politics had gone to Canada's heart in surprising ways.

Examining this frenzied attack on capitalism later, University of Manitoba historian W.L. Morton wrote in, *Manitoba: A History,* that "The Protestant laity were largely indifferent or complacent, ignorant of the theological foundations of their churches, and blinded by the *false doctrine* of the 'social gospel' to the spiritual truths of religion."

He added, "The decline of the Church of England in rural Manitoba and the union of the Presbyterian, Methodist and Congregational churches, consummated in 1925, were...indications of the weakening of the religious spirit as the pioneering years gave way to the years of material accomplishment."

It can be seen now that those crusading social gospellers, with their all-out assault on capitalism and the free market, were oblivious to one vital truth - competition and the free market are the very basis of wealth production and personal freedom. In a calamitous oversight, they held righteously to their ideology.

Sapiro - Like A Meteor Flaring Through The Sky

Drought and collapsing grain prices after World War I brought bankruptcy and despair to many prairie farmers, and demands for new answers. The larger-than-life figure who responded was an American lawyer and perhaps the most compelling stump orator to ever reach the West.

Aaron Sapiro hit Canada in 1923 like a meteor flaring through the sky. Like the social gospellers, he aimed to revoke the market system and transform society. He saw Canada as centre stage in world wheat. He said prairie farmers held the world's wheat surplus in their hands and were the key to transforming the world. He cried out for a government-imposed, wheat-selling monopoly.

"You don't have to be powerless," he thundered, holding up the dream of pooling which some farm leaders were already examining, a dream of farmers using political power to seize control of their crop and somehow sell it outside the marketplace. He suggested they could even extend that control internationally, and then simply declare the price buyers would pay.

Back in his native United States, sceptical growers and the public rejected Sapiro's vision of a world wheat pool, scoffed at this idea of politicians and bureaucrats selling grain. World buyers attacked the idea vehemently. Sapiro's magnificent dream was doomed to failure. But in Canada where the social gospel had taken root, he seduced many prairie farm leaders, helped set in motion a remarkable series of events. The Wheat Pools were formed. The Co-operative Commonwealth Federation (CCF) political party was born and won power. Pastor J.S. Woodsworth led the way in carrying the message to Parliament. Left-wing politics and the church were coming together in a mixture which would transform the industry and reshape the country. Sapiro's legacy and that of the social gospellers hang heavily over Canada even today.

A monopoly Wheat Board was set up during World War II to give Ottawa control over the prairie wheat crop as a vital food source for the war effort. After the war, ruling politicians held fast to that social gospel ideology, even preventing prices rising in line with market forces, and responding to every market problem by imposing more rules on the system. The increasing tangle of controls brought industry gridlock, and the crisis of the late 1960s when Mac Runciman began telling his story of the Wild Hogs of Horseshoe Bend, and when Wally Nelson and his group of growers formed Palliser Wheat Growers' Association.

To understand these events, to learn what went wrong in the West - and in Canada - we must look more closely at events in the development of the prairie breadbasket.

Ed Partridge And The Mother Lode of Pioneering Experience

A United States farm boy of Irish-Scottish descent named Cyrus Hall McCormick had been jeered when he tried to cut wheat with his crude reaper in the early 1830's. But his invention triggered a revolution in feeding the world. As the US began settling the fertile lands of its mid-west, other new farm machines helped make that frontier vibrant with activity. By 1856, wheat was leaving Chicago for Europe.

Some American financiers now saw it as their manifest destiny to seize the North-West and possibly the entire continent. Perhaps they would buy Rupert's Land from the Hudson's Bay Co. The British government's response was to instruct Captain John Palliser to explore "that portion of British North America which lies between the northern branch of the River Saskatchewan and the frontier of the United States, and between the Red River and the Rocky Mountains," to see if it had value.

Palliser and his party left Fort Garry in July, 1857, and after three seasons of study, reported favourably about the park belt but not the plains.

Minneapolis had become a wheat milling centre and stories of an emerging hard spring wheat belt in the North-West including Minnesota and Dakota Territory were reaching Ontario. The Red River Valley running north through Manitoba and the vast prairies to the West held out enormous promise.

Prime Minister John A.Macdonald had turned his eyes west after bringing the colonies of British North America into Confederation in 1867. Those North-West Territories (present-day Saskatchewan and Alberta) had been the preserve of the fur trade for more than two centuries but he terminated the Hudson's Bay Company's charter in 1870 and acquired Rupert's Land for the new Dominion. He lured British Columbia into Confederation in 1871 by promising a transcontinental railway within 10 years. To pay for that massive undertaking he had to find some way to tame and civilize that huge land tract.

The emerging hard spring wheat belt to the south was the evidence he needed. Perhaps the North-West could be transformed into a farming empire. Settlers would generate new wealth to help finance the vast project and provide a protected market for central Canada's industries. Ominously, his National Policy which focused on western settlement and immigration, also included higher tariffs.

Macdonald won the closely contested election in 1872 but he had secretly promised Sir Hugh Allan and his syndicate the contract to build the railway in return for financial support in the election campaign. When it was revealed that Allan was backed largely by American promoters, the Pacific Scandal brought down Macdonald's government in 1873.

American businessmen built a railway from St. Paul, Minnesota, to St. Boniface, Manitoba, in 1878. Macdonald regained power that same year, incorporated the Canadian Pacific Railway in 1881, and saw work begin on it in earnest.

The Dominion Lands Act of 1872 had already caught the imagination of an adventurous generation of Ontario youth by promising virtually free land for homesteaders. John Macoun boasted in his 1882 book, *Manitoba and the Great North-West,* of wheat yielding 55 bushels to the acre. And when the CPR's last spike was driven at Craigellachie, B.C., in 1885, the stage was set.

Land Fever hit the postage-stamp-sized province of Manitoba which would see its boundaries extended in another two years. A time of big and often unrealistic dreams was at hand. Frontier land salesmen turned to hyperbole. The message from one overly enthusiastic pitchman to prospective US settlers urged them to "Buy land in the Canadian west...leave home after Easter, sow your wheat and take in the harvest and come home with your pockets full of money in time for Thanksgiving."

Another's imagination ran wild as he cried, "When you plant wheat, you must be prepared to flee immediately or become entangled and lost in the jungle of the fast-growing and heavy crop."

The new rail line had set the stage for the greatest wheat rush the world had ever known.

Ed Partridge was one of those caught up in the hype and excitement and the promise of the new land. Born in 1861 on a farm near Barrie, Ontario, he was one of 14 children. On completing secondary school, he got a teacher's certificate and taught briefly there. But momentous days lay ahead for Canada and he was destined to be at their heart.

At Christmas, 1883, Partridge was huddled in a little shack on his quarter section homestead in the District of Assiniboia, North-West Territories. He was getting his first taste of the bitter cold and the fearsome loneliness of a prairie winter. He survived his first cruel winter in his little shanty near where the town of Sintaluta, Saskatchewan, stands today. But when he set out to grow his crop, he lacked the money to buy machinery. He seeded 43 acres but his total harvest was only seven bushels. He hung on, began teaching in rural schools and built a sod house for more comfort.

On the Louis Riel uprising in 1885, he joined the Yorkton Rangers to get the 50 cents a day and grub, and credits on his homestead.

He returned from the Riel action to join the myriad other settlers from Eastern Canada, the United Kingdom, the United States and Eastern Europe. They broke their land with oxen and walking ploughs, seeded their first crops of flax, oats, barley and increasingly wheat. They brought in cattle and sheep and hogs to develop mixed farms. And they built their communities. They were making grain the business of the West and of Canada. Wheat and weather became the country's major conversation topics. Those fertile plains were becoming a world breadbasket, bringing undreamed of wealth and becoming the railroad's lifeblood.

The West was "Canada's largest frontier initiative ever," wrote one historian, "and the mother-lode of pioneering experience." It was Canada's linchpin and a world leader.

But Partridge and those other homesteaders were about to become unwitting pawns in Prime Minister Macdonald's nation-building dream. They would soon be engaged in a fierce struggle for freedom and control of their destiny, one that continues at Canada's heart to this day.

2

The Fires of Discontent

A Life-And-Death issue For Every Homesteader - The Sintaluta Victory

The CPR ran up enormous capital costs laying rail line across the West and was soon desperate for revenue so it offered grain companies exclusive rights to grain cars if they would build elevators along its lines. The companies responded, giving growers places to sell their grain and giving the railroad fast boxcar turnaround. But those elevators quickly became a political storm centre that would continue to fester for over a century.

Getting grain to market was a life-and-death issue for every homesteader. A farmer might face a 25-mile trip to the nearest rail delivery point, a 50-mile round trip by plodding horse and wagon with a 50-bushel wagonload which meant a mile of road travel for every bushel. Delivering the grain from a fair-sized farm was like trekking the 5000 miles to Montreal and back.

And when that farmer reached an elevator, the agent often seemed all-powerful and ready to cheat. He might offer Number 3 grade for Number 1 wheat if his number 1 bins were full, or he might even have conspired with nearby agents to be sure farmers couldn't do better going there.

Yes, Macdonald's 1878 National Policy was bringing settlers to the West to produce cash crops, benefitting exporters, railroads and food processors. And those farmers and the West had become a ready market for the goods of Central Canada's manufacturers. But the railroads and grain companies were building an unregulated monopolistic system in which they seemed able to dictate grain prices, grades and dockage. Farmers had become pawns in a cruel game. And ominously, that National Policy increased tariffs on the processed goods they had to buy.

W.R. Motherwell was one of those who had answered

the cry of free land. Raised on a farm at Perth, Ontario, he was 22 years old when he homesteaded in the fertile Abernethy-Indian Head area in 1882 not far from where Partridge would take land a year later. He and his neighbours were breaking the tough sod and seeding and harvesting their crops and building their communities.

Minnesota farmers had already won legislation forcing railroads to give farmers cars to ship their own grain, and allowing flat warehouses where farmers could bin carloads of grain. Now, Motherwell and his neighbours focused on that excessive elevator dockage and on perceived short weights.

They called it a violation of their liberty to have to deal with the elevators and demanded the right to deliver grain over the platform right into the rail cars. They also cried out against depressed prices. They were about to etch their names into history.

They wrote their Members of Parliament in Ottawa, demanding that grain shipping and transportation in Manitoba and the North West Territories be regulated. Ottawa heard their call and set up a Royal Commission in 1899 to probe the grain-handling business. When it urged action, the politicians passed the Manitoba Grain Act of 1900 which became a sort of grain industry Magna Carta - a forerunner of the Canada Grain Act which protected farmers against unfair grading and dockage, and which required railways to supply cars to individual farmers and to provide loading platforms when asked.

But the struggle had barely begun. A big crop in 1901 jammed elevators again and brought a return to car shortages. Farmers who could deliver grain had to buy lumber and run up improvised granaries instead of returning home with needed cash. One thing was clear - the railways had ignored their "Magna Carta."

Then it happened. Those pioneers had endured too much. In December, 1901, according to prairie historian and journalist R.D. Colquette, "the fires of discontent smouldering across the plains burst into flames at Indian Head." A few neighbours met at Motherwell's home and drafted the call to arms - a letter urging farmers to gather for action.

Farmers flocked to Indian Head on December 18 and were joined by political leaders. They presented the evidence, said it was time to set up their own organization and formed the Territorial Grain Growers' Association.[1] This triggered perhaps the greatest farm organization movement the world had ever seen and set the prairies on a course of political action which would shape the West and all of Canada.

Those farmers named Motherwell their provisional president and John Millar provisional secretary, and elected a board of directors. Their idea spread like wildfire. Thirty-eight local associations were formed and each sent delegates to a convention at Indian Head in February, 1902. They wanted sweeping reform and they called on Ottawa to amend the landmark Manitoba Grain Act of 1900. They urged that the railways be compelled to build loading platforms within 30 days of a farmer's request, and to provide cars for loading at every shipping point. They demanded that each station agent be required to keep a car order book recording names of applicants in the order received and to allot empty cars in that order, to avoid favouritism. Ottawa amended the act.

When another bumper crop was harvested in 1902 and station agents ignored the car distribution clause, the group took a case at Sintaluta to court and sued the CPR. When they won their historic Sintaluta Victory, the CPR instructed its agents to strictly observe the Act's car distribution clause. Yes, the farmers had finally found a powerful political voice.

---

[1] Historian R.D. Colquette called the Territorial Grain Growers' Association the beginning of the great farmers' movement in Canada - the first one to endure. Even the great farmers' co-operative undertakings trace back to it. For Motherwell himself and for numberless other farm leaders, it was just another step taking them to the heights of political power and placing their stamp indelibly on the country. Motherwell became Saskatchewan's first Minister of Agriculture when the province was formed in 1905, and was twice federal Minister of Agriculture in governments of Prime Minister Mackenzie King. He was a tireless advocate of better farming techniques for the dry belt. His own place - with its big Ontario-style stone house and the farmstead divided off with garden area, water supply area, barnyard, and shelterbelts to provide protection and attractive landscape and for trapping snow for spring meltwater - became a showpiece in the West. It was designated a National Historic Site in 1966.

"The House With The Closed Shutters" -
A Deep Rage - Action

Ed Partridge had a way that attracted attention in any crowd and after two decades of struggle he was becoming a visionary, injecting a new note into farm gatherings. He was a big man and he now wore a sizeable blond moustache. His eyes seemed to blaze and he had become an impassioned orator, able to coin phrases that stirred his audiences.

He had helped set up the Territorial Grain Growers' and he saw the Sintaluta Victory over the CPR as a historic milestone. He believed utterly that farmers were victims of a grain handling/transportation monopoly and he called this a symptom of a larger issue - the need for a gigantic class struggle with the financial, industrial and commercial interests on one side, farmers and city workers on the other. He told homesteaders their salvation lay in their own hands and he urged, "Don't blame the other fellow for taking advantage of his opportunity. An easy mark is a great temptation to shoot."

He didn't want sympathy. He was intent on changing the very nature of society, righting injustices whether perceived or real, winning freedom and fair play for farmers and shaping a new Canada. His life was about to become a story of dizzying successes as well as devastating failures and tragedies. Everyone - from western farmers and the Winnipeg Grain and Produce Exchange to the milling companies, railways and banks soon knew who he was and that he came from Sintaluta. He was helping set in motion forces that transformed the West and the country, and are at the very centre of our country today, shaping the lives of every Canadian.

By the fall of 1904, Partridge was convinced the time had come for decisive action. His neighbours listened. Twenty of them chipped in $5 apiece, handed him the $100 and sent him on a one-man mission to scout around in Winnipeg's grain trade circles. He bought his train ticket and headed for Winnipeg, arriving there on January 5th, 1905. With what was left of his $100, he got a room at a cheap boarding house.

His arrival at the Winnipeg Grain and Produce Exchange, wrote one reporter, was received "with a courtesy as cold as the air outside the frosted windows." That

strengthened his resolve. He was impressed with how government graders did their job, but with little else. When
the $100 was exhausted after a month, he headed home.

He stopped off at a farm meeting in Brandon to offer
insights of what he had found. Dubbing the Exchange "The
House with the Closed Shutters," he claimed evidence that
five companies controlled the export business - and to some
extent their own profits - by controlling the prices paid to
farmers. He saw smaller dealers sheltering under the big
fellows' umbrella. Most important, he was convinced the
grain trade was exploiting growers.

The Brandon farmers named him chairman of a committee to look into the matter and report at the next annual meeting. That was too slow for the impatient Partridge. He returned to Sintaluta certain that the hubbub
of the Winnipeg Exchange was just sound and fury con-
cealing decisions by those five grain companies which
dominated price-setting. He identified these enemies in
his report to the Territorial Grain Growers' Association
and charged that these companies controlled grain exports
and their profits by keeping out smaller dealers who might
export on their own account.

He also saw some smaller dealers in league with the
exporters, controlling wheat prices throughout the country. They could set special prices at any point by wiring
instructions to operators to pinch independent competition, he charged. He was sure he saw elevator companies
undercutting charges at some points to kill off competition from farmers' elevators, which sold to independent
dealers.

Partridge's remedy was stunningly simple. Farmers
had to escape the clutches of the private companies to get
a square deal. "Go beyond political action," he urged. "Set
up a co-operative grain marketing company where we can
market our own grain, and be on the inside looking around
to see what is going on rather than looking in from the
outside."

Partridge was perfecting his fiery rhetoric. "We farmers are but pygmies attacking giants," he cried. "Giants
may compete with giants, pygmies with pygmies. But pygmies with giants, never!" He charged, "The Grain Exchange is a device for making agriculture profitable for
those who dislike to wear overalls."

He targeted those "palatial homes on acreages facing the Assiniboine River on Wellington Crescent," owned by Grain Exchange members, "some with massive stone walls screening themselves not only from their own ilk, but also from what they considered the lesser breed."

With his formidable phrase-making ability, he was tapping into a deep and growing anger as farmers found that their institutions and the world grain-pricing system often worked against them. That rage was directed towards the seemingly mysterious Grain Exchange, which they accused of producing rich corporate empires but few if any rich farmers. Social unrest was beginning to boil.

The increasing fury of his followers was also directed at the speculative world of wheat futures, of "paper wheat," (in which buyers or speculators bought wheat to be delivered later) which might bring big profits or losses to the speculators if prices rose or fell before delivery time. When farmers occasionally suffered these losses, it was jumped on as further evidence of the deep-seated evil there. [2]

Partridge saw the fight as class warfare and continued his attack. "We are facing the interlocking financial, commercial and industrial interests of a thousand million people," he cried. Appealing to the farmers' pride, he added, "But we are not denizens of a hamlet. We are citizens of a world."

When the grain companies defended their roles by explaining how the markets work, he roared his response, "A lie will travel a thousand miles while the truth is getting its boots on." Broadening his onslaught to the prairie establishment, he charged, "The pious Presbyterian in the employ of the Hudson's Bay Company, who unctuously asked grace over his whisky, or the Psalm-singing Puritan who made it a penal offence for a man to kiss his wife on the Sabbath Day, didn't scruple to buy a five-dollar beaver skin from an Indian for five cents worth of glass beads."

He poured more fuel on the fire at the 1905 Manitoba Grain Growers' Association convention by charging that "Twenty-five years ago smut and other blemishes were removed with the bran. Now, it is the custom to skin the wheat - also the farmer who grew it."

---

[2] Only a few years later, Saskatchewan Wheat Pool's first elected president, A.J. McPhail, told a 1931 enquiry that the futures market offers "very useful protection to the legitimate interests of grain merchants, millers, and bankers." Yet SaskPool continued for decades to attack private grain companies.

Partridge was sure farmers could operate a grain-handling business as well as anyone and send the profits back home. But some farmers were adamant - such a move would destroy their political effectiveness. The debate raged on.

But then, events took over from talk. Certain that the time had come for action, the determined crusader Partridge mailed an impassioned proposition to prairie farmers in 1905 urging them to form their own company. He proposed a joint stock company owned by farmers that would sell their wheat for the highest legitimate price in world markets.

Farmers delivering wheat to their local elevators that fall chewed over his idea while waiting their turn to drive up the gangway, or eating dinner in the hotel dining room, or huddled in groups on the street corner. That winter, Partridge and a few Sintaluta farmers drafted a plan for a farmer-owned grain company. It would handle carload lots on a commission basis. Only *bona fide* farmers could buy shares.

He presented his case to a mass meeting in the Sintaluta Orange Hall on January 27, 1906. The farmers agreed. In a historic act, they set out to establish the Grain Growers' Grain Company - Canada's first farmer-owned grain handling co-operative (it later became United Grain Growers.) Every western grain grower would be welcome to join.

"For God's Sake Kennedy, We're Sleepy!" - Expelled From The Exchange

This idea of a farmers' commission company to handle their own grain caught the imagination of a tough homesteader in Manitoba's Swan River Valley who had gone as a delegate from his local Grain Growers' Association to the Sintaluta meeting. His name was John Kennedy but his friends called him "Honest John." He had grown up on a farm at Beaverton, Ontario.

Ed Partridge was named president of an action committee to sell $25 shares in this new venture and John Kennedy and others threw themselves into the campaign to make it a reality. They spent $10 on a prospectus and $1 for the use of a desk in Wilson's General Store in

Sintaluta. They hung a crudely lettered sign, "Grain Growers' Grain Company," in the window and offered the $25 shares with 10 percent down. The shares would be non-transferable except by a vote of shareholders at an annual meeting.

Kennedy's method of selling shares was simple. Start talking to a farmer, talk for awhile, then keep right on talking. "For God's sake, Kennedy," the farmer might complain, "if $2.50 will stop you talking, here it is! We're sleepy!"

Kennedy would keep everlastingly at it. He was a hard fighter in a quiet way, one who didn't know how to quit. As one historian observed, "Even Fate cannot beat a man like that."

By midsummer, the group had sold 1000 shares and collected $2500. When they paid organization expenses, legal fees, the cost of securing a charter and printing, they had only $1000 left. They needed $2500 for the seat on the Winnipeg Grain and Produce Exchange so Partridge asked, "Will some of the boys at Sintaluta go security for $1500?" Five of "the boys" signed personal notes for the money.

The action committee made financial arrangements with the Bank of British North America, hired an experienced grain man as manager and opened for business in a tiny Winnipeg office on September 5, 1906. The little company started as a commission house handling carlots of grain shipped over the platform by individual farmers. Its first bill of lading came on September 21st. By the end of October, 100 cars a week were rolling in. The future looked bright. the company got larger office space. But the struggle had just begun.

A sort of guerilla warfare erupted that winter against this upstart farmers' company. Even some farmers whispered, "Company men are in it for what they can get out of it." Partridge shot back, "Yes, sir, I have got quite a bit of silver out of this company; not in my pocket book, but in my hair."

But heavier blows were coming. As a cooperative, the company was paying patronage dividends from its one cent a bushel commission. The Grain Exchange called this "splitting the commission," which was contrary to its rules.

"They're after us already," cried Partridge. The Exchange expelled the company from all trading privileges, precipitating a full-scale crisis. It was too weak to export grain on its own account. All exporters were Exchange members. Grain poured in from farmers who had to be paid. The bank overdraft reached alarming proportions. The bank's head office demanded more security. The sympathetic bank manager looked for a way out.

"I will go with you for a bit more if you three executives of your company - Kennedy, John Spencer (Secretary-Treasurer) and Partridge - will give the bank your personal bond without limit as to the amount," he offered.

The three pledged all their worldly possessions. Then their luck changed. The Scottish Co-operative Wholesale Society bought willingly from them. They made big sales direct to Eastern buyers. And in a nip-and-tuck deal with freeze-up near, they sold a 310,000-bushels cargo to American interests. It went on the last ship out of the port of Fort William, saving the company from disaster. The farmers' company could now survive its first winter.

But its troubles were not over. The patronage dividends it gave members were found to contravene its charter under the Manitoba Joint Stock Companies Act. Its directors cancelled the dividend at a December 22, 1906, meeting and a shareholders' meeting confirmed the action. But the Winnipeg Grain and Produce Exchange refused reinstatement, leaving no doubt it was trying to wreck the farmers' company.

Partridge appealed to the Manitoba government. When Premier Rodmond Roblin responded with legislation compelling the Exchange to reverse its position, it restructured slightly, renamed itself the Winnipeg Grain Exchange, and reinstated the farmers' company which dropped the co-operative clause from its by-laws.

With this victory, more and more farmers began to pin their faith in their little trading company fighting on the front lines. By the end of the 1906-07 crop year, the company had handled 2,340,000 bushels of grain, paid off its indebtedness and relieved the Sintaluta farmers and company executives of their liability. It also had a profit of $791. It was breaking the grip of the private grain companies in the Exchange, ending the grain-handling monopoly and proving that a farmers' company could survive. The farmers were making history, selling their own grain and keeping the profits.

By the spring of 1907, with his company launched,

Partridge began to look at his own role. He realized that in popular movements you can't get much light without heat. He had provided heat which led to light. But his contentious personality was a lightning rod that attracted most of the attacks on the company and often engendered more heat than seemed necessary.

Partridge's dream was to end the market economy, defeat capitalists and join with labour to bring a new world of fairness and justice. A tremendous battle lay ahead. But with his high-strung and sensitive nature, his position as a storm centre began to tell. He became convinced a president of a less contentious nature was needed.

He had sought a farmer-owned grain trading company along with an elevator system owned by provincial governments. Ottawa would own the big Lakehead terminals. That's not quite the way it was going to work out. His new Grain Growers' Grain Company was to become a full-fledged elevator company.

3

"TAKE YOUR DAMNED GRAIN HOME" - FARMERS' LUNGE FOR POWER

Young Crerar - "Take Your Damned Grain Home Again"

When young T.A. "Tom" Crerar took his first load of grain to market in the early 1900's, the elevator agent offered him 59 cents per bushel. That was 19 cents under Fort William price. It was virtual thievery and Crerar knew it - the freight rate to Fort William was only nine cents. To rub salt into the wound, the agent also docked him 1 1/2 bushels for supposed screenings.

The mild-mannered Crerar was aroused to vigorous protest, pointing out the injustice of the price offered and the dockage.

"Go to the devil!" shot back the elevator man.

Crerar answered, "There's no use going to the other elevators - you're all alike."

"Then take your damned grain home again!" growled the operator.

Crerar took what he could get. But he needed no further proof. He and his neighbours were price-takers while paying exorbitant prices for supplies. He never forgot that run-in with the private grain buyer. It shaped his long career. He went on to play an extraordinary role in the first farmers' grain company, the West, and Canada itself.

Like most homesteaders, Crerar's family had travelled a long road to this new land. His roots went back to Perthshire, Scotland, from where a load of hardy folk set out in 1832 on a wooden sailing ship to join the migration to the Canadian wilderness. Their Atlantic crossing turned into a 12-week nightmare. The few survivors made their way west to become the first settlers in what is now Perth County, Ontario. Families of Crerars came from Perthshire the next year to join them.

Those pioneers chopped the huge trees, cleared the land, built their communities and began to raise families. When the transcontinental railroad was built, the younger generation became fired with excitement at the promise of free land in the West.

A trek of Perth County settlers to the West began in 1881 when a train-coachful of people "with the pioneer spirit of their Scottish forbears in their very bones" and with two cars full of settlers' effects left Shakespeare, Ontario. Bachelors, newlyweds and families, they all came.

At St. Boniface, Manitoba, they got their oxen and Red River carts and set out on what would be an agonizing trip. They moved through the wide and muddy streets and bypassed the rich black soil nearby, heading northwest on the Fort Pelly trail which for decades had been heavy with the traffic of Metis freighters and their brigades of Red River carts. They trudged along at the oxenrate of two miles per hour, beating off flies and mosquitoes, plunging through rivers and sloughs, fighting weariness. They passed the settlers' shacks and the black squares of ploughed fields and covered nearly 300 miles before coming to Silver Creek near what is now Russell, just inside Manitoba's western border.

It was May 14, 1881. They camped together the first night, then set out to locate their homesteads and build shacks and prepare to break their land with oxen hitched to single furrow walking ploughs. And to build their communities. By 1883, regional picnics had led to the formation of the first agricultural society. Fair buildings went up and the first fair was held that year. Horse racing started. Curling and skating rinks were planned and dances were held where Scottish reels and Red River jigs were favourites.

Sandy and Janet Crerar came to Silver Creek in 1883 with their seven sons and one daughter. Tom was the oldest. With the 1885 outbreak of Riel's Rebellion, a troop of mounted infantry was raised there and two of its members were killed in the ensuing action. With Riel's defeat, the stage was set for orderly settlement.

As a boy, Tom Crerar carried pails of water long distances to the house, shot prairie chickens and occasionally picked highbush cranberries for the table. A crop failure when he was 12 years old forced him to quit school to work at home. Six years later, he went back to Portage la Prairie Collegiate, then to Manitoba College, Winnipeg. He returned to Silver Creek to teach school, boarding at home, helping with the milking night and morning, then walking three-and-a-half miles twice a day to and from school. But he wanted to farm.

He got a quarter section of land, built a shack where he lived with a couple of other young bachelors, began ploughing more land, growing wheat for market and spending many an evening in spirited discussion about issues facing their community. He tried a stint as a sawmill owner and operator. When the mill burned down four years later, he got a job in Russell managing a new farmer-owned elevator for $75 a month.

Now Tom's experience in selling his load of wheat had turned the discussion to political action. Conditions were ripe for social change.

The year before the historic first Grain Growers annual meeting in 1907, Vice-President John Kennedy had gone to the Russell Fall Fair to sell shares in the proposed company. Tom Crerar was the young manager of that new elevator there and he bought one of the four shares sold. He later went up to the Grand Central Hotel to talk with Kennedy and get a good insight into the new company's goals. Kennedy was able to size him up. Crerar was soon sending the company all the grain he could, and sometimes helpful comments.

Partridge and Kennedy decided they must get Crerar to the annual meeting on July 16, 1907, and Partridge wrote to Crerar, intimating they wanted him on the Board. Crerar came and offered plenty of practical suggestions. He was convinced a great future lay ahead for the company. But he protested he didn't want the job of being on the board. He got elected anyway.

Then came the thunderbolt. When the directors met the next night, Partridge made his announcement. He was retiring as president. A younger man was needed to replace him. He concluded calmly but forcefully, "Crerar is the man!"

They all agreed - except Crerar. The 31-year-old farmer/elevator manager turned them down flat. They pressed him. John Kennedy used his most convincing argument. "It ain't hard," he said.

Crerar discussed it with his wife that night and gave his answer the next morning. "Well, gentlemen," he said, "if you want to take a chance on me I'll take a chance on you." He was named President-Manager of the Grain Growers Grain Company, representing a new generation from most of the hardy leaders who had started the company. He was ready to take on its burdens.

The change in style for the young company was startling. Crerar was affable and low-key. Farmers felt at home in his office. But he made no effort to hide his idealism. He and his Board wanted not just a few additional cents per bushel for their grain. They were fiercely committed to some ambitious goals. But Crerar's style was an appeal to reason, not a call to arms.

Another unforeseen blow struck when the company set out to handle the 1907 crop. The Bank of British North America gave notice it was closing out the account. Without bank credit, the company couldn't buy grain. But again, a way out appeared. An eastern savings and loan company had secured a charter as the Home Bank of Canada and opened a Winnipeg branch. It's new manager, W.H. Machaffie, was the former Bank of British North America manager who had fought successfully for the farmers' company earlier. He still believed in it and took its account.

Showdown! A Ready-Made Crusade
For The Farmers' Paper - Expose!

With the crisis past, Crerar and his board had to get out the word quickly that they could continue selling the farmers' grain. One way would be to start their own newspaper. Although Partridge had stepped down as president, he had remained on the board and he had a way with words. His very nature was to express his views, to attack the status quo, to urge change and a new way. He could become editor of the newspaper.

He hesitated at first, but was soon convinced he was the logical choice. He gathered material and got out the first issue of *The Grain Growers' Guide* in 1908 to communicate with members and all farmers as well as the non-farm public. But the radical side of his nature soon burst loose. He wanted to join hands with the labour unions' paper, *The Voice*, bringing farmers and labour together to create a new society. Crerar and the other directors disagreed.

Partridge responded, "I'm too irritable to get along with anybody in an office." He resigned.

In a strange irony, Partridge and the farmers' company he had started had been on separate courses. He broke with it in 1912, organized the Square Deal Grain Company and got a seat on the Grain Exchange. But it got into financial difficulties and had to be wound up. The Grain Growers' Board didn't forget his contribution and arranged needed financial aid for him.

The company grew rapidly as a commission merchant handling and selling grain for its increasing membership. But its uneasy relationship with the Exchange worsened. A dispute over an Exchange rule erupted and Crerar and his directors feared the elevator companies intended to handle grain for half a cent per bushel (instead of its usual one cent) or even for nothing just to take it away from the farmers' company. And they still wouldn't lose because of their "immense profits" from buying street grain and because of storage earnings from their terminals.

The result would be a marketing free-for-all. The only real competition protecting farmers were the commission men and "track buyers" at the local elevators. Elevator companies might kill them off by handling cars for nothing and paying farmers any price regardless of Exchange-established prices.

Crerar and his men didn't back down from the fight. "This is a showdown," they warned shareholders in a letter. "If farmers don't stand together now, we are licked!"

And now they had a potent ally. The new editor of *The Grain Growers' Guide*, George Chipman, recognized a ready-made crusade when he saw one. He waded into the controversy, labelled the elevator companies an "Elevator Trust," charged that "Every injustice and disturbance in the trade that has taken place (to the farmers' company) since grain commenced to be marketed in Manitoba can be traced to the Elevator Monopoly."

Chipman hammered on the issue in column after column and his readers responded with an avalanche of letters. And they shipped more grain than ever through their own company. The victory was total. The Exchange buckled and restored its one-cent commission rule.

Hostilities broke out anew when someone calling himself "Observer" began getting letters published in two Winnipeg newspapers and three farm journals attacking the farmers' company and its leaders. The mystery writer claimed to be a farmer.

Chipman had a nose for news and a detective's instinct. Those letters seemed too well written to be from a farmer. Could it be a professional writer? He found the letters were paid for at advertising rates. He sensed the fine hand of the elevator interests and soon identified a bright newspaper man with some farming experience who had set up shop as a "Financial Agent."

Chipman shut the door to his private office and wrote the story of the deal he speculated had been made. Then, with the expose ready, he invited the Financial Agent to call at the *Guide* office.

On his arrival, Chipman handed his write-up across the desk. "Thought you might like to look over that copy before we use it," he remarked. "I want to be fair and there might be something."

The surprised writer didn't deny the story. He was being financed by elevator companies attempting to erode support for the farmers' company. Chipman carried the story, telling his readers that papers carrying this material were no friends of the farmers. The readers deluged those papers with letters. The columns stopped. To Chipman's satisfaction, "Observer" continued to be paid under his contract by the rueful elevator companies.

For many years, the *Guide* was the country's most militant farm paper and the voice of organized prairie farmers. It went on to flourish as Canada's national farm magazine under the name *Country Guide.*

The Maelstrom Of The Pit - Elevator Ownership - The Die Is Cast

In the early 1900s, rail lines were reaching relentlessly across the prairies, thousands of miles of branch lines were being built and the rail car supply was being increased. Wheatlands were expanding by a million acres a year, and in this explosion of growth, Winnipeg's population soared to 150,000 by 1913, making it the third largest city in Canada. It had become a financial and insurance centre, and as the home of the Grain Exchange, was seen by many as centre of the world's grain trade. Perhaps it was destined to eclipse Chicago.

But no one promised this little Crerar-led grain company the road would be smooth. Early in 1911, Great Britain and Europe seemed to have an oats shortage and export demand for Canadian oats surged. When the Canadian and US governments concluded a reciprocity agreement on January 26th, many grain dealers feared Americans would control the trade. Prices began to fall. The Grain Growers' manager thought overseas demand was too strong for such a drop. He went into the Pit where the grain was traded and began buying, intending to sell for export later to cover his costs. But he was speculating, something the farmers' company opposed. Had he checked with his Board, it would have said, "No!" But he didn't. The Board learned too late.

The whisper went out among traders, "The Grain Growers' are up to their necks in May oats." The company was accused of trying to corner the oats market.

"Bears" are traders on the Exchange floor who take positions to benefit from an expected market fall. They may even try to depress prices to assure their own profits. Now, the bears' response was, "Sell May oats! Sell May oats!" The tiny farmers' company was dragged into the maelstrom of the Pit in an all-out fight for its very life.

Thousands of bushels of oats were offered as the bears tried to load up the Grain Growers', exhausting its line of credit and forcing it to dump the oats back onto the market, breaking the price. The bears would then buy it back at a profit, possibly bankrupting the company.

Rumours flew through the Exchange corridors. "Will the Company go down?" Only the Clearing House and the company itself knew the true figures. The company had no one to blame but itself. And it had no choice but to fight it out.

But it now had good export connections in the Old Country and good relations with its bank. When the grain was delivered May 1, it had the money on hand to pay for every bushel. Half of that grain was riding the waves within weeks, to fill overseas sales. The bears who had sold the oats were soon trying to buy them back.

It was a moment of rare triumph. The company had weathered the attack. And it weathered other storms in those early months. Farmer sceptics were becoming believers. The idea of co-operative grain marketing had come to stay.

Now a new challenge arose. Although the farmers' company had begun purely as a commission house, Partridge had always wanted government to own elevators for the farmers' use. Loading platforms at country elevators had brought competition. But now the company returned to its demand for government-owned elevators. In the 1907 Manitoba election, it bombarded the three prairie provinces with circulars pushing its case.

At the 1909 annual meeting of the Grain Growers' Grain Co., Tom Crerar said, "Experience has shown the elevator system won't serve the farmers completely as long as the elevators are in private hands for private gain."

Rodmond Roblin had been active in the Winnipeg grain trade before being elected premier in 1900 (he served until 1915). He responded to the growers in 1909, saying his government would set up a line of elevators as a public utility. His bill put up money but rejected a key demand - that the elevators be operated by an independent commission without political ties. Control and operation would be through a provincial commission.

Roblin's commission bought 174 elevators between 1909 and 1912. But its plan was flawed. It paid too much for them, bought too many poor ones and tried to cover costs its through storage and handling fees rather than through the more profitable buying and selling of grain. Losses mounted. Roblin wanted out. He said to Crerar and his farmers in 1912, "Try to run 'em yourselves!"

Crerar and his Board never hesitated. They rented the whole system, putting the company into the elevator business, then went on to build or lease another 64. They rented a terminal elevator at Fort William in 1912 and bought an adjacent terminal in 1913. And despite bad crops in 1914 and 1915, the venture succeeded. The company had become a prairie-wide grain handler.

The idea of a provincial co-operative elevator company had caught on in Saskatchewan, where Crerar and other Board members had almost an old boys' network with the government. They began to lobby for support in setting one up. The provincial government answered "Yes!" and acted in March, 1911, setting up the Saskatchewan

Co-Operative Elevator Company. The bill enabled farmers at any point to put up 15 percent of the needed capital in cash and the government would advance the 85 percent as loans. Growers would own and manage the system.

The new co-op let contracts for 40 new elevators and named the Crerar company its selling agent. It built 88 new elevators the next year and bought six more, for a total of 137. By 1913 it had 192 and in 1915 it bought a Regina site to build a modern headquarters for its expanding staff.

The die was now cast. Grain was the business of the West. Growers were entrenching political power and their leaders were about to move forcefully to the very centre of Canada's political and business life as well. General Manager C.A. Dunning of this new Saskatchewan co-op., for instance, soon moved on to full-fledged politics, becoming in 1916 the youngest provincial treasurer in Canada. He became Saskatchewan premier in 1922, then federal Minister of Railways and Canals and later Minister of Finance in Mackenzie King governments.

"The Ominous Rumble Of Distant Thunder" - A Historic Step - UGG Formed

Henry Wise Wood was born into a prosperous American family with farms in Missouri and Texas, and he had developed strong religious convictions as he grew into a lanky and confident young man. The lure of nation-building on Canada's new frontier had caught the imagination of many Americans and it proved irresistible to Wood. In 1905, the year Alberta joined Confederation, the 45-year-old Wood headed north and bought a farm near Carstairs.

Local leadership was desperately needed and Wood was prepared to lead. Wrote one awe-struck historian later, Wood was "a born leader of men. He dominated through the strength of his personality. His impressive figure, his magnificent voice, his philosophical turn of mind, his mysticism, his fervour, his earthiness, his obvious honesty of purpose, his belief in co-operation and his faith in democracy...made him stand out."

An equally spell-bound journalist wrote, "In his voice was the ominous rumble of distant thunder."

Wood and others soon saw the compelling need for unity. In 1909 they merged the province's two farm groups into the United Farmers of Alberta (UFA). Wood was elected vice-president, then president the next year.

The focus of these pioneers was on getting their increasing harvests to market. Wood took up the Crerar cry, and at UFA's urging, the Alberta government incorporated the Alberta Farmers' Co-operative Elevator Company in 1913, along lines similar to the Saskatchewan initiative, and put up cash advances of 85 percent of the cost of each elevator.

Now Wood needed a solicitor. As it turned out, he had a knack for finding good men. John Brownlee was born in 1883 in Port Ryerse, Ontario, son of a small-town merchant and a devout Methodist teacher. He graduated with a Bachelor of Arts from Toronto University and decided to go west in 1909 for a career on the Canadian frontier. He went to Calgary and graduated there in law in 1912.

Wood now chose Brownlee to be solicitor of the new United Farmers of Alberta, bringing him to the very centre of the farmers' movement and of the West's political life. Wood named him solicitor of the grain-handling co-operative as well. Brownlee's career was underway - and he was destined to become a major figure during the next five decades of struggle to build the grain industry, the West and the country.

The new Alberta Elevator Co-op now built 42 elevators and bought another 10. It got Crerar's company to sell the grain that farmers delivered and in that first year, it put through three quarters of a million bushels. By its third season, it had 87 elevators and an active livestock department with offices in the stockyards at Calgary and Edmonton. It also handled farm supplies.

The Crerar-led company had now absorbed the Manitoba elevator system and had member shareholders in all three provinces. The Saskatchewan and Alberta co-ops were marketing farmers' grain and providing supplies, and grain growers' associations flourished in the three provinces. In fact, growers owned and operated over 500 country elevators as well as terminal elevators. Their progress had been breathtaking.

But rivalries and jealousies were inevitable with three separate elevator co-ops. Alberta leaders and those of Crerar's company dreaded dividing the farmers' efforts. They wanted strength through unity, so they devised a plan to make the Crerar company a central agency marketing all the provincial companies' grain. It would also operate the terminals, continue its export business, and do all central purchasing and any manufacturing needed later. And it would continue to publish *Grain Growers' Guide* as the voice of prairie farmers.

Proponents of this plan met in Regina in 1915. Saskatchewan had over half the good farm land in the West and it grew over half the wheat. Its Elevator co-op also had generous government aid guaranteeing its bank credit. Its zealous and confident leaders had less incentive to amalgamate than those in Alberta and Manitoba. They wanted to continue selling their grain separately. Agreement proved impossible.

With this failure, Alberta Elevator Co-op president and general manager Cecil Rice-Jones and Tom Crerar worked out a merger plan for their two companies which led to the formation of United Grain Growers' Limited (UGG) on Sept. 1, 1917. Crerar became President and Rice-Jones Vice-President.

But the die was cast. Farm unity was impossible. Ideological and economic divisions would continue with the three provincial Pools often on one side and the prairie-wide UGG on the other.

The Farmers' Lunge For Power - Crerar's Progressives - Price Collapse.

War was raging in Europe in those momentous days of 1917 and Prime Minister Robert Borden needed strong western voices in his national wartime government. His request that Crerar become Minister of Agriculture left no doubt that Prairie farm groups were gaining a strong voice in Ottawa. The UGG Board agreed Crerar should accept this call despite the challenges facing their company. And it insisted he continue as president, thinking the recent US move into the war would end it quickly and he could soon be back. Rice-Jones could carry the company's burden in the interval.

But Crerar's move into politics would not be brief. Building Canada was going to be a never-ending challenge.

Central Canada's manufacturing interests had powerful voices in Borden's government and on the tariffs issue they favoured high ones. They also had enormous political clout to advance their views. Crerar knew that if the West was to prosper, the farmers' market must be world-wide. Canada's commitment must be to low tariffs. Conflict was certain.

Meanwhile, Central Canada's farmers had also built their political strength and leading farm voices across the country were urging farmers to take direct political action. Crerar resigned from Cabinet in 1919 but remained in Parliament. On January 6, 1920, 100 delegates came to a Winnipeg conference called by the Canadian Council of Agriculture to examine a New National Policy of free trade, nationalization of the railways and "direct democracy."

Alberta's Henry Wise Wood presided and the meeting set out to form a farmers' or agrarian party. Strong differences surfaced. Wood wanted it to express the farmers' view, even at the expense of other classes. "We are now an economic group," he stated. Crerar rejected a class role, warned the party not to stay rigidly agrarian. His view prevailed. The new party's stated goal would be to elect members to bring in the farmers' platform, but it was "in no sense a vocational class platform," nor would it "demand...special legislation to benefit the few at the expense of the many."

Within weeks, 11 independent agrarian Members of Parliament formed the National Progressive Party with Crerar its leader. But still the United Grain Growers' Board insisted Crerar continue as company president.

Arthur Meighen, who replaced Borden as Prime Minister, called a federal election for December 6, 1921. Ontario and prairie farmers and dissident Liberals flocked to this Progressive party which was bringing the farmers' voice to the very centre of Canada's political life. It won 65 seats in the West, Ontario and New Brunswick, becoming the second largest party in Parliament and breaking the two-party pattern of Canadian politics.

Farmers now set out to extend their political power beyond Ottawa to the provincial level. Henry Wise Wood's United Farmers of Alberta seized the initiative again, asking, "Why shouldn't farmers themselves form Alberta's government?" Members answered with a resounding "Yes!" The UFA won the 1921 election, launching a historic experiment in farmers' government.

New Premier Herbert Greenfield beckoned to the UFA's young solicitor, John Brownlee, and he won a seat in a by-election in Ponoka. He was named attorney general, starting a notable political career.

The following year in Manitoba, a cautious agricultural professor named John Bracken was elected Premier, heading the United Farmers of Manitoba party. He went on to lead his province for two decades.

Prairie development had now held centre stage in Canada for four decades and farmers were sending an increasing torrent of grain to world markets. "That Man Partridge" had faded from the scene but growers had built their own grain company and could be confident of honest weights and grades. It might have seemed they had won their fight and achieved their goals. In reality, however, their fierce struggle was only a foretaste of events to come.

In his book, *The First Fifty Years*, R.D. Colquette wrote of perhaps the most momentous event of those times for prairie agriculture. When war broke out in 1914, he noted, the control of materials including wheat, became necessary. Ottawa moved to control materials, including wheat. The crops of 1917 and 1918 were sold under rigid price control, the very short 1919 crop was handled by a national Wheat Board which operated through to 1920 - a forerunner of the Canadian Wheat Board. This controlled wheat marketing, wrote Colquette, "set off a chain reaction which in extent and permanent results, has no parallel in the economic life of Canada."

He could not have known in those early 1950's just how correct he would prove to be.

Trading was restored on the Winnipeg Grain Exchange on August 18, 1920, and "optimism ruled on the trading floor," wrote Colquette. "Prices climbed to a peak of over $2.85."

But those prices were too good to last. When the long streams of wagons began converging on country elevator points in the fall, "prices began tumbling until, by December, they had dropped a dollar a bushel. The post-war depression had set in. Grain prices fell sooner and faster than the price on any other commodity."

Farmers facing catastrophe were desperate to do something. The Progressives' 1921 election success had been helped by that crash. But it had a surprising outcome. The new party faced Mackenzie King's minority Liberal government. Crerar was no radical and some of his members only wanted to shift the Liberals towards free trade. But others wanted to move sharply left. Support for the Progressives dropped.

Crerar made his decision - he became architect of a Liberal-Progressive *rapprochement*. More radical party members remained as Progressives in Parliament and later joined the CCF when it was founded in 1932. It was another stride in the leftward march of Canada's politics.

4

CHEERS FOR THE BOLSHEVIK REVOLUTION - SAPIRO'S STUPENDOUS DREAM

Abolish Capitalism And the Free Market! - The Winnipeg Strike

That 1920 grain price collapse brought desperate hardship to the prairies, destroying the hopes and dreams of many, leaving them ready to grasp at straws. One ray of hope seemed to shine from the new Social Gospel being preached by many pastors.

In researching his PhD thesis in the early 1990s, Paul Earl found that Walter Rauschenbusch and other pastors in the US had convinced themselves they had found a new universal truth - that "corrupt behaviour was merely the product of the system." "Change the system," they cried. "Abolish capitalism and the free market."

When they brought their Social Gospel message to Canada, many farm leaders listened spellbound. It seemed to say that God hated all businessmen - that the Grain Exchange, the railways and the private grain companies were simply there to rip off the farmers. Here was an enemy they could see, and someone to blame for their troubles.

And here seemed to be divine encouragement to wage class warfare and to destroy capitalism. The message seemed too good to be true. Emotion blinded them to reason.

Earl found that the Social Gospel had played itself out in a different way in the US where tradition was to separate church and state. That healthy scepticism saved the US from a costly experiment. But church leaders and the co-operatives and even the public in Canada did not have the suspicion of government that was present in the U.S. He found that "The Canadian Social Gospel movement - and indeed Canadian Protestantism...saw the church as a vehicle for change."

Yes, religion was welcomed into politics in Canada. And the Social Gospel convinced many to sacrifice individual freedom for a much touted "collective good." The stampede of Western farm thought to escape the discipline of the marketplace followed. Left-wing politics and the church were coming together in a volatile mixture which extended its influence into the grain industry and beyond.

The fateful result, wrote religious student William Magney, was that "the Christian calling was vested in the country's institutions in ways...that didn't occur in the US."

Earl's research unearthed another surprising fact. The fierce rhetoric attacking the grain trade in those early days was often wildly and wilfully inaccurate. The Social Gospellers' charges were often based only on imagined evils of the market system and capitalism.

He concluded that those events of the 1920s and later "shaped Canada's grain marketing system for the succeeding half century and shape it yet....The attitudes forged from those debates towards the operation of market forces affected a multitude of...subsequent policy decisions," decisions which go to the heart of today's Canada.

One devastating result was the shift of Canada's attention away from building on its huge resource base. The over-riding issue became an ideology which demanded the country's destiny be given over to Social Gospel-inspired politicians and all would be well.

Parts of the farm movement were not alone in putting their faith in the Social Gospel, a gospel that became deeply embedded in Canada's labour movement as well. According to historian W.L. Morton, the One Big Union (OBU) movement was then emerging internationally as "an attempt to organize labour industrially in one comprehensive union and to convert it to the doctrines of class war and Marxian socialism." He related that this OBU movement and the general strike idea seemed to offer the working class a direct path to better conditions and political power.

This coincided with a passionate and noisy infatuation among some labour leaders with events in Russia following the 1917 Bolshevik Revolution, and Morton added, "The Russian Revolution gave a great impetus to the radical elements in the OBU movement (and)...it also stimulated wild hopes among the immigrant Social Democrats."

These forces came together in a political witch's brew and one result was the historic convulsion described in Norman Penner's book, *Winnipeg 1919, The Strikers' Own History of the Winnipeg General Strike.* [1]

Penner relates that the Winnipeg Trades and Labour Council and the Socialist Party of Canada sponsored a boisterous meeting at Winnipeg's Walker Theatre in December, 1918. Labour activist Sam Blumenberg (who later went to the US rather than be deported) cried out at that meeting, "The Russian question (affects) the workers of the whole world."

When the meeting chairman called for three cheers for the Russian Revolution, he was answered with deafening cries of "Long Live the Russian Soviet Republic!" A labour paper headlined its report "Monster Mass Meeting Cheers the Russian Revolution."

Blumenberg addressed another Socialist Party meeting a month later in Winnipeg's Majestic Theatre and "called upon the returned soldiers, farmers and workers to unite and overthrow the capitalist system." Another speaker, in a fiery class-warfare address, shouted, "prices are controlled by trusts, combines, and banks and milling interests and grain exchanges and pork packers and all the long line of profiteers and parasites."

Within weeks, western members of the Trades and Labour Congress of Canada met in Calgary and laid out their demands: a five-day work week, a six-hour day and abolition of the production-for-profit system in favour of a system of production for use. These labour members were obsessed with events in Russia and they sent "fraternal greetings...to the Russian Soviet Government."

To prolonged cheers they proclaimed "full accord and sympathy with the aims and purposes of the Russian Bolshevik...Revolution," and absolute support for "the

---

[1] Penner writes, "Little was known about the theories of Lenin, whose works had not yet been translated, but there was a widespread feeling that Soviet Russia was a workers' government that should be supported." His book is published by James Lewis and Samuel, Toronto, 1973.

transformation of capitalistic private property to communal wealth."

They went on to approve the One Big Union idea and the General Strike idea intended to lead to labour's seizure of power.

Social gospelling pastors threw their every fibre into this campaign. William Ivens, Salem Bland, R.B. Russell and R.J. Johns attended that Calgary meeting. Ivens had been driven from the pulpit of the Methodist church because of his pacifist wartime views, while Salem Bland was active with the farmers' co-operatives. Russell was a labour radical and he became a strike leader. Johns was a fiery orator and leader of the OBU movement.

But before the One Big Union plan could be acted upon, the Winnipeg General Strike broke out, described by Morton as a "trade-union struggle for very specific economic demands...led by people representing all political tendencies in the Winnipeg Trades and Labour Council from Liberals and Conservatives to single taxers, to radical and revolutionary socialists."

Pastor Ivens had organized the Labour Church in the Labour Temple in July, 1918. Other branches were soon formed, and Sunday night open air Social Gospel church prayer meetings during the strike drew tens of thousands of people. They were addressed by pastors including A.E. Smith, J.S. Woodsworth and Canon Scott of Quebec to raise funds for needy strikers' families.

Ivens was also editing the daily *Strike Bulletin*, which headlined on June 9th, 1919, "Woodsworth Addresses 10,000 at Labour Church." His report went on to say "the greatest meeting ever held in this city was held in Victoria Park on Sunday night. For three hours some 10,000 people at the Labour Church listened with rapt attention to a masterpiece address on the economic situation from J.S. Woodsworth."

At another Labour Church meeting jammed with 8000 people, J.S. Woodsworth said the real test was brotherhood and he endorsed the principle of One Big Union and of One Big Church.

Former Manitoba Methodist Conference President Rev. A.E. Smith charged that it was now "next to impossible for a preacher to preach the genuine gospel of Christ in the churches." He said the Methodist Church had declared at its last General Conference for a radical reconstruction of society, getting rid of the competitive system and replacing it with the co-operative system. But he said the rich Church men had threatened to leave. His own answer was, "Let them go."

These Labour Church meetings raised $4500 for strike funds.

In that strike, added Morton, "the public services, the mails, telephone, street cars, telegraphs and milk deliveries were cut off at once." And this was only the start. "The growing animosity of the public was increased by the fears the Bolshevik seizure of power in Russia was arousing," Morton added.

With the strike at its height, Penner's book relates, Ivens was arrested on June 17th with seven others and "charged by the Government with seditious conspiracy to overthrow the state, etc." These men went before the Manitoba Assizes Court.

Morton summarized these and succeeding events powerfully in a single sentence: "More influential than the Marxian apostles of the OBU were the militant Methodist ministers William Ivens, Salem G. Bland and J.S. Woodsworth....These men, preaching a 'social gospel' drawn from Scripture, from the muckraking literature of the day and from their own evangelical creed, were prophesying a new age and a new order in which labour would come into its own and social justice prevail."

When the strike failed, these social gospellers went on to varied and sometimes unusual careers. Ivens was elected a member of the Manitoba Legislature in 1920 and served many terms. A.E. Smith was elected to the Manitoba Legislature in 1920 and later moved to Ontario where he was elected Ontario president of the Canadian Labour Party. He became a member of the Communist Party of Canada and was arrested in 1934 on a charge of sedition for a speech at Massey Hall in Toronto denouncing part of the Criminal Code. He was acquitted.

Sapiro "Played On That Audience Like An Artist "

But now the ghost of E.A. Partridge returned with a vengeance in an even more charismatic figure. A series of articles in *Grain Growers' Guide* in 1920 turned Western Canada's attention to an American who stumbled into selling farm products and soon became an international evangelist crying out for a marketing revolution.

An emotional frenzy seemed to continually swirl around him. On one occasion in 1922, 2500 farmers followed him through the streets of Abilene searching for a hall big enough to hear him speak.

This was Aaron Sapiro and word of his activities began reaching Canada from every direction. Ontario's agriculture minister Manning Doherty brought him to that province in 1922 to help organize dairymen. On Doherty's recommendations, UGG President Tom Crerar pressed provincial grain grower groups to invite him to speak on wheat marketing in January, 1923. That effort failed. The Farmers Union then asked him to come. Saskatchewan Grain Growers' Association secretary A.J. McPhail also urged his directors to bring in Sapiro.

The *Regina Morning Leader* got into the act as did the *Edmonton Journal.* The Calgary paper offered to sponsor a Sapiro tour. But the United Farmers' Henry Wise Wood was reluctant to have Sapiro in the province and later found he couldn't stand him.

A visit was finally organized and Sapiro came to Calgary and set out his stupendous dream before 3500 assembled farmers and townspeople. He told his audience that Canada was centre stage in world wheat, that prairie farmers held the world's wheat surplus in their hands and that they were the key to changing the world. He went on to three more speeches in Calgary and three more in Edmonton. He spoke to huge crowds in Lacombe and Camrose.

In Saskatchewan, no one had seen his like before - or his equal on a public platform. When he spoke at Third Avenue Methodist Church in Saskatoon on August 7, 1923, journalist Pat Waldron found no standing room within 100 feet of the large church when he arrived. Writing 50 years later, Waldron remembered him as the most inspiring, invigorating speaker he had every heard.

"He moved, he played on that audience like an artist," wrote Waldron. "He controlled their emotions, they yelled and cheered. He could do anything with them. I never saw anything to equal what Sapiro could do on a public platform."

Prairie author James Gray wrote of those early Sapiro visits, "In emotional impact, compelling logic and

sheer inspiration, he far outclassed those legendary re-
vivalists Billy Sunday and Aimee Semple McPherson."

Sapiro cried out to the crowds, "The farmer is the
only man in the world who spends all his time in production without ever thinking where or how or in what way
he is going to sell his product."

Yet he assured them they were only a few short steps
away from an organization that would give them decent
prices and control of their own destiny. And this would be
only the start of a worldwide transformation. His co-operative strategy had helped Kentucky's tobacco growers
break free of large tobacco corporations and take ownership of their own warehouses, raising their incomes by
800 percent. Waves of applause rolled over him.

"I tell you," he roared, "before two years are past,
there will be a pool of surplus wheat between the United
States, Canada, Australia and perhaps even Russia. Even
by itself, the Canadian pool would put 10 cents per bushel
more into the farmers' pockets, Canadian banks would
scramble to help finance a soundly based pool, and if they
didn't, American bankers would lend them the money."
Sapiro had no doubt that times were indeed changing, that
"earlier distributing and marketing systems will go. Men
will be wise to recognize and stand up to the new align-
ment. If not, they must also go."

Said one Saskatchewan Grain Growers' Association
official later, "Sapiro resembled a missionary...he passed
like a brilliant meteor from point to point, leaving behind
him as it were, a trail of light stretching like the tail of a
comet across the heavens."

Just who was this charismatic man? Aaron Sapiro[2]
was born in 1884 to a Jewish family so poor it had no
home. He was delivered on an aunt's kitchen table in
Oakland, California. By age six, he was on the streets selling newspapers and matches to help support the family.
At 10, his widowed and impoverished mother put Aaron
and three other children into an orphanage. Recalling

---

[2] Sapiro's story is told in detail in Garry Fairbairn's book, *From Prairie
Roots*. He served as artillery Sergeant-Major and officer trainee in World
War 1; Chairman of the National Legislative Committee of the American Legion, 1923; President of the Motion Picture Exhibitors Association, 1928; President of Journal Square National Bank, N.J., 1928;
and President of the Midtown Bank, 1929.

those desperate days later, Aaron said he was "...a puppet in a cold, unfeeling system that tended to squeeze the joy of living and the individuality out of any child."

He began to make his mark early, organizing small boys to fight off any bully who tried to pick on them individually. Sheer academic brilliance and intense study rescued him from poverty. He took eight years of rabbinical studies, then a law degree. He was appointed to the California markets board, learned about farm poverty and about agricultural co-operation. He co-authored a marketing bill that included radical ideas to battle poverty.

Then he drove himself hard, crisscrossing the country, speaking virtually everywhere, ignoring threatening letters from right-wing or anti-Jewish elements. He organized California prune and raisin growers; Washington apple producers; cotton farmers in Arkansas, Georgia, South Carolina and Albabama; dairy producers around Chicago; wheat growers in the northwest; potato farmers in Maine; tobacco growers in Kentucky; and others. His idea was adopted in 41 states. He became consulting counsel for farm groups with membership surpassing 650,000.

Pools had already been set up in the US for some farm crops, although these eventually disappeared. Serious articles in the Stanford Food Research Institute paper discussed national marketing organizations similar to the pools. Later the Institute would study the Canadian Pools.

Sapiro had come to show prairie farmers a way out of their gloom. And with his 1923 arrival, many caught his dream. The furious fight to bring pooling to Canada's wheat erupted with a vengeance. It would sweep the prairies, shaking and reshaping the country and catapulting its burgeoning wheat industry onto the world's political stage. It would also, at times, trigger massive reaction against some of these radical ideas.

The Furious Fight For Pooling -
A Mighty Crusade For Justice

Author Walter P. Davisson had no doubt at all. Wheat was the central factor in Canada's economy in those early days, and he wrote in his 1927 book, *Pooling Wheat In Canada*, "Winnipeg has been known as the greatest pri-

mary wheat market in the world...a greater volume of new
wheat direct from the producer, passes through the Winnipeg market than anywhere else, not even excepting
Chicago where the first grain exchange to reach international development was established in 1848."

Davisson saw the prairies as a huge and fast-growing world breadbasket and he said building it was "an awesome achievement in only 25 years," giving Canada an
"immense responsibility," calling it to "world leadership
in bread-grain....As the Wheat Crop goes, so goes the Dominion's commercial pulse." Booming wheat exports
showed "the dominant position of the Canadian west in
the Wheat world...indicates a vast prophecy of the Canada
of tomorrow!"

He saw the effort to set up a pool as a mighty crusade for justice, virtue, right - a reshaping of the role of
man - and he wrote, "the objective is a better distribution
of the wealth which comes up yearly out of those Prairie
farms." The rewards would be "happier homes and a
brighter and better rural citizenship!"

He seemed to scoff at the work of earlier pioneers
who had built the co-operative elevator systems, labelling
their achievements "the tender beginnings...(of)...an effort
to sell wheat as cleverly as it is purchased; to meeting
buying intelligence with selling intelligence; to counter
information and experience with information and experience - to put the growers on a trading parity with the men
who use their grain; a courageous attempt to close up the
wide chasm between the wheat dollars and the bread dollar."

He called the first wheat shipment through Vancouver Port on January 6, 1921, "the opening up of a vital
alternative grain-channel, almost synchronized with the
coming of The Pool Way....(and lowering)...the terrific
grain-pressure on the terminal spouts at the head of the
lakes...(and this) made the Orient strategically pervious
to Canadian grain."

Davisson cried out for a world wheat monopoly to
bring full justice to farmers, give them a fair market price,
and eliminate the evil private grain trade from the face of
Canada and perhaps beyond.

But it was Sapiro who lit the pooling torch and so
often carried it high. When grain prices hit disaster levels
in 1923, many farm leaders were intent on making the

Sapiro dream a reality. A provisional board of directors was named for the Saskatchewan Co-operative Wheat Producers (to become the Saskatchewan Wheat Pool) on August 25, 1923. It set the goal to sign up farmers to deliver half of the province's acreage - 6.1 million acres - into a pool to be sold collectively by farmers.

The campaign got a rousing reception. Banks, boards of trade, retail merchant associations, municipal councils and service clubs joined in. Newspapers got caught up in the crusade. Saskatchewan Grain Growers' Association secretary and farmer A.J. McPhail urged clergy to preach supporting sermons. Proponents launched *The Progressive* newspaper in August 1923 (renamed *The Western Producer* in 1924) as a propagandist organ and to publicize the sign-up campaign.

Sapiro's rules were clear, simple, uncompromising - the Pool must be non-profit, non-speculative, exclusively focused on one commodity. Absolute democracy meant one man, one vote. Directors must be chosen in geographically-defined districts to prevent centralized control. Every member would be "bound by a written contract more sacred than matrimony" to deliver all his wheat for a full five-year period. No operations would start until half the wheat acreage was locked up in such contracts.

He decreed that the Pool should own elevators as soon as possible and that there should be only one pool organization per province. The three provincial pools would sell their wheat through one central sales agency, forming one united powerful wheat pool.

No open opposition emerged in that 1923 campaign. But by the mid-September target date, contracts covered only 3.5 million acres, 29 percent of total wheat acres. The Saskatchewan campaign had failed.

When the Alberta sign-up drive concluded on September 5 just short of the 50 percent, MLA John Brownlee of the farmers' government there stepped in to help design the Alberta Wheat Pool's structure, and to draft its membership contract and the plan by which United Grain Growers and private elevator companies would handle Pool wheat. The Alberta government gave guarantees to banks financing the Pool, and elevator companies fell into line. Everything was ready to go for the 1923 crop and it started operations on October 29.

In Saskatchewan the Pool directors decided to struggle on, trying for the 50 percent target. Crerar's UGG contributed $5000 to help out and the Saskatchewan government put in $45,000. With momentum from Sapiro's first visit subsiding, the provisional Pool board overcame some internal squabbling and invited Sapiro to return in early 1924.

But then the *Regina Morning Leader* launched a series of articles attacking Sapiro for supposed fraud and dishonesty, and condemning the pool idea. The *Edmonton Morning Bulletin* ran scathing attacks, calling the Sapiro idea a financial dictatorship which would concentrate unbelievable economic power in the hands of a few pool directors.

When Sapiro returned to answer the charges, thousands had to be turned away from Regina's Metropolitan Church on February 20, 1924, and from further meetings in Saskatoon, Kindersley and Weyburn. He described how his work for co-operatives had brought him death threats and health problems and he said he had not received a penny beyond expenses for his gruelling 1923 prairie tour.

He urged the farmers on with their pool idea and said farm leaders throughout North America expected a Canada-US-Australia-New Zealand pool to be organized within three years, with a joint Liverpool sales agency that might also handle Argentine wheat. If and when that office were set up, he boasted, "it would name the price of wheat for the entire world production."

But dissenting voices warned that such a world monopoly was unlikely and would bring strong response from consuming nations.

Sapiro proceeded to sue the *Leader* which settled with him out of court two years later, retracted its stories and printed an apology. A Royal Commission drew Sapiro to Winnipeg on April 28, 1924 and he was forced to recant statements that Alberta Pool members were getting eight cents a bushel more than their neighbours. He also admitted a Canadian wheat pool alone would be unable to control world prices. But that Commission also boosted the pool campaign when a Port Arthur terminal manager said his terminal shipped out 1.8 million bushels more Number 1 wheat than it received, thanks to the profitable practice of mixing grades.

The Alberta Pool was now operating profitably, bypassing the Winnipeg Grain Exchange and selling 80 percent of its wheat directly to export customers. In Manitoba the sign-up campaign ended on April 1, with less than 30 percent of the acreage, but organizers went ahead to set up a pool for the 1924 crop.

The Saskatchewan sign-up campaign continued through winter and spring. Farmers were apprehensive about a contract clause stating Pool directors could order a farmer to deliver his wheat any time, any place; they had to take on faith that directors would be reasonable. When the campaign went over the top on June 16, 1924, hitting the 50 percent mark, Saskatchewan Wheat Pool set up its democratic membership structure and put in a Regina office. New president A.J. McPhail resigned as secretary of the Grain Growers' Association on 16 August and delegates were elected from across the province. Then 16 directors were elected to the permanent board.

Saskpool's Rambunctious Start - Speculation - Near Disaster

Exhilarated by their achievement and by the challenge ahead, and certain of the rightness of their cause, directors of the three Pools set out to get elevators of their own to handle their grain. An attempt to purchase UGG with its prairie-wide elevator system failed, for its delegates had earlier decided to continue in business, offering farmers an alternative.

SaskPool then signed an agreement on August 24 to market its grain through UGG. To get more control, it turned to the Saskatchewan Co-operative Elevator Company to handle some as well, but its directors were soon outraged to find the Co-op charged one cent more a bushel than the privately-owned line elevators. When their attempt to buy the Co-op was rejected, the Pool began building its own elevators, opening its first one on July 1, 1925. When it released its first annual report in October, it had 86 elevators built or bought on a cash basis.

Meanwhile another watershed event was playing itself out in Alberta when a "well-mannered back-stairs revolt" led to Premier Greenfield's retirement in November, 1925. The precocious John Brownlee replaced him and was soon asked to help in this dispute between SaskPool and the Co-op. The pragmatic Brownlee urged compromise. "Have the Pool manage the Co-op elevators!" But the Pool demanded control.

When the three Pools met for talks with UGG, SaskPool "demanded" (as reported in *'From Prairie Roots'*) the older Cooperative drastically cut service to farmers who were not Pool members. UGG's answer was a resounding "No." It insisted on serving all farmers "without discrimination." The three Pools tried again in late 1926 to buy UGG elevators but delegates to the UGG annual meeting rejected the offer by a four-to-one margin. Continuing competition between UGG and the Pools was now certain.

Sapiro was still being consulted by the Pools and he now urged SaskPool to try again to buy the Saskatchewan Co-operative elevator system. At a special meeting in late 1925 the Co-op delegates finally fell in line and the Pool purchased it in early 1926 to become the province's major grain handler with 451 elevators, two Lakehead terminals, a transfer terminal at Buffalo and a lease on a third Lakehead terminal.

The expansion-minded Pools now found a clause in members' contracts authorizing them to retain up to two cents on every bushel of wheat sold. They used this money to begin building their own elevators. Pool historian Walter P. Davisson called this deduction "a giant builder of money reserves," adding that from four crops "including the 1926 crop, the organized growers of Prairie Canada have paid in a total of $10 million."

Pool leaders were now determined to finally escape the Grain Exchange and the private trade. Again they turned to John Brownlee and in a fateful move that would trouble prairie farmers and provincial and federal governments for years to come, he helped draft an agreement setting up the Central Selling Agency (CSA) in July 1924 to sell grain direct to buyers. Each Pool got an equal number of directors.

CSA began selling Pool grain into an uncertain market. It was soon bypassing the Winnipeg Grain Exchange, sending every possible bushel direct to export customers and domestic millers. But it still had to sell some remaining grain through the Exchange and the futures market. In deciding when to sell there, it was inevitably speculating. Some Pool leaders wanted it to go further, buying speculatively at times to firm or boost market prices. This caused more conflict. CSA sales agent D.L. Smith favoured occasionally buying wheat futures to slow sharp price declines. Cautious and puritanical agency head A.J. McPhail (who was also SaskPool president) accepted limited use of such tactics, but insisted the job was to keep wheat moving toward consumers, not to speculate seeking large profits.

In speculating at all, the Pools were living dangerously. Prices were slipping in early 1925. Alberta's Henry Wise Wood opposed selling below $2 a bushel, urging at a January 31 CSA directors' meeting that the agency buy May futures. Exchange prices fell to $1.88 by March 7. Wood wanted to buy futures instead of reducing agency selling prices, hoping to profit as prices bounced back. By April 3, prices were down to $1.38, just three cents above what the Pool had paid farmers. The situation was ominous. The Pools' future hung by a thread. The CSA stepped in the next day and bought speculatively for six weeks.

Then fortune smiled. The price turned. Winnipeg prices rose quickly to $1.69. A mighty sigh of relief was almost audible from the agency, the Pools and the farm community. The agency made a profit of $485,508 on its futures trading. But it had tasted the future.

By 1927, with the CSA's efforts in danger of faltering, its president A.J. McPhail set off to Europe accompanied by Premier John Brownlee to consider opening CSA offices there. Brownlee's cool eye observed many things. A practical man rather than an ideologist, he came home with a frank and ominous assessment - the CSA could have made more sales by dropping prices five or six cents.

A World Wheat Pool? - The Big
Dream Dies - Price Collapse

That magnificent orator Aaron Sapiro had stirred the souls of many growers when he cried out, "The wheat pooling movement of the world cannot be started anywhere else except in Canada. You are the key to the surplus exports of the world," adding, "the one place where it ought to be done...is Saskatchewan where you raise more than one-half of all Canada's wheat."

Western growers were now on the world's centrestage, their time of destiny seemed to have arrived. A world pool was within their grasp. In a sense, the world's fate was in their hands.

Pool directors planned a world conference of wheat growers' associations "to consider what might be done," a euphemism for seizing control of all wheat and ratcheting up prices. But that goal was to prove elusive. Leaders of the three Canadian Pools set out for a first International Wheat Pool Conference in St. Paul, Minnesota in early 1926. Four Pools from Australia and 10 from the US were represented, along with two observers from the Soviet Union. The Central Selling Agency's directors displayed unbounded optimism, seeing no limit on what could be accomplished.

Henry Wise Wood thundered, "These three great English-speaking countries can raise the price of wheat at least 50 percent...without the assistance of any other country." Manitoba Pool director W.G.A. Gourlay added, "The object of this pool is to raise the price of wheat."

But caution prevailed, the moment of triumph was delayed. Delegates agreed only to hold another meeting the next year. And the run-up to that second conference in Kansas City in 1927 hit an unexpected roadblock. The previous year's talk of boosting prices had set alarm bells ringing overseas. Mussolini himself had called a meeting in Rome to seek ways to boost European wheat output to counter any world pool. Now, in Kansas City, Henry Wise Wood gave up on the dream, admitted it would be impractical to merge the world's wheat pools into a centrally managed unit. The dream was dead.

By the time of the third International Wheat Pool Conference in Regina in 1928, Sapiro's vision of a giant world pool had collapsed. Yes, the Pools "controlled" a tenth of world wheat trade - half of Canada's one-fifth share. But to suggest they could control prices was a pipe dream. The only way was to hold wheat off the market, and this would see foreign and domestic competitors take over.

Yet enthusiasm for the pooling idea seemed undiminished in Canada. Ontario-pooled wheat came into the CSA in 1927. But when the CSA set up a London office in a move to bypass European traders and make direct sales, a storm of international opposition erupted. Proclaimed the *Birmingham Gazette*, "Housewives will Not Benefit," charging that any savings from direct sales would not be passed on to British consumers. British co-operatives saw the move as high-handed and the Pools as "food trusts organized to oppress the consumer," according to a Canadian there.

Growing divisions surfaced in Canada too. One author grumbled, "Orderly marketing...is one of the popular catch phrases of the co-operative charlatan."

Yet the Canadian public was increasingly fascinated with the wheat industry's high profile and rapid growth and the foreign earnings it brought in, began to see the Pools as a new giant on the scene.

Maclean's called it, "The colossus of the prairies...an infant prodigy" sprung from "the dreams of prairie farmers." The magazine labelled their joint elevator system "a veritable Gargantua, the like of which mankind has never seen." It noted that pool wheat now accounted for a big part of world wheat trade, waxed, "In five years, the pool has made the Man Behind the Plow the mightiest merchant in this Dominion."

For a brief shining moment, it seemed the prairie farmer had finally won a favoured place in society. Some farm leaders let their optimism run wild. An over-zealous Manitoba Pool director declared, "We are going to put fur coats and silk stockings on every farm woman."

SaskPool supporters called on Sapiro again to launch a "100 percent Pool" campaign in a series of July, 1927 speeches. The aim was to get legislation forcing every farmer in the province to deliver to the Pool. Sapiro obliged, crying out that so long as any wheat remained outside the Pool, it could be used to damage the majority's interests.

In February, 1929, Alberta's United Farmers' convention voted decisively for compulsory pooling legislation. But in June, even Pool delegates rejected compulsion by 120 votes to 25. In September, an Alberta Royal Commission on grain condemned the compulsory pool idea. Within days, Sapiro was back ridiculing "the Umbrella Man," the non-pool farmer who would "sneak under the pool umbrella in bad weather," but wouldn't help hold up the umbrella. That campaign was never concluded.

Relations between UGG, with its unshakeable commitment to personal freedom for farmers, and other cooperatives were strained to breaking. Saskatchewan cooperative leaders accused UGG of not being a "real" co-operative. When consumer co-operatives attacked UGG's role as a purchasing service for farmers, UGG officials labelled it a "routine of petty persecutions," and took the farmers' company out of the Co-operative Union of Canada in 1929.

The impossible dream of a world pool had died a noisy

death. But now another vastly more sinister event loomed. Heavy shipments of low-priced Argentine wheat flooded onto the market early in 1929. On May 7th, prices broke eight cents in one day. A US wheat surplus was growing. To slow the price decline, the Pools' Central Selling Agency again dipped its toe into the black waters of speculation, held back its own wheat and bought wheat futures.

It was a fateful and curious move. At the heart of the Social Gospel faith was absolute rejection of the marketplace. Yet here was the CSA speculating in that "evil" place.

Surpluses piled up. Other countries sold into the market. The moment of truth was at hand.

In July, the CSA set an initial price of $1 a bushel for the coming 1929 crop which turned out to be a desperately short one. On August 31, the CSA owed $68.2 million to banks and $6.7 million to the three Pools. It held wheat valued at $105.3 million. Canada's grain supply was rising. The CSA refused to sell. Sapiro predicted in a Regina speech September 20 that the crop carryover into the next year would be "sold at a magnificent price with a profit."

Black Tuesday hit with devastating fury on October 29th, 1929, bringing financial chaos. Stock market prices dropped, banks collapsed, fortunes were lost. The CSA held on through the new year and into summer, fighting to stave off bankruptcy. European buyers had no sympathy. The *London Daily Herald* wrote on March 20, 1930, that the National Association of British Millers was fighting "one of the most ruthless world wars in commercial history" against "the price-fixing attempts of the American and Canadian Pools."

There was now no escape. The Pools buckled and sold wheat left over from the 1929-30 pool. Returns were unlikely to cover even the initial payment on the 1930-31 pool. The Pools' Central Selling Agency was essentially bankrupt.

Prime Minister R.B. Bennett's new government was hardly sworn in in August, 1930, before the three western premiers as well as CSA Head A.J. McPhail, were in his office seeking federal guarantees. The provinces continued their support for the CSA, but the situation deteriorated further.

Bennett approved a bail-out - an Ottawa guarantee

of half of any bank loss up to $10 million. To placate those banks, he named veteran grain trader John I. McFarland general manager of the Central Sales Agency. The Pools' humiliation was now complete. Their CSA was virtually a government agency.

Sapiro's big dream that had fuelled the euphoria and the purpose of Pool leaders and others for so long had collapsed, perhaps proven to be a hoax. Many of those Pool leaders had developed a lasting distaste for this man who in so many ways had been their spiritual leader. They accused him of stirring up trouble, of championing internal critics from 1924 to 1929. The question was raised, had he really been a charlatan all the time?

Another side of Sapiro soon began to emerge. Publicity swirled around his high fees, his legal work for a Chicago laundry-owners' association dominated by Al Capone, his New York state disbarment on charges of witness tampering and his later career dabbling as a middleman in the shadowy world of high finance.

Appalling Ignorance - Hounded Out Of The Movement

In his Social Gospel thesis, Paul Earl found that farm leaders who led the attack on capitalism often turned on any of their own members who didn't live up to their crusade as they saw it. But they sometimes were hard-pressed to document their case. J.B. Musselman, for example, had been a director of the Saskatchewan Cooperative Elevator Company. He wrote articles in the *Grain Growers' Guide* explaining futures markets. But, wrote Earl, in the view of co-operative leaders "he failed...to condemn the open market in terms (co-operative leaders) thought it deserved...and thus lacked ideological purity."

Because of this failure, Musselman was "hounded out of the movement." When he retired from the Co-operative board in 1925, Musselman cited a "campaign of misrepresentation, innuendo and vilification" which had been carried on against him for several years. The Grain Exchange had been "the central target" of those attacking Musselman and in their wrath, they ignored his "objective accounts."

George Langley had been a vice-president of that

Saskatchewan Co-operative Elevator Company. He had also been a member of two Royal Commissions and, wrote Earl, was "presumably knowledgeable about the industry's workings." In campaigning to set up the Saskatchewan Pool, Langley claimed that if Western Canada's farmers had sold the previous year's crop through their own Pool direct to Liverpool, instead of at Winnipeg, they would have received $27 million more for it. He accused the Winnipeg grain man, the middle man, of getting this difference.

When challenged, he offered an explanation that undoubtedly revealed the thinking of most of those who then hated the Exchange. He testified, "A member of the Exchange told me that for every seller, there was a buyer. Mr. Chairman, I have never believed it. I believe there is an arrangement by which operators on the Exchange can sell without having a buyer. I have held that opinion for many years."

The grain trade called Langley's statements incorrect and a grave reflection on every grain-trading concern. The Stanford Food Research Institute analyzed the spreads between the two markets from April 1921 to November, 1925, and according to Earl, their charts showed "no consistent price spread between the two markets to give exporters a guaranteed return over the costs of transportation and handling, as the Pool leaders had claimed." He found that neither Langley nor anyone else ever presented "a shred of evidence" to support that claim nor a theory as to how such a system would work.

Earl had worked in the grain industry for years and he suggested that futures marketing is much simpler than is commonly supposed. "The 'mystery' the farmers seemed to see in the futures market," he wrote, "arose because farmers failed to inform themselves about its workings and often expressed the most appalling ignorance of the institution they condemned."

He added that "the contrast between the fiery accusations of manipulation and dishonesty made to the 1931 Royal Commission and some of the almost bumbling responses to the questions of clarifications posed in cross-examination" were quite embarrassing.

Earl identified one more profound consequence of the attack on capitalism. When the Pools were being set up, their leaders advanced their case with a fierce "moral fervour," and acted with a "self-righteousness" bordering on fanaticism. He said the Pools' attempts to buy UGG elevators showed that "self-righteous intolerance...lay behind the Pools' adamant refusal to see Pool wheat and non-Pool wheat occupy the same elevators." And this led Pool leaders "to cling to a set of theories about the futures market that did not stand up to scrutiny...and it led them to ignore all the evidence that their marketing operations did not do what they claimed they did."

Earl said the importance of this ongoing attack on capitalism can hardly be overestimated. "The events of the 1920s and 1930s shaped Canada's grain marketing system for the succeeding half century, and shape it yet in the enduring presence of the Canadian Wheat Board." And this "burdened (farmers and industry) with costs at the very time the industry should be at its most lean."

He added, "The attitudes forged from those debates towards the operation of market forces affected a multitude of other subsequent policy decisions...explained why the handling and transportation system has been so slow to evolve towards...larger elevators and more efficient use of rail facilities."

Thus Canada had diverged dramatically from the United States. As J.H Nichols[3] wrote, "By the mid-thirties the most conspicuous feature of the American theological scene was revolt from 'social gospel' liberalism, without diminution of Christian social responsibility and action."

---

[3] *History of Christianity, 1650-1950*, by James Hastings Nichols, Professor of Church History, University of Chicago. The Ronald Press Company, New York, 1956.

5

POOL DECEPTION -
DEPRESSION'S ONSLAUGHT -
GRAIN AND WAR

What! Cheating Grain Companies?

Manitoba's Premier John Bracken was working to soften the onslaught of depression in 1931 when he received an open letter that quickly flared into a political firestorm.[1] Fallout from it offered some astonishing insights into happenings in the province and the country.

The letter-writer charged that the Manitoba Wheat Pool had been "foisting...the most expensive system of country elevators ever built in Western Canada on farmers" who had been "inveigled into forming elevator associations...by hopes impossible of fulfilment."

He accused the Pool of paying for the resulting financial losses by overdocking, short weights and undergrading, and by excessive overages and special year-end charges. And the Pool had concealed from farmers the true costs of the elevator system and the losses "by lavish expenditure of money (extracted from the farmers) on propaganda work." Further, he charged, after 1928 its "financial statements...have not been filed with the Registrar of Co-operative Societies" as required by law.

The letter suggested it was "a fair assumption the Pool management was afraid to have the 1929 and 1930 figures analyzed."

Here was an amazing charge. For years some farm groups had been waging an intensive campaign accusing

---

[1] As reported by Paul D Earl in his 1992 PhD thesis for the University of Manitoba.

private elevator companies of failing to provide fair weights and grades. Now this letter said the Pool was guilty of those very misdeeds and more.

And the letter-writer was not some crackpot. He was Vice President and General Manager J.R. Murray of Alberta Pacific Grain Company. Murray had won respect earlier as General Manager of United Grain Growers and as secretary of the Winnipeg Grain Exchange. He would later be asked by Prime Minister Mackenzie King to take over as Chief Commissioner, Canadian Wheat Board.

An irate Manitoba Pool President C.H. Burnell demanded an inquiry to clear the Pool's name.

Premier Bracken was an Ontario-born and educated agricultural scientist who had gone west in those early years and become a professor at the University of Saskatchewan and then at the Manitoba Agricultural College. He gained prominence writing books on scientific farming and he joined Tom Crerar's Progressive movement. (Years later, in 1942, he would be named national Conservative leader but not before insisting the party blunt its right-wing, big business image by adding the prefix "Progressive" to its name.)

By 1931 Bracken had risen to the political heights. He was a cautious man, but he responded to this letter quickly and decisively. Within five days he named Winnipeg lawyer and University of Manitoba lecturer Esten Kenneth Williams, KC, a Royal Commission to investigate those charges.

Williams found that, yes, the Pool had built a system of elevators that were larger and more elaborately equipped and hence much more costly than was intended by the elevator policy; that the resulting financial losses were indeed being covered by overdocking, short weights and undergrading; and that the accounts provided to the local associations concealed from members the proportion of the elevators' costs covered by overages and grade gains. He found a final charge that the farmers could have received a better deal at competing elevators was vague and not proven.

Williams noted that the whole structure of the Pool organizations was said to be based on service at cost, and concluded, "Mr. Murray would seem to be justified in his assumption that for some reason the Pool management did not wish to have the figures analyzed."

The Manitoba Pool slammed that scathing report as a slur on its good name by an urbanite who simply didn't understand what the Pool was all about.

Curiously, while this was going on, another startling event caught media headlines. With the failure of their Central Selling Agency, the debt-laden Pools were seeking some villain to blame and had been attacking the line elevator companies, searching for evidence of Exchange "skulduggery" and demanding an investigation.

Sir Josiah Stamp was an economist, chairman of a British railway and a Bank of England director. [2] He had successfully chaired two Royal Commissions in Britain. Prime Minister Bennett now lured him to Canada and set up the Stamp Royal Commission to unearth how both the Grain Exchange and the Wheat Pools carried on business.

In Stamp's 1931 hearings, Exchange lawyer Isaac Pitblado presented a Reader's Digest condensation of an article written by SaskPool's public relations head which talked about manipulation on the Exchange and charged "Skulduggery has been practised in the market to depreciate the value of the Pool's wheat supplies." Pitblado asked SaskPool President A.J. McPhail if he hadn't had three representatives on the Exchange since the Pool had been in existence?

"Yes" replied McPhail.

Pitblado asked if any of them had found evidence of this skulduggery which his public relations man referred to.

They had made "no definite report," answered McPhail. Nor had they made any complaints to the Council of the Exchange.

The Pools, in fact, had no evidence to support their charges of Exchange wrongdoing, and Stamp reported he could find no evidence at all of unfair Exchange practices.

These findings of the Williams and the Stamp commissions were a devastating repudiation of some Pool activities. Paul Earl concluded "The Williams commission... proved that the Pool engaged in undergrading and overdocking which the farm movement had condemned in the private trade for three decades...(that it) had concealed these practices, and had not been fully open and honest with its members on the Pool financial results which these

---

[2] As reported in A Century of Grain, by C.F. Wilson.

practices were used to hide."

Earl added that Pool officers and directors "had gained sufficient power to practice a deception against farmers from which they personally stood to gain...and they had succumbed to the temptation to do so." They had, in fact, "confused self-interest with the broader interests of society" and from 1924 on, while fighting to do away with futures trading on the Winnipeg Grain Exchange, "the three wheat pools conducted a sustained polemic against the grain trade and its practices," focusing on the Exchange itself.

Finally, said Earl, Pool advocates "claimed a centralized marketing body would do a superior job of price discovery and would share the risks of price change among grain producers." But when the results from this marketing agency were found wanting, "they either ignored it (as with the Stanford work) or reviled their opponents (as they did constantly in the debate on who got the better price,) or denied that such comparisons were valid (as they did with the Williams Commission.)"

"To some extent," Earl concluded, "the Pools sold their ideas on the very premises that they elsewhere scorned." He asked rhetorically why Manitoba Pool members were not outraged at Williams' findings, and why had they not deserted the Pool in droves?

His response undoubtedly explains it all. Pool achievements were not trivial, he wrote. "They built powerful organizations which handled about half the Western wheat crop and over which they exercised democratic control," and which gave them strong voices in the ongoing grain policy debates about how much individual freedom would be allowed in the grain system. And through these, "they gained the confidence and status which SaskPool President A.J. McPhail had so perceptively identified. Control over the source of their livelihood and the dignity to stand as something other than a hapless price-taker was the real issue."

Farmers wanted a "social position...a pride of place," so they stood by their Pools, said Earl.

Crerar Retires To Politics -
Law, From The Spice Trade To Depression, War

The spotlight had focused on the Pools in the turbulent years leading up to the 1930s. But the Crerar-led United Grain Growers had continued to build, gaining controlling interest in Vancouver's Burrard Terminal in 1926 to get access to the Pacific markets and then putting up its large Terminal "A" at Fort William in 1927.

A miserable short crop was hardly in the bins in 1929 when the Wall Street crash hit North America and the world. The Great Drought was on and Depression lay ahead. The virtual collapse of the Pools' Central Selling Agency in 1930 further signalled the fearful times to come. Prairie farmers and their companies would be challenged as never before.

Tom Crerar had served as UGG's president/general manager for 23 years, and now, on January 16, 1930, 10 weeks after the Wall Street crash, he decided it was time for new leadership. He resigned.[3]

---

[3] Crerar returned to public life and was named Minister of Railways and Canals in the Mackenzie King government. That government was defeated nine months later by R.B. Bennett, but with King's 1935 re-election, Crerar returned as a cabinet minister and held that rank until 1945. Then he was named to the Senate where he continued as an unrelenting political activist.

But what was this man who served Western farmers and his country for so long, really like? "He was genuine through and through," said a later UGG president, Mac Runciman. "He had the knack of being friendly, genial, without being phoney. He was a man of substance and influence. If he had been a small man, he would have been dapper. But he was rangy and gaunt. He dressed well for he liked to look well.

"He and his wife travelled to Britain for the Coronation of George V. He had the required clothes tailored for the occasion and on my first visit to his house, he took pride in having his wife bring out that finery to show me.

"And," recalls Runciman with some satisfaction, "Crerar would reminisce more freely about his work with UGG than about his life in politics. He attached more significance to it."

Honours cascaded in on Crerar in later years. His leadership of the Progressive party, which he had taken reluctantly, had been criticized vigorously by many. But he had taken it to Ottawa in 1921 as a free trade party and he was not one to shift his views with the political winds. When it became clear that some of its members had a different agenda, he and others decided there was no continuing role for their Progressives. The party fractured, and he and his group went back with the Liberals. Some of his political supporters accused him of betrayal. But his position has stood the test of time.

UGG Vice-President R.S. Law was an English-born scion of an old family in the tea and spice trade. He had agricultural interests early in life and had become a local official of a major English farm group. He came to Canada as a young married man in 1911, farmed at Claresholm, Alberta, for 10 years, served as a director of the Alberta Farmers' Co-operative Elevator Company for two and managed the Claresholm Co-operative Farm Supplies Company for a time.

UGG directors spotted Law's impressive record, brought him on board, and he was later named secretary, then Vice-President. He won the directors' confidence and they named him President.

Law was honest, low-key and deliberate. His first annual report to members in November, 1930, came at a fiercely difficult time. After the bumper 1928 crop, the short 1929 crop had halved UGG's grain handlings. The company had also lost money carrying unhedged grain. Drought was beating in on growers. Prices on the Winnipeg Exchange broke to 37 1/2 cents on Dec. 13, 1932, the lowest recorded on the international market in 400 years and a price at which prairie farmers would receive nothing at the elevator. [4]

Crerar was later named a director of several companies. He was the first politician to be named companion of the Order of Canada (1974.) And he became the senior Privy Councillor in the British Commonwealth (The Privy Council is a body of officials and dignitaries chosen by the British monarch as an advisory council to the Crown.)

A 90-year-old Tom Crerar was invited back to speak at UGG's annual dinner in 1966. Then-president Runciman, who introduced him, remembered the evening vividly years later. "Crerar was the only survivor of the pioneers who founded the company. He was still energetic and lively. He described the events of his early life, and the totally unacceptable conditions in grain marketing and the spirit of the men who founded UGG.

"His memory was sharp, he spoke with passion and his words were spell-binding."

In Runciman's view, there would be no United Grain Growers today had it not been for Crerar. "His leadership enabled the little company to grow and achieve so many of the farmers' goals. People recognized his qualities and tried to use them as UGG President and as a cabinet minister in two wars. But he has never been fully recognized for the power he wielded in building Canada."

---

[4] *The Canada Year Book,* 1932, reports, "The average price per bushel received by growers for their wheat in 1931 was estimated at 38 cents, compared with 49 cents in 1930 and $1.05 in 1929."

As Law and his board faced depression's onslaught and a squeeze to more frugal operations, stories of hardship and worse were coming out of every community. One farmer recalled later taking "a jag of wheat" to the elevator that December and receiving a little over $7 for 60 bushels, or 11 cents per bushel.

A gallows humour story told of a farmer who delivered a wagonload of barley to the elevator only to be told by the agent that handling and freight deductions totalled more than the barley was worth and that the farmer owed him 50 cents. Lacking the money, the farmer agreed to bring in a dressed chicken to square the account.

When he returned in a few days with two dressed chickens, the agent said, "I told you I would settle for one chicken."

"Yes, but I brought in another load of barley today," he replied.

Big new government bureaucracies were inevitable to deal with this catastrophe. And the UGG Board had to intensify its efforts to give government its best advice to help the West and Canada meet that crisis. It resisted the cry of some farm groups for more government controls and blamed the wheat problem on lack of markets, not on failing marketing machinery. It opposed restrictions on farmers' freedoms except in emergencies, saying wheat required attention separate from domestic food products because it was an export crop.

Instead of controls, Law asked for government-guaranteed advance payments to wheat growers. And he urged Ottawa to create a board with power to buy and sell wheat and to underwrite its operations and any losses.

Conditions were desperate in the summer of 1935 and when an army of unemployed marching from the West to Ottawa paused in Regina, a riot broke out. A policeman was killed and 42 other persons were injured. The R.B. Bennett government, in one of its final acts, legislated a Canadian Wheat Board with unlimited power over the grain trade. But the bill didn't save his government. The next year, UGG urged the Mackenzie King government to "Retain the Wheat Board! But leave farmers free to sell to the Board or on the open market."

By early 1937, Mr. Justice Turgeon was conducting a grain inquiry and the unpretentious R.S. Law, absolutely untainted by the siren song of the social gospellers, was in the witness box. His testimony fascinated *Winnipeg Free Press* reporter J.B. McGeachy who perhaps caught the real drama of those times:

"Mr. Law farmed in glorious Devon before coming to Canada in 1911, which would account for his slow soft speech," wrote McGeachy. He noted that UGG did not pool wheat, and went on "Mr. Law's idea is that pooling is for farmers who don't want to do their own selling, don't want to take a chance in the market and will be content with the season's average price - say $1.25 if the market ranges from $1.50 to $1.00 in a crop year.

"The trouble is, in Mr. Law's opinion...the pools of 1924 departed from this sound and simple thought...."

"The non-poolers, Mr. Law and the UGG insist, must be left free to sink or swim at their own risk. There must be no coercion of them....But Mr. Law also thinks the Dominion should guarantee a minimum price - not to the poolers only, but to all farmers - as it now does.

"Mr. Law has been a unique witness," McGeachy reported. "He is the first to say that he is no authority on the grain trade. He is the first to announce that he does not know the answer to the farm problem. Mr. Law's disclaimer of both expertise and wisdom, from which he could not be budged by questions, proved a little baffling to counsel.

"Mr. MacPherson, KC, counsel for Saskatchewan pool elevators, tackled him on his point...that pool marketing should be available to farmers who want it...Mr. Law had suggested that a pool's objective should be to get the average price which it could do by selling the same amount of wheat every week in the year. Was this, asked Mr. MacPherson, a practical plan? Could any pool really operate on this basis? Would such a pool, in short, be a sinking or a swimming pool?

"Mr. Law in reply said he really had no idea. This endeared Mr. Law to observers who had been listening to experts for a month but it mildly exasperated Mr. MacPherson. Mr. Law's position, however, looked sound. He noted that James R. Murray, one of the original inventors of the 1924 wheat pools, believes a 10 percent pool could work whereas George W. Robertson, a pool official since the start, thinks only a 100 percent pool will be any good.

"'When experts disagree,' says Mr. Law, 'how should

I know, in view of the fact that I've no experience at all in pool business?'"

Meanwhile, a better 1938 crop signalled the drought was ending. But world prices were low. War broke out in Europe and the 1939 crop soared to nearly half a billion bushels, the second largest on record. A mounting grain pileup threatened prices and challenged the entire industry. Western farm leaders including Law met with Ottawa and fought hard to hold a 70-cent initial price for the 1939-40 crop year and thus stave off a disaster.

With war raging, UGG launched a huge building program to help handle the growing grain carryover. It built 357 temporary country annexes with over 10.5 million bushels' capacity by 1941, and added two terminal annexes, each holding two million bushels. Two years later, with wheat markets in occupied countries shut off, the carryover ballooned to nearly 600 million bushels.

Mackenzie King's government responded by closing the futures market and directing the Wheat Board to take over as an instrument of government policy. When wheat reached $1.23 1/2 at Lakehead on September 27, 1943. The Board bought all unsold wheat in commercial positions at about $1.25 and continued buying until July 31, 1945.

At war's end, the industry faced the monumental challenge of feeding the world's hungry. Surpluses ebbed and by mid-1945 most of UGG's annexes were empty. The big Lakehead annexes were scrapped the next year. The British Wheat Agreement was signed and Ottawa acted to guarantee a minimum price of $1 up to July 31, 1950.

By 1948, R.S. Law's financial and management skills had carried the company through depression, war and the impact of wartime taxation. It had dealt with nearly 600 wartime orders-in-council affecting the grain crop; had dealt with two surpluses piling up and the building of massive emergency grain storage space; and had counselled government on ways to protect the farmers' interests and urged policies by which farmers could contribute fully to the war effort. The company's financial structure withstood the test of those times.

Law had served as president for 18 years and played a crucial role in building the company, the industry and the prairies. But now his health was failing. At his 1948 retirement, Ottawa was ending price controls, freeing up the tightly-regulated economy, confronting farmers and grain companies with the full shock of inflation - and higher costs. Bumper crops and surpluses were ushering in a time of momentous change.

Brownlee's Political Career Ends In 'Scandal,' A New One Begins - Massive Post-War Expansion

When Ottawa brought Saskatchewan and Alberta into Confederation in 1905, it diverged from earlier practises, retaining its control over their public lands and thus over their enormous resources wealth - oil, minerals, forests and agriculture. Alberta's farmers' Premier John Brownlee had taken office in 1925, and the long-headed lawyer-politician knew these resources were the bedrock of the Western economy. If the region was to prosper, Ottawa's grip would have to be broken.

Brownlee showed the way, drafting an historic agreement to transfer control over Alberta's resources from Ottawa to the province. He negotiated it and signed it December 14, 1929. It changed the country's destiny. One need only ask, "Without that agreement, could Alberta and the West have had their energy and resources booms? And their breathtaking economic development in post-war years? And could they have made their massive contribution to building Canada?"

But as depression slammed into the prairies in the 1930s bringing misery and frustration, the cautious Premier held to fiscal restraint. Voter disenchantment with his conservative aid programs grew. And now a messiah named William Aberhart proclaimed a Social Credit doctrine. Brownlee became a lonely voice against this new tide. He was further undermined by a charge under the Alberta Seductions Act. He left office in 1934. The United Farmers of Alberta government was devastated in 1935.

Brownlee's trial grabbed national headlines and was confusing in the extreme. Many believed the charge was nothing more than political dirty work. A later UGG president A. M. Runciman, who worked closely with Brownlee and got to know him well, recalled him as a family man devoted to his wife.

"He was charged under an Alberta seduction law, not a Federal law, with seducing this Vivian McMillan on various dates," recalled Runciman. "Yet it was revealed without contradiction that on a number of occasions Mr. Brownlee was not even in Edmonton when some of the offenses described by her were alleged to have taken place. Yet the trial went right ahead as if that information had never been revealed.

"I am left with a strong feeling that the case was contrived, that he was innocent but was framed for political reasons. That interrupted a remarkable political career that would have greatly benefitted Canada.

"And consider another of his achievements as provincial premier," said Runciman. "He played a leading role on a Royal Commission that recommended the Bank of Canada be established to control banks, assure financial stability and stabilize inflation."

Despite the downturn in his political fortunes, Brownlee's career was not over. He simply redirected it, opening a law office in Edmonton. When Hitler set Europe aflame, the call came to him again. He had worked closely with UGG over the years and he now became its legal counsel. He was named to the Board in 1942 and became first Vice President and general counsel. His talents were quickly directed to strengthening the company's financial structure and he reorganized the capital stock and led the application to Parliament amending its Act of Incorporation.

At Law's retirement in 1948, John Brownlee had four decades of experience in the business and politics of grain and he had the Board's confidence. It named him President/General Manager.

Under Brownlee's vision and leadership, the company began a massive expansion increasing its fixed and working capital, building larger more efficient elevators and annexes, buying others from line companies and closing smaller ones. Brownlee now saw the need for more professional field services workers to serve farmers, and he personally interviewed and hired a group of university agricultural graduates in 1950 including Jim Mants, Gordon Moss, Don Fraser, Dusty Titheridge and others. He turned them over to a remarkable member of his management team.

Fred Dickinson had been in the Canadian army in World War 1, going over the top 19 times and eventually suffering a nervous breakdown. He had farmed and had once been named world oat champion. He was an old associate of Crerar and had become UGG field services head leading up to WW II. He enlisted again and after the war ended he returned to UGG as head of field services. One company director who knew him well said Dickinson was so loyal he "would have thrown himself down in front of a train if he thought it would do United Grain Growers any good."

Dickinson responded to Brownlee's command to upgrade his unit, and this new team helped lead the company into the post-war world. Wages were modest then. These men were paid $225 to $250 per month. Even Lou Driscoll had started as Treasurer in 1955 at a modest salary of $6500.

By then, Canada was "falling in love" with big government, as author William Morris observed in his book, "*The Canadian Wheat Board.*" So farm policy and farm politics took much of Brownlee's and the Board's time. The Liberal government had amended the Wheat Board Act removing prairie-grown oats and barley from the open market and turning them over to the Wheat Board and the tender mercies of the politicians. For anyone who wanted to look, Parliament was controlled by populous Central Canada. Brownlee had been fighting for prairie farmers from the beginning and he understood only too well the dangers of Ottawa having too much control over the prairie farmers' destiny.

Export demand was brisk and prices good at first. Then, inevitably, Eastern Canada's meat producers complained - the prices they paid for Western feed grain were too high. They wanted government-administered cut-rate prices. Eastern politicians joined the clamour. Prairie growers were under attack from within Canada.

Brownlee and others fought back, insisting the Wheat Board was the growers' selling agency. Its job was to sell for the best price, whether in export or at home. They prevailed this time.

Another long-simmering issue came to the boil in 1949. A Royal Commission on Transportation took dead aim at the statutory freight rates which compelled the railroads to haul prairie grain at low rates.[5]

---

[5] The Crow's Nest Pass Agreement of 1897 between the CPR and Ottawa provided for the railway to build a rail line from Lethbridge to Nelson, BC to take advantage of rich mineral deposits discovered there.

Ten years earlier UGG had opposed an attack on the Crow. Now Brownlee reminded that Royal Commission that the prairies and its grain industry had been developed as *a matter of national policy* - and that if the Crow subsidy ended, the railroads would inevitably raise rates for they faced no competition. Because farmers had no one to pass rail costs along to, they would be certain victims. Brownlee insisted the Crow rate remain statutory and his logic resonated like thunder. The battle was won. For now. But the debilitating Crow struggle continued as the longest-running farm policy issue in Canada's history and led to a transportation crisis in the 1970s. It was finally resolved in 1995, but not without bitterness.

Now came another taste of the bitter medicine ahead. The four leading wheat-exporting countries along with the United Kingdom had expected huge post-war marketing difficulties. They wanted to know how Europe's war-devastated countries would pay for wheat. Prices might collapse. A 1933 International Wheat Agreement to stabilize world markets had crumbled. A 1947 London Conference failed to agree on minimum prices.

Two years later, 46 countries including Canada, the US and Australia - signed a four-year agreement setting minimum producer prices and a putting a cap on British consumer prices. But growers were left out of the negotiations. Market prices soared and consumers got a bargain, costing growers dearly. Brownlee and other leaders lobbied hard for compensation, arguing that growers were sacrificing present income for future security. Ottawa finally paid $65 million, far short of the $300 million some thought justified.

The CPR was to get a subsidy of $11,000 per mile. Farmers were then complaining about high rates charged by the CPR so in return, among other things, the railway was to reduce rates on specified westbound goods by 10 percent mostly, and to reduce eastbound rates for grain and flour by 3 cents per hundredweight and to charge no higher rate thereafter. The CPR further reduced rates in 1903. Ottawa agreed in 1918 to rate increases. In 1925 Parliament specified that the Crow rate applied to all grain and flour going to the Lakehead and from all western points. Now, it was a statutory stabilization of rates binding on all railways. The Crow rate paid only a fraction of what it cost to transport grain. The Western Grain Transportation Act of 1983 replaced the Crow and allowed grain-shipping costs to increase gradually, but never to exceed 10 percent of the world price for grain. Ottawa paid the rest of the grain transportation costs. The Crow was discontinued in 1995 and a one-time cash payment made to farmers.

In another ominous signal of things to come, wheat-importing countries which had been scarred from war-time food shortages began subsidizing their farmers, aiming for self-sufficiency. World bumper crops further depressed prices. The US government guaranteed its farmers high prices, aggravating the problem still more. Envious Canadian growers applauded. But US growers, enticed by those higher prices, ploughed and seeded more acreage and soon had a two-year wheat supply pileup. The US government took the next inevitable step, subsidizing its exports and further undermining world prices.

The weather smiled on prairie growers in 1955 and they harvested over a billion bushels of grains, including 476 million of wheat, almost twice the previous year's crop. Although price prospects remained bleak, it confirmed that UGG's expansion strategy had been sound. It now had 691 elevators and capacity for 55.1 million bushels.

Ahead for farmers and their industry lay unimagined growth - along with fierce unending challenge, political conflict and frustration as Canada rushed blindly into the world of big government.

6

SASKPOOL CCF'S HEART AND SOUL - THE POLITICS OF GRAIN - THE CHINA SALE

From Scotland - To The Freakish Fury Of Prairie Depression

Alexander Runciman grew up and was well-educated in Scotland and managed sizeable estates there until 1921 when he and his wife Evelyn opted to farm on their own. But when they found their small operation could not be viable, they faced a major decision. Alex was 45 years old. He had family in Canada and Evelyn had already lived in Saskatchewan (her brother was secretary to the Lieutenant Governor then) and had enjoyed farm life there. It seemed a logical destination and they made their wrenching choice.

They set out from Scotland in 1928 with children Mac, Jim and Joan, planning to go to the Peace River country. On reaching Saskatchewan, they settled on a half-section in the Balcarres district not far from Sintaluta, only a few miles from where E.A. Partridge had taught at the community's first school 40 years earlier. They paid $5280 on a 25-year payment plan.

Thanks to good wartime wheat prices, many farms there had fine homes, excellent buildings and equipment. Good crops were harvested in 1928 and prices had not yet collapsed. But oldest son Mac, who would go on to become a well-known leader in the prairie grain industry and in Canada itself,[1] still carries vivid memories of what came next.

---

[1] Mac Runciman's grandfather had worked in the Register House (Scotland's vital statistics) in Edinburgh for 43 years and bore the high-sounding title "Depute Keeper His Majesty's General Register of

The first of the hot dry windy years hit the Runcimans with freakish fury. On April 5, 1931, a fire of unknown origin, whipped by northwest winds, flared in the sawdust banking around their house. Their own frantic efforts and the timely arrival of neighbours saved it.

Two months later, a stovepipe fire broke out when Mac's mother, Evelyn, was home alone. It almost got out of hand. Again, the arrival of a cool and capable neighbour saved the home.

Then in mid-July a cyclone ripped through the yard. It almost wrecked the house, tore the roof off a new barn,

---

Sasines" at his 1921 retirement. His three sons, like their friends of the day, went to good schools and then to university. For recreation they played British rugby and golfed. One of them, Mac's uncle, Jimmy Runciman, became a lawyer and migrated to Saskatchewan in 1912. Mac's father, Alexander, aimed to become an estate manager (or factor as it was known in Scotland) and took post-secondary education that included courses in agriculture, law, architecture, management and accounting. He later assumed charge of the large estate of Sir Hector McLeod of Cadbole in the north of Scotland.

Meanwhile, William Anderson and his brother ran a tailoring business in Edinburgh which had been in the family for generations. He and his wife Jemima had fourteen children of whom eleven survived and grew up in relative affluence. When both parents died young, the eldest son had already gone into the family business. (As this book is written, the firm, founded in 1868, is continued by family members.) The other ten children had to make their own way in the world. Daughter Evelyn Hope Anderson was well educated in private schools and she chose to become a governess, "employed in a private home to train and instruct children." She migrated to the United States with the family of an Armour meat packing empire officer, then later moved to Saskatchewan because a brother and three sisters lived in Regina. Many rural areas there were still without schools and Evelyn worked as a governess with a family on a farm north of Grenfell.

After going back to Scotland for a short stay, Evelyn returned to Saskatchewan. Her brother was then secretary to Saskatchewan's Lieutenant Governor and a sister was a clerk in Government House. Evelyn found employment with a farm family at Craven, just north of Regina.

Alexander Runciman had known Evelyn since their school days in Edinburgh and he was then managing the extensive Cadbole estate headquartered in the village of Invergordon. He now telegraphed her a proposal of marriage. She accepted and returned to Edinburgh to be married late in 1913. Mac was born in 1914. Alex served in World War I, then returned to estate management in another part of Scotland.

Because of Scotland's dire post-war manpower shortage, youngsters learned at an early age how to work. Mac was paid for picking potatoes prior to starting school on his fifth birthday.

blew away all the granaries, and strewed shingles and lumber scraps for over half a mile.

"The eye of the storm must have gone right through the yard between the house and barn," Mac related, "because the house shuddered, the old two-holer outdoor toilet went southeast and the barn and granary wreckage northwest."

But the ordeal wasn't over. In early November they were wakened by a pounding on their door and a neighbour shouting that a stack of sheaves was blazing behind the barn. The year's meagre grain harvest was there as well as the straw, hay and sheaves for the livestock in the coming winter and for the next spring's feed for the horses. For the third time that year help was at hand. An entire highway construction crew came and saved the farmstead from disaster.

"I'm sure that summer's exposure to the danger of fire is why I never became a smoker," Runciman admitted later.

But now, drought and collapsing prices had ushered in the dirty thirties. Farm gate prices dropped as low as nine cents a bushel for rye and 20 cents for wheat. Eggs went to five cents a dozen, cream to $2 for a five gallon can. Life for many across the west became a struggle for survival. Farm women strove to feed and clothe their families and maintain decent standards in their homes.

Runciman was taking a load of grain to the elevator on one occasion and the shortest route was through neighbour Tom Townsend's yard. Tom was over at the pigpen, throwing something to the pigs which were squealing so hard Tom didn't hear him. Runciman was curious.

"I stopped and walked over to see what he was doing. A grumpy Tom explained his actions. 'I was over to Patrick (a nearby village) this morning, and they offered me five cents a dozen for eggs.'

"An enraged Tom had brought his eggs home. He told me, 'Before I'll insult the hens by asking them to stretch their butts to lay eggs for five cents a dozen, I'll fire every one of them into the pigpen.' Tom was doing just that - throwing those eggs to the pigs.

"But those adversities often brought out the best in people," Runciman remembered. "Folks learned again how to make their own entertainment, to have fun without money in their pockets.

"The focus of social activities became the school. The local orchestra beat out dance tunes. Admission was 25 cents for men. Ladies brought cake or sandwiches. Card parties and the annual Christmas concert brightened winters. Summer brought softball games and the school picnic with lots of homemade ice cream. Church services in the school brought neighbours together. A travelling library which was exchanged for another from time to time offered a wide range of books.

"People felt genuine concern for friends and neighbours then," he recalled later with some nostalgia. "A flu epidemic hit our Craneshill district one cold winter sending whole families to bed. Many lacked phones. Yet well neighbours would ride to do chores for stricken families, to brew tea or make hot soup. Human qualities shone through, giving a quality of life that is sometimes missing today."

In 1932 the Runcimans went into sheep and made a few dollars to buy their first radio. They read the *Western Producer* and other papers to keep up on events but "without a full understanding of what some of them really meant." Stem rust struck wheat hard in 1935, turning a bumper crop into feed and signalling the end for Marquis wheat.

For many local families, Balcarres was an hour or two away by team. But they made the trip once or twice a week for mail and groceries and to recharge the "A" radio battery. In summer it was a buggy ride, or for a few, a car ride. Stores stayed open Wednesday and Saturday evenings. People would stay in town later on Saturdays socialising along Main street till after midnight because they could sleep in on Sunday.

"We farmed with horses up until the war," he said. "In busy seasons you got up before 5.00 a.m. to feed them and take them out of the barn at 6.50. We were ready for bed by eight or nine at night."

Hockey took over in the late 1930s. Communities put together teams to play on outdoor ice, and Mac and his brother, Walter, joined in. As roads improved, cars and trucks could run later in winter. But much of that travel was by team and cutter or sleigh. Some people travelled 15 or 20 miles to town for games. Often some unexpected event stuck in their memory. At one outdoor skating party when the Runciman dog, Peter, kept chasing the skaters they shut him in the car. In trying to scratch his way out he tore the stuffing out of all the cushions and seat backs.

In 1936, Mac's mother, Evelyn, fell while wall-papering, breaking an arm and a hip and putting her in a toe-to-armpit plaster cast for the summer. "Thank goodness it didn't matter to mother if she was well off or not as long as she could be with her family and see the day clear in front of her. She was a remarkable woman."

Even at the worst of the drought in 1937 they had grain to thresh, feed for the livestock and a good garden - more than many had that year. Everyone pitched in then. Mac's father was active in community affairs, served as a trustee on the local school board and as a municipal councillor in 1935 and '36. He and Evelyn left the farm when he became secretary-treasurer of a rural municipality. He stayed at that occupation until he retired.

Mac, Jim and Joan were still on the farm, with Mac furthering his education by correspondence. He got his grade 11, intended to go to veterinary college at Guelph. But it was the fateful year 1939.

With war's outbreak, depression-devastated prairie communities galvanized for action. Huge numbers of young people rushed to join up, while those remaining behind set about growing more grain than ever to feed the war effort. The Runciman's hometown of Balcarres was typical. It had a total population of only 550, yet 285 people enlisted from Balcarres and district before the war was over. Nearby Abernethy had only 300 people, yet 186 enlisted from that community.

Mac and Jim Runciman were among the first to join up. Mac quickly arrived in England and became a sergeant-major, served in North Africa, Sicily and Italy. He returned home in 1945. Four years later he and Marjorie Dick, who had grown up on a neighbouring farm, married. They built a new house on their farm in 1950 and looked forward to a lifetime there.

"The depression was a harrowing time for mother and dad," explained Mac. "But I don't know what harm it did to us kids. Except I had absolutely no knowledge of how to use credit when I started up. Mother hated owing money. We never owed anybody any longer than we could help. Fear of debt was a Scottish trait. You don't owe anybody. But I could have done a lot of things easier with credit."

He started off with a little 26 h.p. tractor "not much more than you would use for a garden tractor today. I paid $1274.85 for it, farmed with it for years."

SaskPool The CCF'S Heart and Soul - Ignoring The Facts Of Life

Mac Runciman was growing grain on his Abernethy farm in those post-war years and shipping it through both SaskPool and Reliance Grain Co. when UGG bought Reliance in 1948. Politics was at the very heart of selling the prairie grain crop, and Runciman soon found there was something he liked about selling through the UGG.

"My mind-set to the Grain Growers' was right,' he explained later. "I felt comfortable with the people there, became a 100 percent customer. I never delivered anywhere else."

Looking back later, he explained he didn't know the Pool story from personal experience because of his Scottish birth and his youthfulness. "But there was too much Aaron Sapiro in there, a fanatical flocking to hot gospellers. I didn't like the battling that went on for a compulsory pool. Some members were committed to a 100 percent pooling, to single-board marketing and to a central selling agency. That was going to be a way to dictate prices, to make buyers pay more.

"We growers needed more money. Wheat got down to 32 cents at the Lakehead. But this wasn't the way to get it. I just couldn't believe you could set up a system in the middle of North America that the rest of the world would accept."

Runciman had been in Italy when the 1944 election of Tommy Douglas' CCF government signalled that historic left turn in Canadian politics. But he soon got a memorable introduction into the fiercely partisan politics of Saskatchewan and Canada. At a farm meeting he was chatting with SaskPool's Field Services Department head when that official "bragged to me that his group had committed itself to social politics, to the CCF. And in fact that *he* had elected the CCF in Saskatchewan in 1944.

"In effect, he was telling me that SaskPool had become the heart and soul of the CCF movement. It was a distressing discovery. He was a rabid CCF'er. He left no doubt, SaskPool had played a powerful, perhaps decisive role, in this turn of events."

Runciman never forgot that incident. "I felt the Pool had really come unstuck when it became the prime mover of CCF socialist politics. If one of its main functions was to run the province's government and to also try to run the country's, that didn't make sense to me."

Mac had a warm and energetic nature, and he was soon active in his UGG local and was named a delegate to the 1952 annual meeting in Calgary. "Marjorie and I had never been to Calgary," he recalled. "We didn't know where to stay. Head office sent a list of hotels and their prices. The banquet was in the Palliser Hotel, the meeting in the Paget Hall. We added up the prices of all hotels. The St. Regis had the average price, so we went there. It was only two doors from the Paget Hall.

"I had never experienced a meeting of that sort before," he recounted. He was elected secretary of the UGG local the next year.

His nearest UGG director waś Sveinbjorn "Sonny" Loptson of Bredenbury, east of Melville. Loptson was of Icelandic descent and his father was a member of the Saskatchewan Legislature.

"When Sonny resigned from the Board in 1955 to become a commissioner of the Canadian Grain Commission, there seemed two prospects to replace him," remembered Runciman. "Jim Snedker was a good UGG customer and an aggressive man who later became a Liberal MLA and speaker of the Legislature. Tom Neal was a quiet but high-profile fellow like Snedker. And a Conservative."

UGG district manager Joe Busch came calling on Runciman one day and talked about an upcoming celebration at nearby Indian Head for the province's 50th anniversary. A cairn commemorating the 1901 establishment of the Territorial Grain Growers Association was to be unveiled. UGG President John Brownlee, SaskPool President Jack Wesson and Premier Tommy Douglas would be there along with Senator Tom Crerar.

"Joe Busch asked me, 'Are you going to Indian Head that day?' I replied, 'Oh, I don't think so, there will be a lot of speeches and so forth.'

"Joe came back to the subject a few times. I played a little coy. I guess he had his orders. He asked again as he was leaving, 'Are you coming to Indian Head?'

"I replied, 'Joe, you've been pretty persuasive. I'll go.' He answered, 'I think you better, because if you are not smart enough to figure out what's going on, you're not smart enough to be a director of UGG.'

"The UGG board met in Regina on that anniversary occasion, went on to visit elevators at Abernethy and one or two other points, then finally arrived at Indian Head. It was a hot August day. Over 2,000 people came out.

"In addition to the local politicians and community leaders, Liberal federal Minister of Agriculture Jimmy Gardiner was there. My wife Marge's father, Mr. Jimmy Dick, came. He was a personal associate of W.R. Motherwell who was nicknamed Billy Goat Motherwell because of his blunt direct approach to problems.

"Mr. Brownlee approached me and said, 'I have the board's authority to invite you to become a board member. Would you be interested?'

"I answered, 'Yes.'"

Runciman heard nothing more till September when he was invited to a board meeting in Winnipeg. He got a $3.75 per night room at the Marlborough Hotel. Alberta director J.J. McLellan had resigned that summer so his successor Lester Snyder and Runciman were appointed together. It was the first meeting for both.

In the evenings, Runciman began to get to know other directors, found them "sensible people who had done well in their own right. We all got along well. Bob Wilson from Gladstone, Manitoba, and Harold Staples, a quiet unassuming fellow from Benito, Manitoba, usually stayed at the St. Regis Hotel.

"Albertans Snow Sears from Nanton, Hugh Allen from Huallen in the Peace River country and Lester Snyder stayed at the Royal Alex Hotel because their train came in there. Don Trapp was an agricultural engineer who taught at the University of Saskatchewan in winter, farmed at Marriott and had come onto the board in 1952. He and I often stayed at the Marlborough. Mr. Brownlee always stayed at the Royal Alex Hotel.

"There were no clear cut groups or cliques. Three of us would eat supper together one night, two of the same group and somebody else the next night."

Runciman found that none of the directors seemed to be socialists. "Our directors didn't see it as a role for a farm organization to run the government. It wasn't the

Grain Growers' way. Our founders had a simple idea. Build a sound industry. We never veered. We kept following what they saw as the farmers' and the industry's best interests.

"These socialist theories were held out. What was promised was economically impossible but people ignored the economic facts of life, probably didn't understand them. They thought, 'This could be a lot better than what we've got.' No wonder Saskatchewan became the first home of the CCF."

These left wing politics led to some curious events. "A prairie delegation was down to see Prime Minister Diefenbaker in 1961," said Runciman. "SaskPool president Jack Wesson normally had quite a presence. He was the main spokesman on that occasion. A couple of things he said offended the Prime Minister.

"Dief's eyebrows arched, he fixed his eyes on the SaskPool president, his egotism surfaced. He growled, 'Mr. Wesson, I'll have you know that I did never on any occasion say either of those things. Those are false statements. I don't want to hear them repeated.'

"We hardly heard from Wesson again that day, which was uncharacteristic."

The Bitter Politics of Surplus - Brownlee A Marvellous Teacher

Canada's grain industry was moving into troubled times in Runciman's first full year as a director. Growers harvested a huge crop in 1956 which was UGG's 50th year. Russia and Poland bought heavily and early. World wheat exports hit a record 1.1 billion bushels. But the US with its export subsidies grabbed almost half the total; Canada's share fell to less than 25 percent - only 263 million bushels, 45 million below the previous year. Europe's heavily subsidized farmers were making that once-huge market self-sufficient.

Prairie grain wasn't moving and Runciman's Abernethy elevators were plugged. He and his neighbours didn't deliver a bushel for the last five months of 1957. "I had a barn full of grain, every bin full. Grain was sitting in piles, running out of my ears. Yet I couldn't sell enough to pay my taxes and the fuel bill.

"This crisis hit our farm community hard. We finally

appealed to Agriculture Minister Jimmy Gardiner who was
our MP. The message got through. He got a few cars which
arrived at our shipping point on January 14th, 1958.

"We came to the elevator with truckloads of grain
and found ourselves in long lineups. We could only deliver
100 bushels of wheat per farmer, not our full 300-bushel
quota. A few years later, when I had rented out my farm, I
got more income from my one-third of the crop than I was
getting in those years for all I could deliver."

John Brownlee's nature was to face adversity directly, and he focused on what he believed was causing
the crisis, attacking the "economic madness" of high guaranteed prices (even for inferior wheat) to farmers in the
U.S., France, United Kingdom, West Germany, the Neth-
erlands, Belgium and Argentina. Those subsidies were
triggering rising production, making the region a strong
exporter, and he protested that US-subsidized dumping
along with barter deals and foreign currency sales were
hurting Canada's sales as well.

He added, "Even Canada's high hopes for the International Wheat Agreement have been disappointed."

A massive prairie wheat buildup would soon hit 481
million bushels, heralding a return to tough times which
would lead to fierce and divisive farm politics with all the
bitterness UGG so disliked. In a speech ringing with logic,
Brownlee said, "The cost of this price competition falls
squarely on Canadian wheat growers who are guaranteed
only an initial payment. The answer to subsidies must
come through international political action in the General Agreement on Tariffs and Trade."

Brownlee saw Canada well-placed to lead the fight
against subsidies and he advised Ottawa's politicians to
"Attack dumping! The word has a defined technical meaning in legislation. And state-subsidized dumping is considered reprehensible."

His foresight was 20/20. But he could hardly have
imagined it would be 30 years before a successor, UGG
President Ted Allen, could say that dumping subsidized
food products on world markets "is finally on the agenda -
the issue is being addressed."

But UGG still saw a strong role for government and
Brownlee drove home the company's unyielding position:
Canada's welfare required a healthy western economy. If
emergency government aid was needed at times "It is a

proper government function to help share the burden of carried-over wheat."

Ottawa was already providing several millions of dollars in cash advances on farm-stored grain. It brought in the Temporary Wheat Reserves Act in 1956, paying storage and interest costs of about $30 million annually on Wheat Board stocks over 178 million bushels. But this meant Canada was being dragged into a time of massive payouts to farmers because of other countries' subsidies, and because of its own distrust of the marketplace and its commitment to big government.

An alarmed Brownlee cautioned, "These are only temporary measures. The only solution is more wheat sales."

But now, selling grain had been taken out of the hands of growers and the trade and given to the government Wheat Board. Brownlee left no doubt what that meant. "It is primarily Ottawa's responsibility to develop new approaches...and new sales techniques."

He stated, "We must recapture our share of the world grain trade, find new or expanding markets." And with telling foresight, he pointed to increasing Japanese purchases, saying they showed the rising potential of Oriental markets.

UGG's confident directors had built the company's country elevator capacity to 49 million bushels by the 1958 crop year-end and would boost that to 70-million-bushels a year later. But even that wasn't enough. Despite a poor 1958 crop and low prices, slow movement left the company storing grain in rinks and sheds. Brownlee offered one glimmer of hope. Wheat exports were up by 53 million bushels in the 1957-58 crop year to 315 million, and the US share had fallen.

But now a disruptive policy issue arose. Farm groups in the Canadian Federation of Agriculture (CFA), with their roots in the Social Gospel and the resulting distrust of markets and profits, demanded deficiency payments. Ottawa turned them down. Press reports said SaskPool planned a mass delegation to Ottawa to petition for those payments.

"Our board didn't shrink from tough decisions," recalled Runciman. "But we agonized on some. We disliked attempts to intimidate politicians. We preferred to present reasoned arguments."

Here, in fact, was the crux of Canada's ongoing farm

problem - the seemingly irreconcilable differences among its farm groups. The goal of some was to force government to set prices at levels high enough to give farmers what they called "parity." UGG rejected that totally. "With government setting prices, prairie farmers would be certain to get hurt," said Runciman.

On the other hand, UGG and most cattle producers' groups and others believed in markets and profits and individual freedom and were moving away from the CFA.

Runciman found Brownlee, "with his political skills was good at covering such questions." And he was a "marvellous teacher" on dealing with such issues.

"His mind was uncluttered with ideology. He looked clearly at the issues and based his judgements on what he thought best for prairie farmers. Watching him, working with him, I tried to comprehend farm policy needs, think of possibilities.

"Mr. Brownlee was tall, well-built, statesman-like - a dominant figure and an awesome presence. He had a well-trained encyclopedic mind. He was an orator. He inspired. Nobody could jolly along with him. Few people, especially in the company, ever thought to challenge him on a debating basis. He was 70 years old with a mane of snow-white hair but nobody was gunning for his position. Some people in the country thought we should be looking towards a replacement, but no one around the board thought that.

"He had good political instincts. He would invite heads of farm groups like the Farmers' Union for lunch so he could stay conversant with policy matters. At board meetings he could discuss any issue that came along - conflicts among the farm groups, the drive for cash advances on farm-stored grains, or subsidies. He kept his board informed and held nothing back, for he respected us.

"He had his own style and was totally engrossed in his work. He lived in Calgary but he and his wife had suite 298 in the Royal Alex Hotel when they were in Winnipeg. He was there every night answering every piece of mail. She would knit. He would drive to the office in the morning with his dictaphone belts for Miss McFadyen to type. I don't think he ever went to a movie or a theatre.

"At elevator managers' meetings, he would listen quietly, then do a five-minute wrap-up that seemed to say all that was needed. General Manager Bill Winslow used to say, 'If we could get him to country meetings, let the farmers meet him and see what he is like, it would be so good for the company's business.'

"One meeting proved how right Winslow was. Brownlee came to a delegate report meeting in the Wilkie, Saskatchewan, elevator office. The chairs filled up and more people crowded in. Five-gallon cans were brought in and planks put across them - not the most comfortable seats ever invented. Mr. Brownlee talked for over an hour. The crowd forgot how hard the seats were. He could really get an audience - not in the hot gospeller sort of way. He spoke quietly."

But now some farm groups planned to march on Ottawa to support their demand for deficiency payments. UGG would have to take a tough stand.

"I wrote confidentially to Brownlee in November, 1958," Runciman remembered, said if the cause of deficiency payments did not have sufficient merit to ensure its adoption after careful thought, I couldn't feel that a delegation would sway the government. And it could create real resentment among the public.

"Brownlee agreed, said an Ottawa march 'would cost from $80,000 to $100,000.' He doubted 'sheer numbers can impress the government when representations from farm organizations cannot...Reasonable representations by farm leaders will get just as far.'

"We decided against the ultimate gesture - refusing to go," said Runciman. "A couple of board members went, but I didn't. None of us felt it was the thing to do."

Meanwhile a new International Wheat Agreement, aimed at stabilizing prices through long-term contracts, was signed in early 1959 with slightly lower maximum prices and similar minimum prices. It offered some relief from the gathering gloom. But buyers simply agreed to take specified percentages from member exporters. Brownlee said Europe's increasing prosperity offered some hope.

Terminal Collapse - Operating From Strength

Despite the fierce struggle to find ways to soften the impact of the grain cash-flow crisis on growers, every grain company had to deal with its day-to-day challenges. Sometimes a bad day will come along. The worst day of all for United Grain Growers was September 23, 1958. Directors were on the train enroute to Fort William for a Board meeting, to inspect the terminal there and talk to staff. At the Kenora stop, a message was delivered to Assistant General Manager Peter Watt who took it to Brownlee's compartment and read its stunning news. The company's main 30-year-old Port Arthur terminal elevator annex had collapsed into the water in a pile of rubble and grain.

A shocked Brownlee responded, "Peter, I wonder if this means the end of the old company?"

Runciman was on that train and described the event later. "The terminal went into the drink about 8 o'clock in the evening. No one was hurt because it was in the evening. If it had waited until 10 o'clock the next morning, the board of directors might have been on the annex and gone with it.

"Only one person was affected. A watchman in the Abitibi lot across the inlet was enjoying a quiet time, looking out across the water. When the annex went, he couldn't believe his eyes. It flopped into the water and created a tidal wave.

"He saw this wave coming at him and he started to run. It caught up to him, knocked him down and rolled him up the shore. Then the wave came back and left him lying there. He wasn't hurt. But can you imagine what was going through his mind? He must have wondered if he had gone crazy."

Brownlee's fears were greatly exaggerated. The elevator workhouse and inshore storage bins were undamaged. And the farmers' company now operated from strength. The directors were already buying the Canadian Consolidated Grain Company Limited elevator system with its Lakehead terminal along with 129 Manitoba and Saskatchewan country elevators. They soon directed grain through that terminal and proceeded to rebuild and expand the collapsed terminal.

"A head-on battle with the Wheat Board followed," said Runciman, "when it demanded we hand over the quantity of grain in the elevator before it collapsed. Mr. Brownlee and Peter Watt and Harry Griffin and Lou Driscoll worked under intense pressure for months with Wheat Board Minister Gordon Churchill and others.

"Eventually we got a $750,000 settlement out of a

Wheat Board holding fund. This drew fierce criticism from the farmers' unions and remained a sore point with them.

"Lou Driscoll (who would later become company general manager,) had talents just ideal for working on that issue and really won his spurs there.

"Cause of the collapse was never agreed upon. The soil supporting the annex may have slipped on the bedrock but the engineers were never sure."

System Breakdown - Hamilton's "China Sale" Biggest In History

As grain piled up in those late 1950s, the Americans faced many of the same frustrations as Canadians, and Runciman and others began looking south for answers. "A number of us went down to Fort Collins for talks with US wheat growers. We met some nice folk there. Carl Bruns from Idaho told us horrendous stories of how hard up American farmers were because their wheat wasn't being sold. I asked him that night at dinner, 'Carl, you painted a pretty black picture this afternoon. Is it really that tough?'

"He had a wry sense of humour. He looked at me and said, 'Mac, it's really bad. I'm down to my last Cadillac.'

"He went on, 'It got so bad we figured we had to get out of wheat. We tried potatoes, went in heavily. It worked out beautifully. We sold $285,000 worth the first year and it didn't cost us a cent more than $325,000 to grow them.'"

As Runciman chatted with more and more grain people at meetings across Canada and abroad, one thing became clear. The cause of the Canadian grain pileup was no mystery. The problem was lack of shipping capacity. And the cause was no mystery. Farmers had let grain marketing get bogged down in politics. Selling grain was an ideological struggle - not a hard-nosed business of getting it to market.

"The obsession with politics is why the Wheat Board enjoyed the sway it did," said Runciman. Ottawa's game is politics. It couldn't respond to the pile-up with aggressive marketing programs. Instead, it tried cash advances and the Temporary Wheat Reserves Act and other Band-aids.

Runciman came to a sobering realization. Even if a

big market did open up, our system was incapable of moving grain to fill it. The whole marketing/shipping system needed overhauling.

He began saying in speeches, "Farmers should mind their own business and get involved to see that the decisions made serve their best interests." Momentous political events ahead would prove him correct. Diefenbaker's minority Tory government replaced the Pearson Liberals in 1957, and an historic election campaign was underway a year later.

"John Diefenbaker had a mass meeting in Winnipeg one night when our board of directors was in the city for a meeting," remembered Runciman. "After dinner, our director J.D. MacFarlane said, 'Let's go over and see John tonight.'

J.D. MacFarlane had been a Liberal, but Dief had done legal work for him. They knew each other well. "A huge lineup greeted us at the Winnipeg auditorium. We worked our way through it and got within a person or two of Dief. MacFarlane said, 'Hello, John Diefenbaker.'

"Dief responded, 'Oh, hello, J.D. How are you?' And Dief was shaking hands up to the elbow. J.D. then introduced me - it was the first time I had met the Chief.

"The Diefenbaker campaign caught fire that night and raced across the country. He won his landslide. But in succeeding months grain remained piled up and prices low. The US continued to subsidize exports through Public Law 480 and other programs and to boost its market share despite a new International Wheat Agreement. And the European Community's Common Agricultural Policy (which showered big subsidies on farmers,) was moving that once-huge market towards surpluses of its own."

Frustrated farmers in Diefenbaker's prairie homebase became increasingly impatient. The Prime Minister had to respond. He turned to another Saskatchewan politician who, as it turned out, was the right man for the job.

Alvin Hamilton was an entrepreneurial guy who had run for office many times before finding himself an MP in Diefenbaker's government. On October 11, 1960, the Prime Minister named him Minister of Agriculture replacing Gordon Churchill. Dief gave him the Wheat Board too and directed Hamilton to "sell more grain!"

World wheat and coarse grains production were then on the increase. But trade was also increasing. China had bought Canadian wheat two years earlier and rumours said the Chinese would be short of grain.

A few weeks earlier at a meeting in Ottawa, Wheat Board Chief Commissioner W.C. MacNamara had suggested that Canada's Hong Kong trade commissioner apply for visas so Board officials could visit China. His Minister Gordon Churchill concurred. [2]

MacNamara visited Hong Kong and Canton in late 1960, and an official from each of the Departments of Trade and of External Affairs went to Peking to ask the Chinese to consider 'mixing our wheat with your wheat.' They reported back that the rumours were true, that poor 1959 and 1960 harvests meant China would face acute food shortages within six months. China had already begun negotiations with Australia, had placed no grain orders, but would soon be a volume buyer.

Days later, on January 3, 1961, a China Resources Company delegation arrived in Toronto and was met by Wheat Board personnel ready to start serious negotiations. But this was a delicate situation. The two countries lacked diplomatic relations. The Chinese would not go to Ottawa and Canadians could not officially go to Beijing. And the Wheat Board could not make credit sales without government approval.

To the Wheat Board's surprise, the Chinese asked to be taken first to the Royal Bank of Canada. Their purpose, as it turned out, was not to arrange credit or any such worldly matter, but to locate the grave of former Royal Bank head James Muir who had been the only senior Canadian banker to visit China. Muir's visit had been seen by the Chinese as an important courtesy. They now placed flowers on his grave, then were ready for business.

A deal was signed on January 27 for 260,000 tons of barley and 750,000 tons of wheat. Of course the financial arrangements were made through the Royal Bank.

The Chinese demand for secrecy while it completed freight bookings hit a snag when an over-eager Wheat Board Minister Hamilton announced the sale in the House

---

[2] These events are related in Bill Morriss' book on the Canadian Wheat Board and in Patrick Kyba's biography of Hon. Alvin Hamilton, PC. Although the two accounts seem to sometimes diverge, the events as I have described them consider both as well as discussion with people who were close to those events.

of Commons on February 3, saying China had taken 28 million bushels of wheat and 12 million bushels of barley, for $60 million. The Chinese alleged a breach of a gentleman's agreement, but the ruffled feathers were smoothed. Now, evidence mounted that this was only the start. China wanted a long-term agreement. The Wheat Board's Doug Treleaven and Frank Rowan flew to Hong Kong on February 16 and were told on the 23rd that China might buy three-to-five million tons of grain over three years if it could get payment flexibility.

Alvin Hamilton was a man of big dreams and absolute determination. When he got this news in early March, he told Cabinet that history was in the making. China would buy 190 million bushels of wheat and 47 million of barley over a two-and-a-half year period "if flexibility in payment arrangements could be negotiated."

Cabinet divided and deadlocked on ways to give China gifts or credit. A venturesome Hamilton was ready to try anything. He threatened to resign from Cabinet if credit was refused. The Prime Minister got the deal through Cabinet - 25 percent cash, the rest payable in nine months.

On April 22, after 31 days of negotiations with China Resources in Hong Kong and Peking, Wheat Board Chief Commissioner MacNamara signed the first long-term agreement with China (all details were not yet worked out). It was the first agency-to-agency long-term agreement negotiated solely by the Wheat Board backed by an Ottawa guarantee on bank loans for the credit. And it was the biggest grain deal ever - but no announcement had yet been made.

Diefenbaker told the Commons on April 26 that Hamilton was en route to Hong Kong to discuss a sale. Hamilton made his brief (one-and-a-half days) but famous visit there seeking whatever political benefits he could garner. He waved a piece of paper before the TV cameras and proclaimed, "We've got a deal with the Chinese."

Treleaven and his party left for Canada on April 27 carrying the signed agreements. Hamilton returned to tell Cabinet that China would buy $362 million worth of wheat and barley over the next two-and-a-half years and announced the sale in the House on May 2.

C anada's huge grain industry was in crisis in the late 1960s when President **Mac Runciman** of farmer-owned United Grain Growers took the message across the West and to the rest of Canada, "Red tape is strangling the cash flow needed to make the industry viable ... The system is 20 years behind the US."

In researching his Ph.D. thesis in the early 1990's, **Paul Earl** stumbled on a stunning phenomenon - a century earlier, Protestant pastors had convinced themselves they had found a new universal truth, cried out, "Abolish capitalism and the free market." Their message shaped the grain industry and the country.

International evangelist **Aaron Sapiro** hit Canada in 1923 and like the social gospellers, aimed to revoke the market system and transform society. He became godfather of the Wheat Pools, but his dream of a world wheat pool failed. It turned out he had close ties with Al Capone and was disbarred in New York state on charges of witness tampering.

During the 1919 Winnipeg General Strike, the daily *Strike Bulletin* headlined, "Woodsworth Addresses 10,000 at Labour Church." Preacher **J.S. Woodsworth** went on to become the CCF party's first leader.

A.J. McPhail was president of the Wheat Pools' Central Selling Agency (CSA) which tried to evade the open market and set prices itself, paying growers an initial price. When Black Tuesday hit with devastating fury in late 1929, the *London Daily Herald* called "the price-fixing attempts of the American and Canadian Pools ... one of the most ruthless world wars in commercial history." The Pools buckled, and Ottawa and the three provinces bailed them out.

Palliser Wheat Growers' Association President **Ivan McMillan** found the prairies frozen in policy deadlock and in crisis, explained, "We have two diametrically opposed philosophies. Some groups are passionately committed to supply management ... others, like Palliser, want producer freedom which leads to ... an expanding industry."

With wheat sales strangled from over-regulation, journalist and commodity marketer **James McAnsh** saw rapeseed, which could be sold outside Wheat Board regulations, as a potential winner. He played a leading role in building the crop to rival wheat in value.

Andy McMechan was martyred when he was arrested in 1996, handcuffed and marched off to jail for trucking his own Manitoba-grown grain to waiting buyers in North Dakota, pocketing the money and returning home to buy groceries, pay his bills, repair his machinery and educate his family.

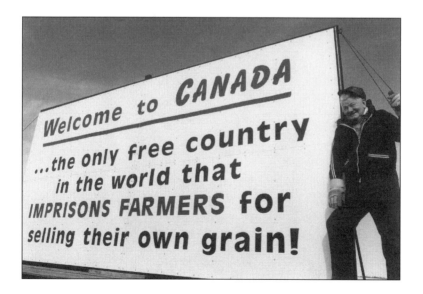

With McMechan languishing in jail, Farmers for Justice members displayed this sign on a truck flat bed along prairie highways for months. Grower **Clarence Taylor** is seen with it near Regina.

Hard-nosed, no-nonsense overachiever Wally Nelson cropped the deep black soil south of Regina and was building the province's biggest John Deere dealership and a General Motors one as well. But he and his neighbours couldn't sell their big crops in 1970, their cash flow had stopped. They began meeting, found they "had gone for years with no idea of how our grain was marketed." They formed the Palliser Wheat Growers' Association to fight for farmers' freedom.

Five past presidents of Palliser (now Western) Wheat Growers seen at their 1995 annual convention: Wally Nelson, Ivan McMillan, George Fletcher, Harvey McEwen, and Hubert Esquirrel.

7

FROM SOARING SALES TO BULGING BINS - A NEW MONOPOLY - POLITICAL PRICING

John Brownlee had been UGG's president and general manager for 13 years by early summer, 1961, and the company had grown rapidly under his leadership, boosting its country elevator numbers by 50 percent, doubling its capacity and enlarging its terminals. Like Partridge and Crerar and Law before him, the former Alberta premier had recognized that golden rule of prairie grain - "Keep your eye on grain politics and policies." Influencing them had required all his skills.

But now his health was failing. His resignation as general manager was accepted at an early June Board meeting and at his urging, treasurer Lou Driscoll was named to that post. He resigned as president on July 1st at a Calgary Board meeting, died two weeks later.

"The place wasn't really teeming with candidates to succeed him," Runciman said later. "It wasn't in my mind that I wanted to be president, or that I would be considered. I had never done speeches and was apprehensive about them. I wasn't good at debating. And I had a terrible time making myself mouth some of the conventional wisdoms of the day on farm policies."

But Brownlee had grown to respect Mac Runciman's judgement and trust his advice, and he had nodded towards the Abernethy farmer before he resigned. As it turned out, Runciman's fellow directors shared Brownlee's views. They knew him as a man who loved chatting with neighbours at local meetings, making friends, soaking up information and remembering everything. And he had a set of principles that were right next door to sacred. They saw him as a warm and sociable but intensely committed board member.

Fellow director Bob Wilson emerged as a leading figure as the Board faced that decision. "Wilson was a sensible conscientious and devoted director," Runciman recalled. "In keeping with those times, he was almost parsi-
monious. When director per diems were $10, he would take
only $5 if it was an evening meeting."

Wilson had become a farmer by a circuitous route.
He joined the ambulance corps in World War I and won a
bravery medal for saving lives. On his return, he graduated from university and began working on fruits and or-
chards at the Central Experimental Farm, Ottawa. When
he came to the government research farm at Morden,
Manitoba, he brought 20,000 seedling apple trees. Most
of them died, but he developed a hardy apple crab as well
as others.

When he began farming at Gladstone, Manitoba,
Wilson grew huge apples which he would bring to Board
meetings for his fellow directors to munch. He was recognized as a leading citizen and farmer/fruit grower, and a
man of character.

He now became the liaison between the board and
Runciman. "He led the delegation that asked me if I'd take
the presidency," remembered Runciman. "I said 'Yes.' But
I would not be general manager as well."

Mac Runciman was elected president in Calgary on
July 1, 1961, "dropped into this job at the age of 46," doing
something which he insisted was foreign to his nature and
training and background. He saw no way he could continue farming and take over his new role. He expected
those early days to be "a formidable period for the whole
company, with an absolute greenhorn out there who never
chaired a meeting in his life."

He would face his first annual meeting within four
months. "Members had to ask, 'And what is he going to do
when he gets up there?'" Runciman knew.

They left the farm they loved and moved to Winnipeg. "I had backing that if it didn't work out or if I was
defeated in an election, Marjorie and I could go back to
the farm, which is what we wanted to do in the first place."

"That summer of 1961 was dry. My cattle were short
of pasture. I sold the 43 head to a neighbour who had cou-
lee pasture, and rented the farm to Marjorie's nephew
Garry, who later bought it. I never farmed again."

The rookie president got his share of free and sometimes fatherly advice. Director J.D. MacFarlane sidled up to him and cautioned, "Watch the booze! Too many good men have gone down on the booze when they get into a position like yours. Leave the booze alone! You will be alright."

Chuckled Mac later, "I was fortunate. I never had a booze problem. Oh, I drank a bit. I always said I would quit if I got ugly when I drank like some people do. I went the other way - happy, relaxed."

More good advice came at a meeting in the elevator office at Macklin on the Saskatchewan-Alberta border. "A fellow with a cowboy hat and boots looked me up and down and asked, 'Have you got big feet?' I said, 'Pardon?' He asked again, 'Have you got big feet?' I said, 'Yes, very good-sized feet.'

"'Well that is a good thing," he responded. "If you are going to fill John Brownlee's shoes, you will need big feet.'"

But decisions had to be made in Winnipeg. "UGG head office had a bit of an ivory tower image then. Mr. Brownlee was 76 years of age when he left. Assistant G.M. Peter Watt was 72. Economist Harry Griffin aided Lou Driscoll in many ways so we kept him until he was 82, and trading chief Jerry Bell until he was 69.

"A few country people would say 'Those guys in the ivory tower don't know what goes on.' I had the advantage of coming right off the farm. Many of our members saw this as a departure and they were out to see that I got along. I decided we were going to enforce a normal retirement age, to give young people a chance to come up."

Times were changing in Runciman's favour as the annual meeting approached. His lack of speaking experience could be a benefit. "In earlier days," he said, "if a dinner speaker didn't go on for an hour, he was thought to have neglected his function. Now, thanks to radio and television, if he spoke for more than 20 minutes, people would get up and walk out.

"As it turned out, every single delegate came that year prepared to make sure the meeting went well and that the new president made a go of it. The sentiment was fantastic. If I had got lockjaw that morning and couldn't speak, the annual meeting would have gone off successfully."

Runciman was ready to accept all the luck he could

get. And now fortune smiled. Record-breaking Russian sales followed the recent China sale. Prices soared. "Nothing clears the air of contentious subjects faster than lots of grain moving," he recalled.

"These sales were from heaven...just too good to believe. The new three-year International Wheat Agreement further brightened the outlook. The grain business suddenly looked good again, and farmers made big commitments that led to huge crops in the 1970s."

Close Down Rail Lines? - Russian
Wake-Up Call - Greatest Wheat Year Ever

With sales brisk and the world's population increasing, UGG's directors almost dared to believe a new age had arrived, that a ready market awaited every bushel growers could harvest. The company was expanding and upgrading its system. Its new 4.25 million bushel Port Arthur annex (to replace the smaller one that had collapsed) was nearing completion. By 1962 UGG had 55.4 million bushels of capacity. It had also bought Canada West Grain Company to get more fully into grain and forage seed. The road ahead seemed clear.

Then ominous news hit. Canada's wheat exports fell to 328 million bushels in the 1962-63 crop year. Elevators were again jammed with grain. Farmers' cash flow tightened up. Uncertainty gripped the West. Some way had to be found to get more money back to growers.

It was no secret that the West had too many rail lines - the cost of maintaining them to serve small and obsolete elevators was simply too high. The 1961 MacPherson Royal Commission on Transportation had found farmers could easily haul grain longer distances. Get rid of some lines (rail line rationalization, it was called) as a way to get more dollars to growers, it urged.

Brownlee said this would free up UGG and the other companies to improve their systems. But the uproar from left-wing farm groups and from the Pools, which owned most of those smaller elevators and didn't want to lose them and the customers shipping to them, was deafening. Moving grain was a political issue, and the country's Social Gospel heritage with its hatred of capitalism, was alive and well.

Ottawa backed away. Getting change would be a daunting task.

Runciman gave speeches on this in 1961, '62 and '63. "But I got sick and tired of the Farm Union people going into their song and dance, their teary, weary story saying we couldn't abandon any rail lines because farmers hauled their grain to market with little half-ton trucks - that they couldn't afford bigger trucks. And besides, it would destroy municipal roads.

"That plea didn't hold water. At harvest time you would see farmers hauling grain from the combine in three-ton trucks. If I had stayed on the farm, my travel on municipal roads after rationalization would be identical to that before it. It would be the same for every farmer who lived off black top. Economics said it had to be done.

"But the politics being played made it difficult. SaskPool labelled it an attack on small farmers, called it unthinkable to deny farmers those rail lines and the little old elevators on them. SaskPool President Charlie Gibbings threatened to play the Pools' 'Quebec card' if he didn't get his way, enlisting Quebec's farm groups to bring political pressure on Ottawa to help stop it. And he did."

That issue was destined to preoccupy Runciman and UGG and the whole industry and indeed the country for decades. But just then an astounding piece of good news hit, driving rail rationalization right off the front pages - and the back pages too. Soviet Union grain buyers arrived in Canada in September, 1963. Drought was devastating their crops. They needed wheat. And in *the biggest single wheat sale in Canadian history* they bought 239 million bushels for shipment by the following July 31.

As luck would have it, farmers grew a record 793 million bushels that year. Runciman told delighted delegates at his 1963 annual meeting that Canada's exports could soar to a record 550 million bushels. Hopefully a new day had come and future sales would take all the grain farmers could grow.

"Reclassify that wheat surplus into an important national asset - a world food reserve," he suggested, praising the company's earlier directors who had the courage to plough back earnings into the elevator system.

With that massive sale, exports hit almost 600 million bushels, more than twice the average of wheat and flour prior to 1963 when 300 million was considered good and 350 million extraordinary. Carryover fell to 461 million bushels from the 579 million 10-year average. At his 1964 annual meeting, Runciman called the year ending July 31, *the greatest wheat year in history.*" The company had set new records for handlings and for earnings.

"All Canada is acclaiming the grain industry for its contribution to the national economy," he told delegates. "Those massive sales...point towards continued good times. The world will need all the food prairie growers can produce," he beamed.

Uncertainty crept in again in late 1964 when the wheat crop hit 578 million bushels, surpassing the 453 million bushels 10-year average and threatening new surpluses.

Then history repeated. Soviet buyers returned in 1965 with open order books and took 187 million bushels of wheat and flour. Trade Minister Mitchell Sharp, who had begun his career with the James Richardson Grain Company, glowed with optimism as he announced that total demand was greater than in that astounding year 1963. He predicted another export record for 1966. Once again, prairie farmers seemed to be living a charmed existence - with an assured market for every bushel they could grow and the railroads could move in the next 12 months.

Soviet buyers returned in June, 1966 for a record-shattering $800 million of wheat - the *largest grain sale in history*. The deal called for delivery of 336 million bushels of wheat in the three years beginning August 1, 1966, and brought Soviet purchases from Canada since 1963 to 814 million bushels.

Farmers harvested a record 824 million bushels of wheat in 1966, 60 percent over the 10-year average. The UGG Board reported "the greatest grain export year in history," with 1965-66 exports hitting 670 million bushels. Wheat and flour exports at 580 million bushels were double the long-term average.

A new day seemed to have dawned. Despite a series of bumper crops, rising exports had cut into surpluses. Demand for livestock was growing too so the West would be challenged to boost beef and hog output. The impossible dream of all-out production had become reality - the Wheat Board in effect was promising farmers they could continue growing big crops.

UGG spent heavily to upgrade and expand its system in 1966, buying 87 country elevators and a terminal at Port Arthur from McCabe Grain Co. Ltd. Wheat exports ran at record levels in that 1966 year. Farmers' cash receipts had nearly doubled in the decade to a record $4.232 billion. They rose 11.2 percent in the previous year alone to 28.5 percent over the five-year average. Farmers were clearing hundreds of thousands of acres of land, investing heavily in new machinery and buying fertilizer and chemicals. The number of commercial farms was increasing.

The world media began focusing on what it called the population explosion and the War on Hunger. Headlines screamed that per capita food output was failing to keep pace, and asked anxiously, "Can famine be staved off? Or must tens of millions of people die?"

The House of Commons Agricultural Committee placed an official stamp of approval on what seemed the unlimited market for food, stating in May, 1967, that Canada would need billion-bushel wheat crops by 1980 to meet growing demand. Industry leaders at a Saskatchewan meeting set their sights on that magic billion-bushels crop. The 1967 Kennedy Trade Round of GATT promised to pry open the rich US and other markets to more food products. And a new International Wheat Agreement boosted wheat prices for the next three years.

Wonder of wonders, prairie farmers now seemed to face unprecedented prosperity - they could grow their crops, confident of selling them all at good prices. A kind of euphoria gripped the prairies. But it would soon vanish. Other forces were at work which would lead to a far different outcome. A market roller coaster was about to shake the grain industry to its very foundations.

Bulging Bins - Near Bankrupt Communities - Monopoly Time Again

Prairie grain had come a long way since Ed Partridge made his historic trip to Winnipeg in 1905 to peer inside "The House with the Closed Shutters." But less than two years after the euphoric news in 1967 that world hunger heralded a new day, the dream had died. Farmers' bins were bulging with record inventories as winter 1968-69 set in - 1.5 billion bushels of wheat and 1 billion bushels of coarse grains.

Allan Coulter of Stranraer, Saskatchewan, voiced the fear felt by every grower. "We faced a four bushel wheat quota, no barley sales to speak of, staggering 24-cents-a-bushel carrying charges. Our community was near bankruptcy."

Yet one thing puzzled growers. Why was US grain moving when their's wasn't? They couldn't get clear answers. A harsh reality gripped them. World farmers were producing more food than seemed possible. And soon would come the shocking realization that Canada's grain handling/marketing system was failing. The industry began moving into and out of the spotlight, despised as a political burden one day, acclaimed as a saviour the next.

In fact, ominous signs of the pileup had appeared following the 1963 and 1965 Soviet sales when the grain system was unable to handle the huge movement. The industry was dominated by politics. As Paul Earl concluded in his 1992 PhD thesis, the social gospellers' attack on capitalism in the 1920s and 1930s "shaped Canada's grain marketing system for the succeeding half century and shape it yet..."

In the resulting tangle of regulations, the Wheat Board, elevator companies, individual country elevators and railways all had separate responsibilities. But the rules were seldom in harmony. Long-term planning was impossible. The rail system couldn't be rationalized, nor needed improvements made to the handling system. Government/Wheat Board subsidy programs on grain storage often rewarded companies for storing grain rather than moving it to export[1] and shaped a storage-oriented system.

Several studies had documented the breaking crisis. Tom Kerr of the non-political Agricultural Economics Research Council (funded by industry and government) showed in a 1966 study that the policy mix-up was shutting grain out of good markets and shifting hog and cattle and turkey production from the West to politically favoured

---

[1] This muddle is explained in detail in "State Of The Industry," Grain Handling and Transportation, a special committee report by J. Candlish, A. Mills, R. Martinelli, and P. Earl, done in 1973 by the Canada Grains Council.

Central Canada. This was costing tax-payers money but wasn't bringing more income or jobs to Canada's economy.

The answer? Scrap those subsidies! said Kerr. But do it gradually to give people time to adjust.

A 1967 Task Force urged Ottawa to *abandon its paternalistic management of the industry.* "Don't depend on government," it urged industry people. "Work together! Take more responsibility!"

With the US mounting a frontal attack in 1972 to gain more access for its farm products into Europe, Dr. Sandy Warley called upcoming Common Market negotiations, "The most important political event of our time." The University of Guelph economist advised Ottawa, "Urge the U.S. on and cling to her coattails....Let's not withdraw into 'fortress Canada.'" He was certain we would find growing markets there, in Japan and Eastern Europe for feed grains and livestock.

Market economist Dr. Walt Anderson urged, "Join the US in pressing for longer-term world trade liberalization." Dr. Gordon Dobson noted that Australia and New Zealand doubled or tripled their agricultural exports to the US in the decade, calling it the biggest meat consumer in the world. "We could double or triple our exports to the U.S. in the 1970s," he said. "But we will have to work at it harder...to develop a strategy." For we lacked the supplies to do it.

Some deep-rooted problems lay outside Canada. A series of International Wheat Agreements from 1949 to 1967 had set minimum prices to support farmers, but the U.S. had quit co-operating by early 1965, using export subsidies to boost market share and triggering a price war. Canada's 26.3 percent share of world wheat trade in 1966-67 fell to a new low of 17.9 percent the next year.[2] And an International Grain Arrangement that pushed up prices about 21 cents per bushel in 1968 was crumbling under the grain surplus as all countries ignored its minimum prices.

One thing was clear. Food was a growth industry, but despite Canada's huge breadbasket, the country couldn't fully participate. Government policy was the Achilles heel.

---

[2] William E. Morriss, in *Chosen Instrument - A History of the Canadian Wheat Board,* provides more detail on this.

"No wonder panic struck," said Runciman later. "Rail rationalization was blocked, the branchline system was failing. Canada's *share* of world wheat sales had tumbled. Marketing failures and the inability to move grain had the industry at a crossroads."

History had come full circle. UGG had been formed half a century earlier to break the railway/grain company monopoly and free up farmers to work in a fair environment. Tom Crerar had fought as UGG president and then as a Cabinet minister and Senator to preserve freedom of choice in marketing. He had acquiesced to a monopoly Wheat Board in 1943 because of the wartime emergency. But Prime Minister King's cabinet amended the Wheat Board Act four years later to give the Board permanent status and complete control over interprovincial and export wheat movement, and to permit Ottawa to extend the Board's authority to other grains by order-in-council. As a Cabinet wheat committee member, Crerar spearheaded a revolt by some Liberal senators to stop the bill but it was unsuccessful.

Now, in the late 1960s, overregulation had left it another monopoly like the one farmers faced 60 years earlier. And this one, bogged in bureaucracy, couldn't even move the grain, let alone adapt to the changing world market place. Needed investments couldn't be made.

When the Wheat Board tried a block shipping system to slash rail car in-transit time and give faster turnaround, the Crow rate forced railways to lose money on every bushel. Disillusioned, they didn't replace their aging boxcars. The number in use fell by half in the 10 years ending 1973. The industry was in full crisis.

"Too many people other than farmers are deciding the producers' future," said Runciman in 1969. "The Wheat Board is selling grain 'in the best interests of growers,' yet nobody asks a farmer what is his interest. Red tape is strangling the cash flow needed to make the system viable, smothering initiative, leaving it unable to respond to world markets. Farmers' earnings were managed by government in every sense at desperate cost to them and the grain industry and the country."

Business wouldn't invest because regulations precluded any return on investment. And besides, business was vilified at every turn. The industry faced a near impossible[3] struggle to build a new system for a different world.

"The sheer number of elevators was too high," recalls Runciman. "No company could afford to upgrade all of them, or even to man them." A few ad hoc improvements were possible. "We had to close old ones and we targeted those in smaller points served by too many companies. We would sit down with a line company or a pool and say, 'If you get out of this point, we'll get out of that point.'

But grain politics stood in the way. "Many good customers didn't want to lose their nearby elevators. When we announced a closure, we got letters, many of them quite bitter....But the industry lacked a strategy to reduce rail lines, so we couldn't plan which elevators to upgrade or where to build new ones....We could only whittle away at it."

The car shortage reached desperate proportions. Ottawa finally responded, buying 2,000 modern 100-ton steel hopper cars in late 1972 to be held by the Wheat Board. Then Wheat Board Minister Otto Lang announced in March, 1974, that Ottawa would rehabilitate 2,400 boxcars. Within two months the Board used farmers' money to buy another 4,000 hopper cars, 1,600 of them 70-ton aluminum cars to cope with load limits on secondary branch lines. It continued buying, pushing the Board-administered fleet up to 19,000 cars by 1985. And the Saskatchewan and Alberta governments each bought 1,000 cars.

"But serious reforms were needed," said Runciman, to break loose from the red tape and vested interests that had sapped the food industry's energy for so long. He urged growers to find a way to get changes that served growers themselves rather than the bureaucrats or the ideologists.

"Set up a wheat commodity group to lobby for growers' interests....Become personally involved in how and why wheat marketing decisions are made," he urged every

---

[3] This was a classic result of socialism becoming embedded in a political system. Thanks to the Social Gospel's penetration into Canada's political life and the resulting fierce distrust of capitalism by Canada's political and social elite which was taking over the country, individual freedom was being eroded. The style of government was moving towards management from above rather than the English system based on Magna Carta with its deep respect for the individual and the philosophy of individual freedom and responsibility. As William D. Gairdner wrote in 1990 in *The Trouble with Canada*, "with no common moral vision, political, economic and social life becomes a war of all against all in which interest groups contend for ever-diminishing tax dollars to fund their morally conflicting causes. The rules of the game no longer ensure fairness; they favour those with power."

grower. His words were prophetic. Massive change lay ahead.

Love Big Government -
Political Pricing Of Feed Grains

Anyone who wanted to look could see Canada's love affair with big government was taking its inevitable toll. Tom Crerar had warned UGG members in 1920 about Canadians' desire to give government more and more duties. "We are a much-governed people. It is a *disease* in the nation's health that if not eradicated may bring it to disaster," he said.

Crerar predicted with ominous accuracy, "people can do most things better for themselves, through co-operation, than can be done by government agencies." People need "more freedom...to buy and sell where they please, freedom to order their daily lives as they wish so long as they do not overstep...the rights of others."

Runciman repeated those prophetic words 55 years later in his 1975 annual report. "In the past year, UGG along with the Western Stock Growers' Association and the Palliser Wheat Growers' Association has written to all MPs cautioning, 'Commodity by commodity, we are developing...policies that will create an inefficient inward-looking and government-dominated industry, cut off from world markets and increasingly dependent on taxpayers.'"

Here was the heart of Canada's farm problem. Policies were not based on boldness and economic logic, nor designed to strengthen the economy. They were pork barrel politics, pitting one farm group or region against another. Politics, not the marketplace, ruled. The Farmers' Union (it passed resolutions for a few years attacking UGG for its open market support,) the Wheat Pools at times and socialist political parties with their unthinking hatred of free markets favoured heavy government controls.

The "disease" Crerar identified was reflected in another long-running nightmare that Runciman labelled "the unending struggle over how Western feed grain was made available to Eastern Canada." Feed Freight Assistance was a wartime subsidy paid to Quebec and Ontario livestock and poultry producers on western feed grain shipped east to encourage them to produce more meat for the war effort. But it denied prairie producers a matching subsidy on livestock or meat shipped out of the West. It was government interference at its worst and should have been killed in post-war Canada when markets for livestock products were expanding fast. It became a massive ongoing burden to the prairie economy and an endless issue of dispute.

That feed freight subsidies damage was aggravated by another policy. Very little prairie-grown feed grain moved to export in the early years of settlement. Growers were free to sell it to anyone. Even when the Wheat Board was entrenched in post-war years, feed grains sales were left outside it. When prices dipped, western growers could feed cheap grain to cattle and pigs, then ship the meat to the big Ontario and Quebec markets. But this might erode prices in Toronto and Montreal and Ottawa. Livestock and poultry groups there had the votes to count in Ottawa. They had already won feed freight subsidies to give them cheap feed. And Ottawa had given them marketing boards and supply management programs to shield them from market forces. Now they demanded further protection - they wanted to shut off meat from the West. And they had a surprising card to play.

Many in the wheat Pools with their Social Gospel distrust of markets, chose ideology over economics. They backed this Eastern demand. Yes, it would restrict prairie meat output.

Together, these groups dominated the powerful policy-making Canadian Federation of Agriculture (CFA). And through it they now demanded that prairie coarse grains sold in the West be yanked off the open market and placed securely under the Wheat Board where prices could be set politically.

An appalled Runciman called it a betrayal of Western farmers. "If Western delegates in the CFA had been battling for Western Canada, they would have absolutely turned thumbs down on this," he said.

UGG's unwavering policy called for less interference, saying Canada's "traditional principle of free enterprise" is in the western farmer's interest, that he is better to "solve his problems, first, by himself, and second, through action of his own organizations."

Runciman had seen this betrayal too often. "When these CFA farm leaders faced a practical situation in grain shipping or handling or production or crop management, they would stand up and offer a philosophical argument...They went to Ottawa....with proposals that hurt western farmers. They knew better. But they let their members down."

This devastating move to political pricing of coarse grains prevented western feed mills from buying grain direct from farmers, added needless costs and further hurt prairie livestock men.

An outraged Senator Crerar saw it as a flight from common sense and he again led a revolt of Senate Liberals against the move.[4] But most politicians bowed to the "big government" lobbyists and handed the Board control of oats and barley.

Other perverse Wheat Board regulations had often damaged the West. UGG had commercial seed oats available in Alberta to meet a shortage of seed oats in Manitoba and Saskatchewan in the months prior to 1962 spring seeding. But it couldn't ship that non-Board grain between provinces without Board permission. The Board adamantly refused.

"SaskPool President Charlie Gibbings would say, 'If that prohibition is ever removed, it will be the end of the Wheat Board,'" recalled Runciman. He called this "sheer obstructionism by farm groups. When the prohibition was later removed, not a word was heard about it.

"But it had left the prairies with a hidebound system. We couldn't move the crop for a time because it wasn't being sold. All grain companies were building storage. But we had been locked into old, outdated elevators by years of restrictive handling tariffs and Wheat Board handling contracts. Then when grain began to move in 1961, we couldn't move it fast enough because the system was obsolete."

---

[4] These actions of some prairie farm groups had distressed Brownlee too in his final days. He wrote confidentially to Runciman a few weeks before his 1961 retirement, "I am completely disappointed with the present leadership for the farm organizations across western Canada. When I think of the energy devoted by the farmers' unions to the trivial question of the sale of feed grain to feed plants, and the fact that they do not seem to be interested in such important items as the closing of branch lines and the complete loss of the Crow's Nest Pass rates, I find myself at a complete loss...."

The problem extended beyond grain. With their vast land resources and leading edge technology, Canada's farmers could have greatly increased their food output. Yet they weren't even meeting Canada's own needs. Food imports had doubled to over a billion dollars from 1950 to 1965, climaxing a six-year, 10 percent annual rise. Half of these imports came from the US and many of them could have been produced right at home.

But the game was politics and Canada seemed determined to ignore and waste the rich potential of its farming industry.

8

RUNAWAY CANOLA SUCCESS -
SACRED COW DEFEAT -
HORRIFIED TRADE MISSIONS

A Ray Of Light - Cinderella Crop - Industry-Wide Council

One ray of light began to glimmer in that blackness of the late 1960's. U.S. farmers were writing a breathtaking success story with the vegetable oil crop, soybeans. Exports hit a modest 40 million bushels by 1953. But by 1965, a dozen years later, they had surged, reaching a value of $200 million. The next year they soared to over $1 billion. And that seemed barely a start. World demand for edible vegetable oils was booming, yet Pacific Rim countries with their teeming populations had hardly tasted them. Soybeans had become the US glamour crop.

Canada's farmers now got lucky. Plant scientists seeking new crops in the early 1950s had focused on a plant that produced an edible oilseed. The seed had industrial uses as well, including one as a marine engine lubricant. A little had been grown for the war effort beginning in 1943 but interest sputtered. It had the curious name rapeseed.

A few growers who now tried the new varieties found them too good to be true. Rapeseed thrived in the prairies' northern conditions. And it could be marketed outside the regulation-stifled Wheat Board. Farmers desperate for cash flow could use their own ingenuity to sell it to the highest bidder.

Growers barely hesitated. They seeded a million acres in 1965, found cash markets for every bushel, and sent acreage soaring by 80 percent in 1966. Processors and margarine makers seized on it, finding found ways to make rapeseed oil competitive with soybean oil. They saw unlimited prospects and began putting together an industry-wide coalition.

"US soybean growers credited much of their success to their Soybean Council of America which brought growers and the trade together to plan for their industry's future," explained Mac Runciman. "We wanted to learn from them."

Now, an unusual man came onto the scene. Scottish-born Jim McAnsh had joined his army regiment as a boy in World War I and on his discharge came to Canada. He became a reporter under the legendary *Winnipeg Free Press* editor John W. Dafoe and was soon a protege of the trail-blazing woman farm journalist there, Cora Hind. He later moved into the commodity exchange business.

After WW II McAnsh got a call to go down to Ottawa. He left home one morning and returned four years later, having gone to Rome with the United Nations Relief and Rehabilitation Agency. He later moved to New York with Merrill Lynch to work on the commodity exchange in oilseeds. On his 1966 retirement, he bought a marvellous home in Vancouver. But his retirement was short-lived.

With his journalism background and his knowledge of commodity markets, McAnsh saw rapeseed as a winner. It would soon be dubbed "the Cinderella crop." A rapeseed futures market had been set up on the Winnipeg Commodity Exchange in 1963. But the industry faced growing pains. It needed to set quality standards and find ways to price, market and ship increasing volumes. And it had to co-ordinate market promotion, get out information to growers and establish research projects to improve the crop's quality.

An excited McAnsh began publishing *Rapeseed Digest* from Vancouver under his own name, urging an association be set up. Interest grew. UGG's marketing director in the West, Harry Francis, foresaw real growth. Bernd Weinberg, who headed Fats and Oils for Canada's Department of Trade and Commerce, urged action because he had research money he couldn't use until an association was in place.

United Grain Growers, the Wheat Pools, other grain firms and private traders were then holding annual Barley and Oilseeds Conferences, alternately in Winnipeg and Minneapolis. Their leaders listened to McAnsh's call, put up the funds and planned a conference for the Royal Alexandra Hotel in Winnipeg with McAnsh as co-ordinator and Runciman as chairman. Interest soared - 180 people came. Guest speaker was Soybean Council of America President Glenn H. Pogeler who related that Council's successes.

Pogeler helped sweep aside any doubts. The meeting voted unanimously to act, shamelessly fashioning a new Rapeseed Association after the American Soybean Council. It was set up in early 1967, with 22 provisional directors representing most industry segments, including farm groups.

Mac Runciman had the confidence of most trade members and much of the farm community. Those first directors thought he could bring together this group's sometimes distrusting members. They named him president. Jim McAnsh was named executive director and he quickly put together an office and staff and began getting out information to growers and consumers.

The new board set up committees of growers, processors and marketing people. "People joined in this crusade to build a new industry," said Runciman. "The Pools, the Farmers' Union and just about everyone else came to the early meetings.

"Our first Vice President, Mike Macdonald, was an extraordinary man. He was Vice President and Managing Director of Canada Linseed Oil Mills Ltd., Montreal, the first Eastern company to begin processing rapeseed into oil and meal. He was a Protestant Scot who had pulled off the remarkable feat of serving as Chairman of the Montreal School Board. He undoubtedly spoke French. He walked with a limp from war wounds, was close to the shipping industry and had insights on getting the commodity on board ship. He brought a vision for the industry."

That breadth of representation from government, industry and growers meant that "everyone and his dog who had anything to do with rapeseed had a say," said Runciman.

The US soybean industry pushed production to over 1 billion bushels by 1971 and U.S. soybean oil dominated world vegetable oil markets. Runciman and his board targeted that success story as their goal.

Getting Growers to "Mind Their Own Business" - World Crusade

The new Rapeseed Association now faced a crucial challenge. "We had to get more growers to join us - to 'mind their own business,'if we were to fully succeed," Runciman recalled.

"But Prairie farmers weren't used to this radical approach. In pioneer days, farmers got up before five a.m. to feed the horses, didn't finish evening chores til eight o'clock or later. That didn't leave much time for thinking about marketing problems."

Runciman remembered those days well. "We had grown quality wheat for decades. 'Grow it, and everything else will take care of itself,' we thought. Our attitude was a by-product of the Wheat Board and the Pool systems. When a farmer dumped his grain into the pit, he felt he was done with it, his responsibility over.

"To make matters worse, growers were conditioned to see the trade as the enemy, to trust only the government....But the spark for this new association came from the Grain Exchange. Some growers thought it a heresy to give the Exchange any credit. Yet we were asking farmers to join the trade. Our goal was to build the industry to benefit farmers.

"Farmers really had no choice. We kept repeating at meeting after meeting, 'We've got to get farmers out and onto our board to make this work.'

"Then a grower named Forrest Hetland and a few others began drifting in. After one meeting, he came over, sat down and asked interested questions. He and his wife, Doris, ran a model farm operation at Naicam, Saskatchewan. They were Master Farmers and good citizens. And they were growing rapeseed successfully.

"The first farmer to sign up as an individual member was an elderly gentleman named Mr. Jamieson who grew rapeseed at Nipawin. He believed something could be done. Another was Bert Summerfeld who grew 2,000 acres of it on his farm east of North Battleford. Gordon South was a Carrot River Valley grower and a Pool director who got interested and showed real leadership.

"Saskatchewan farmer and industrialist and member of parliament J. Gordon Ross had helped form Prairie Vegetable Oils Limited in 1945, two years after rapeseed was first grown. He had chaired the the first Canadian Oilseeds Trade Mission to Europe in 1961. He joined us." Growers were becoming intrigued. Three hundred came out to a meeting in Tisdale's rapeseed country organized by growers in April, 1969 and Jim McAnsh's enthusiasm rubbed off. They launched a Saskatchewan growers association and set out to get a check-off for development work. McAnsh reported back jubilantly, "We got 135 new grower members from this and another meeting."

"More good people kept popping up from the industry as well," said Runciman. "UGG's Harry Francis was named a director and chairman of our executive committee and he helped organize the first research projects. Within months, Trade and Commerce's Bernd Weinberg had his research underway.

"Ken Sarsons was SaskPool's flour milling and rapeseed crushing man, an independent-minded guy with a strong personality who was held in awe by some people. He supported sensible suggestions and became an important team man. He and I had a good relationship.

"Jack Reynolds who managed SaskPool's Saskatoon oilseed crushing plant chaired our technical committee dealing with the erucic acid and glucocinolate problems and others. John T. Dallas of Continental Grain, Winnipeg, was a hard-working, progressive guy with a sense of humour who represented the exporters and shippers. He handled the finances, twisting arms and getting the money when I didn't think it could be done.

"Hilmar K. Moen from Alberta Pool Terminal in Vancouver was an early activist and worker. John J. Banfield of Lethbridge Canbra Oilseed Crushing Plant, which was the earliest to market the oil with a rapeseed tag (Westoil) on it, helped bring in the crushers' and retailers' viewpoint which many participants had never heard. Cargill's Dick Dawson brought in the industry side."

People from every part of the industry were joining this crusade to build a new industry. The Winnipeg Grain Exchange opened a new Futures based at Thunder Bay to help speed the crop to markets in Europe and Eastern Canada. The first trade mission went to Japan in 1968.

In the 1968 federal election a lawyer named Otto Lang won a seat in Saskatchewan as a Liberal. Grain politics was part of Lang's heritage for he had been born and raised in the wheat province. He had become a Rhodes

Scholar and was a former University of Saskatchewan Dean of Law. The Prime Minister named him Minister without Portfolio and then in 1969, Wheat Board Minister under ranking minister Jean-Luc Pepin. Later he became full-fledged Wheat Board Minister while Pepin remained Industry, Trade and Commerce Minister where he could continue to support change.

Lang could recognize a winning horse when he saw one. He insisted that the Wheat Board be fully on side with this new crusade and that it adjust rapeseed quota levels to meet the crushing industry's needs. He also pledged Ottawa's support for a massive marketing effort to double rapeseed exports from the previous years's 22 million bushels.

Ottawa was soon sponsoring missions to Europe and Asia, introducing quality standards and bringing foreign buyers to see how the crop was grown and processed. Mission members brought back some astonishing findings.

"We often didn't know what buyers used rapeseed for," said Runciman. "Japanese buyers didn't consider rapeseed meal a protein supplement at all. They used it as a fertilizer for crops like tobacco and citrus fruits instead. We had to respond. And we later found that rapeseed meal wasn't being fed to livestock because it wasn't as good for some classes of livestock, and because its high glucocinolate content gave a less-desirable spicy flavour."

Runciman recalled an earlier UGG experience. "We were selling buckwheat to Japan. Demand peaked twice each year. We didn't know why, and asked, 'What do they use it for?' We found they used it celebrating the New Year, and in hot months as a cold noodle for a cool meal. We could then plan more effectively.

"Richardson Grain's West Coast man Torben Hoyer grew up in Denmark and his wife was French-Canadian. Torben represented the shippers very well. When he and I went to Japan on a government rapeseed mission, he carried his heritage with him. Each morning he wanted toast and Danish blue cheese for breakfast."

But there were rocky moments. "Grain Exchange President J.E. McWilliam was too abrasive for the National Farmers' Union. I expected its President Roy Atkinson to walk out, and he did, making his exit as dramatic as he could. As he walked, I thanked him for his contribution and regretted he couldn't stay. Then, I got on with the meeting.

"The Pools could see the need for industry groups working together. But they were itchy, too, and I had sympathy with them. McWilliams carried his open-market convictions so fanatically he antagonized people. The mood changed when Jim Clark replaced him at the Grain Exchange and on the Rapeseed Board. Next to the Farmers' Union, the Pools were the most difficult to accommodate."

Grower Forrest Hetland's involvement gave Runciman some fascinating anecdotes. "He was a positive onside guy, a strong businessman who saw the need. He staged seminars on how to grow rapeseed. Ottawa soon named him Commissioner of the Canadian Grain Commission and he left the farmers' ranks. But his talents weren't lost. He worked closely with McAnsh and went on missions to places like Russia.

"And his abilities were recognized. He came to our house on New Year's Eve, 1975, as a Grain Commissioner and left after midnight, in 1976, as a Wheat Board Commissioner. More recently his son Bill was President of the Saskatchewan Canola Growers' Association."

Health Scare Crisis - Scramble To Canola

The maple trees on the rolling hills and mountains around Ste. Adele, Quebec, north of Montreal, turn a breathtaking scarlet each fall, making this one of the world's beauty spots and a mecca for conventions and meetings and holiday outings. The Rapeseed Association and the Canada Department of Industry, Trade and Commerce planned an international conference for late September, 1970, and they succumbed to the lure of this splendid location.

Four hundred scientists, businessmen and others from 20 countries converged on this spot. The goal was to identify industry problems and set the stage for further growth, and speakers reported startling progress. Rapeseed acreage had doubled in each of the past two years to 4 million - 11 percent of seeded acreage. The 80 million bushel harvest was worth $200 million. Rapeseed oil was fast becoming Canada's most important vegetable oil.

Plant breeders reported on new improved varieties. Enthusiasm pervaded the sessions. Buyers from Japan and other countries addressed the meeting. A European participant said no conference he had attended in 20 years compared to this.

It was a milestone, showing that growers, crushers, grain handlers and government could work together focusing on marketing and setting up seminars and education programs in Canada and abroad.

Then the euphoria was shattered. A research report which said rats that were fed rapeseed oil had developed dangerous fatty heart lesions caught media headlines.

"Overnight we had senior people come down from Ottawa," recalled Mac Runciman who was Conference Co-chairman. "An Oils and Fats Division official told me rapeseed's high erucic acid content was deemed to produce high fat levels in the hearts of rats fed it. 'If it's bad for rats, it's bad for humans,' he declared. He said his group was going to put us out of business.

"That scared the hell out of us. This was a full-blown crisis. Our executive stayed up until 4 a.m. with some government people considering what to do. Dr. Bert Migicovsky of Canada Department of Agriculture was jointly chairing the Conference with me. A dramatic debate was certain the next morning. Bert chaired that session and I was thankful he was there.

"Bert began with a beautiful slant, saying, 'Look, gentlemen, most of us here are scientists. We must look at this in the clear cold light of science and recognize it isn't enough for us to just do the research and publish it. We must be concerned about how that knowledge is interpreted and used by the public and the media. If the facts say we have to ruin the rapeseed industry to prevent hazards to the human population, so be it. But let's not ruin an industry because of too few facts or a misinterpretation of them.'

"To make his point, he told a story of a hunter who had 'a very very very clever hunting dog. He went hunting, shot a duck and it fell into the lake. The dog simply ran over the water, picked up the duck and brought it back.

'The proud hunter couldn't wait to take his friend out the following morning. When they shot a duck, the dog ran across the water, got the duck, and ran back.

'What do you think of my dog?' beamed the hunter. His friend answered, 'I don't like to criticize a dog to his master, but I can see your dog can't swim.'"

The point of the story was clear. "The facts were the

same, but the two people interpreted them differently," said Runciman.

The best scientists in the world on this issue were in attendance so the meeting could draft a statement that reassured the public, yet gave the industry time to devise a strategy. "We said the high erucic acid oils fed in this research...were much higher than you'd get in the human diet. And no hazard to human health has been attributed to rapeseed oil now, or throughout its long history," said Runciman.

Plant breeders had new varieties with low erucic acid and higher linoleic acid levels. A gradual changeover could be made, and the regular rapeseed oil used until then.

But the industry had to go further. It had to change to new double zero varieties which contained neither erucic acid or glucosynilates. This was the historic shift to canola.

"We had to ask, 'How long will this changeover take?' said Runciman. "Garnet wheat was a precedent. This variety couldn't grade above Number 3 Northern but it was early-maturing. Growers in the Alberta foothills hung onto it for years to feed to livestock. They didn't care if it wasn't a high protein milling wheat.

"But occasionally one of them would dump some into the local elevator. That created a bad carload of milling wheat. Officials tried for years to stamp out Garnet. We wondered, 'Will people do the same with rapeseed?'

"A few of us went to Ottawa to discuss it with Agriculture Minister Bud Olson and his staff. Canada Grain Commission Chief Del Pound was there. We outlined our program and said 'We can make the switch in two years.' Olson and Pound were willing to back us. What a pleasure it was to sit down with a minister and his senior staff who knew what they were talking about and where they wanted to go.

"The switch was done in two years. Absolutely amazing. Our Association was paying off, getting people to sit around a table trying to understand each other's problems and develop an industry attitude."

Defeat For The Holiest Of Sacred Cows

By 1971 rapeseed acreage had increased fivefold in four years. Each year's crop had been sold before the new harvest began. Unlike wheat and barley which sold under the Wheat Board, rapeseed was not plagued with on-farm surpluses. Support prices were unknown.

But here were seeds of trouble. Those soaring sales were being led by the efforts of growers, the grain firms and other industry players. This success story was being written outside that holiest of sacred cows - the Wheat Board. And this was a constant rebuke to compulsory marketing fanatics.

Inevitably, Saskatchewan Wheat Pool - and others who were still gripped with blind animosity to the open market and to farmers making their own marketing decisions - found this intolerable. SaskPool President Ted Turner, reaching back to the old Social Gospel rhetoric to support a little scare-mongering, intoned, "Private concerns can make huge profits at the farmers' expense under the present system, especially in rapeseed."

A campaign to bring rapeseed into the bosom of "orderly marketing," and securely under the control of politicians was underway. A crescendo of speeches shouted the message that Wheat Board control would even out price fluctuations and give producers more stability. Wheat Board Minister Otto Lang bowed to the pressure and called a rapeseed vote.

It was Runciman's nature to seek compromise unless on an issue of principle. He had the utmost respect for several Pool people he knew from farm meetings. He absolutely believed farm groups should seek common cause on important issues. Yet distasteful confrontations were too frequent. This was an issue of principle. The battle would have to be fought.

The Pools and the Farmers' Union now demanded of Lang that all Wheat Board permit holders get a vote, whether they grew rapeseed or not. The normally unflappable Runciman was incensed. "If *I'm* growing rapeseed and *you* never grew rapeseed and don't intend to grow it, why should you have a vote in deciding how I am going to sell my crop?

"This illustrated perfectly the left-wing philosophy that griped me intensely," he said. "I always believed the farmer who puts his life and his bucks into farming should have an absolute controlling input into how his business is handled. A bunch of guys in Ottawa with indexed pensions shouldn't be telling him how to run it.

"If non-growers got a vote and the results favoured bringing rapeseed marketing under the Board, it would have been absolutely unjust to growers.

"Look!" he reasoned. "If single desk selling is so essential, how did canola get to where it is today? Canola went from nothing to a great success based on open-market selling. It never had a monopoly selling agency."

In the campaign leading up to the vote, the Rapeseed Association's Jim McAnsh drove home that point with cool logic. "How will Board control improve anything?" He wanted "a lean, aggressive industry able to address every challenge and keep growing," not one tangled in the Wheat Board bureaucracy.

"Consider the competition we face," McAnsh urged. "US soybean growers have a river system with barges and many more gateway ports to move their crop than we have for rapeseed. They are free to sell soybeans in the open market, or if they don't like the Chicago price, to put them into the government loan program and redeem them later when the market changes. That free movement helped in their industry's fantastic growth.

"Compare that to what rapeseed growers face. Canada has only two east-west transcontinental railway lines. Our long haul to tidewater is in boxcars. No rapeseed can move by rail without a Wheat Board permit. The Wheat Board's delivery quota system starts right at the farm and applies to all grains going to commercial storage or to processors. Our block transportation system's restrictions can distort prices, restrain rapeseed movement, impede the future market operations and reduce its effectiveness at hedging."

McAnsh's message was unequivocal. "It's not more restrictions we need. It's fewer impediments."

Wheat Board Minister Lang finally rejected the every-farmer vote demand and confined it to rapeseed growers.

That vote was a turning point not just for rapeseed, but for the entire prairie grain industry. If growers had turned their backs on their astonishing success story and voted for monopoly selling - in effect turning their crop over to the politicians and bureaucrats - it would have been a devastating setback for prairie agriculture.

When the dust had settled, growers had voted 52 percent to 48 percent to keep their crop on the open market, clearing the way for further rapid industry growth.

But little could they have realized then just how rapid that growth would be. By 1994, canola acreage had soared and the harvest rivalled wheat itself in dollar value.

Council Breakthrough - Pepin's New Day - Together In One Room

When Pierre Trudeau hit the campaign trail for the 1968 election after succeeding Lester Pearson as leader of the Liberal Party and Prime Minister, he addressed a rally at Winnipeg's International Inn. World farmers were then pouring out more food than had been thought possible, collapsing prices. Canada's grain pileup and the lack of cash flow were of crisis proportions. Grain was the West's most pressing issue.

The open-market canola industry was writing a glittering success story. But the Wheat Board monopoly for wheat, barley and oats remained unbroken, holding the grain handling/transportion systems virtually frozen in time. Farmers and the trade were stymied, blocked from devising initiatives to find new markets and strengthen the selling effort and deliver the grain when buyers wanted it. Good markets were being overlooked. Much of the world's wheat surplus was piled up in Canada.

"The Wheat Board's attitude was reflected in Chief Commissioner Bill McNamara's apparent belief, 'We are a monopoly, we control the world,'" said Runciman. "He seemed to feel, 'Who is going to sell wheat at a dollar and a half a bushel? We'll wait till it's at $1.75, then sell some.'

"He felt, 'You sell wheat when prices are good, store it up when they are bad, sell again when prices are good. And farmers make a lot of money.'

"Wheat Board Commissioner Larry Kristjannsen thought the same way. He might be heard to say, 'We can't get the price right now, but they are going to have to come to us one of these days, and maybe we'll get the stuff moving and the farmers will get some money.'

"That's fine if you're getting paid to run the Wheat

Board," said Runciman. "It doesn't work worth a damn if you are running a farm and have bills to pay every day of the week. One summer our family bought groceries on time because of that idea. Having come through that, it didn't sit well with me to let some Wheat Board bureaucrat decide when farmers were going to get income.

"A farmer's income is bushels times price. If his grain didn't move, he had nothing to live on. He just sat there and twiddled his thumbs and hoped some day he would get a quota and sell a few bushels."

On this 1968 campaign stop in Winnipeg, Trudeau had been well-briefed by advisers outside Ottawa's grain bureaucracy and by others not committed to monopoly selling. He offered a momentous suggestion.

Why not set up a national grains council where leaders of the railways and the elevators and farmers and processors and unions can come together to plan overall industry strategy and to provide government with leadership and advice on needed measures? he asked.

Here was a blinding insight. And it couldn't have been more timely. Runciman was convinced the idea was right. The industry desperately needed new initiatives like rail line abandonment and system rationalization. The idea caught on.

"Manitoba Pool President Bill Parker and National Grain President George Heffelfinger were leading Liberal lights. Both favoured it. So did I and others," said Runciman. "It became an election ploy and a government commitment."

Trudeau won the election and his Cabinet appointments brought a refreshing new face to the prairie farm scene. Jean-Luc Pepin had been first elected to the House of Commons from Quebec in 1963 with the Pearson government. By 1967 he was Finance Minister and Receiver General. Trudeau now named him Minister of Industry, Trade and Commerce. He also gave him perhaps the most formidable challenge of all - the Wheat Board.

Runciman found him willing to listen. "He began to recognize the grain industry's huge potential, the need to market grain aggressively rather than cutting back production....He had the wisdom and the guts to tackle sacred cows, and the clout in Ottawa to get the critical things done. He was prepared to attack the status quo.

Pepin got the ball rolling so we could begin to build

a system to move all the grain we could grow. His arrival in that dark period was like the dawn of a new day."

Twenty-seven organisations, including UGG, named members to be appointed by Ottawa. Many didn't know one another and thought they wouldn't like each other. Pepin wanted a chairman who could bring them together. Runciman's work as Rapeseed Association president was now widely praised. Pepin named him to the post.

The group met in Winnipeg on February 3, 1969 to set up the Council. "The idea wasn't new," said Runciman. "A UGG Board had considered it years earlier. Harry Griffin had recorded in 1931 how such a body would bring groups together to talk and plan, giving marketing leadership and advising government. We located that old document and took our goals from it almost word for word."

The Council set out to hire staff and plan the work ahead. Dr. Don Dever was a Canadian working in Ontario for an American firm which had asked him to move to the US. He applied for the manager's job of this new Council. "He was flown in from Ontario," Runciman remembered. "Manitoba Pool President Bill Parker and I interviewed him with a flourish, dined him at the Manitoba Club, found he was highly qualified. We hired him."

The Council was launched on April 1, 1969, bringing together for the first time people from just about every group in the grain industry. To break the tension, Runciman tried a little humour, jokingly telling the crowd how they had decided on a name.

"We first thought of calling it the National Grains Council, but rejected that because it might be confused with George Heffelfinger's National Grain Company. We considered calling it the Federal Grains Council. But that might be confused with Federal Grain Company. We finally decided on the Canada Grains Council."

Runciman admitted later, "That didn't set off gales of laughter. Everybody seemed serious - they didn't get it."

Horrified Trade Missions

Despite the grain pileup, Council members rejected the tired old knee-jerk Canadian response that growers should slash their acreage, or launch a raid on the federal treasury. They wanted fresh approaches. And now the world market for coarse grains caught their attention.

"That feed grains market has increased 25 percent in 10 years and trade has nearly doubled," Runciman told one early meeting. World production was over 48 percent of total grain output. Yet Canada's tightly regulated industry had virtually ignored it, focusing almost exclusively on the slow-growing quality protein bread wheat market. It was even failing to meet Canada's own feed grain demands.

Runciman urged farmers, "Feed out more cattle or hogs to use up the grain." He called coarse grains "a vast market that could absorb Canada's production if our prices were competitive."

The Council raised funding for four teams of five people each to examine the world feed grains market. These missions visited 26 countries in the Americas and in South and Southeast Asia. They talked to farmers, governments, feed mill and grain trade people, processors and anyone else they could find.

They found the Southeast Asia market beyond comprehension. Over 300 million people and a soaring birth rate in fast-industrializing countries. Most were short of animal proteins. On their visits the Canadians kept bumping into US and Australian salesmen. Corn was the basic feed grain because US salesmen got there first. Most buyers had never heard of Canada's feed grains. Mission members in Mexico found grain brokers lacked confidence in Canada's grain system. They didn't believe we would meet delivery dates or provide post-sales service.

The horrified Canadians returned with the devastating news - we lacked an effective marketing presence. And with the US so well entrenched, we faced an uphill struggle. Runciman reported, "This is the very heart of our problem - our failure to open markets means we are losing too many farmers off their farms."

He asked the only question that mattered. "Why do we phase out a Canadian farmer who can grow wheat for, say, $1.20 a bushel when a European farmer's costs are $2 or more?"

Part of the cause lay beyond Canada's border. "European Common Market support prices were too high with soft wheat at $2.77 per bushel, barley at $2.14 and rapeseed at $4.60. Policies that ignore markets are hindering world development and could provoke more trade wars." He called on all countries to act.

But Canada had to act on its own as well. The new Council drew up a master plan focusing on feed grain and including projects to breed and develop new grains; to improve the barley grading system; to set up overseas market information and development offices; and to bring people from these countries to Canada to see how to feed these grains to livestock. And much more.

Canada-Japan Trade Council President R.L. Houston, who knew Japan well, told an early Council meeting that Canada's best hopes for new food markets lay in the Pacific basin. Japan was the hub. But he challenged, Let's be honest. We Canadians can't make up our minds to serve these markets. How can we compete with Australia, the US and New Zealand who are already there, when we haven't yet seen the need for personal salesmanship?

Japan Consul-General Eiichi Uchida brought a Regina audience the same message. Japan must import feed grains on a massive scale and produce its own meat, or else increase its meat imports while increasing its feed grain imports less rapidly, he said. Either way, you Canadians stand to gain. But you must produce at competitive prices.

Uchida also predicted the Japanese wheat market would expand just as rapeseed markets were doing. "If Canada could provide feedstuffs at competitive prices, and market aggressively, it could make huge sales there," he promised.

The Grains Council did bring people together to develop an industry attitude, as the Rapeseed Association had done earlier. "But it had anything but smooth sailing," said Runciman. "Ottawa's bureaucrats acceded to Trudeau's campaign promise, helped set up the Council. But they didn't want big parts of the grain business running loose outside their control. In time they seized tight control of the industry, too often victimizing the Council."

The Council had foreseen a major role in educating customers about grain products. The Wheat Board was to put up money. "But the Board was always an enemy of the Council, wanted to kill it," said Runciman. "Chief Commissioner Bill McNamara gave it token service because Mitch Sharp was his Minister. But the Board didn't want to finance anything influenced by this too-independent

Council which it saw impinging on some of its policies.

"And Ottawa bureaucrats saw the education budget as too big a plum to hang on the tree for this upstart. The Council was hardly up and going when the Canadian International Grains Institute was set up to control the money and do the education job." The bureaucrats soon muscled in again, setting up a Grains Group as a sort of think-tank with a concept of inland terminals in mind. But this think-tank idea was to have been part of the Council's mandate, Runciman remembered.

"The bureaucrats weren't going to let those powers and budgets go to the Council - they were robbing it of intended functions and left it as a sort of shell."

The Council faced other trials. At an early meeting, some members were accused of trying to make agricultural policy. "The minutes show we passed a resolution to stay away from policy," Runciman said. "But no matter, the National Farmers' Union walked out. Again this was partly triggered by J.E. McWilliam's extremism."

Human Foibles In Buying Grain Companies

When Otto Lang was named Wheat Board Minister in 1969, he faced an insurmountable backlog of unsold wheat but his mind grasped the big picture. Prices were deteriorating. Payments to farmers under the Temporary Wheat Reserves Act were at record highs. The industry had been studied to death but action never seemed to follow. He summed up the challenge succinctly, "Grain has been a national problem needing a solution."

Reform-minded farm groups were mounting intense pressure for Wheat Board change. And now cracks in the gridlock appeared. Board Chief Commissioner McNamara retired and was named to the Senate on October 5, 1970. He was replaced by career grain salesman Gerry Vogel from the private trade.

"Vogel sharpened the Board's focus on selling and set about tightening up its operations," Runciman recalled later. "He once bragged very happily to me that he had reduced the Board's administration staff by 25 percent. So the Board had been a pretty affluent bureaucracy."

Farmers were already shifting out of wheat and Lang tried to further restrain the flood swamping the country with his famous, or infamous, "LIFT" (Lower Inventories for Tomorrow) program which paid farmers to cut back on wheat in favour of forage crops and summerfallow. This slashed the 1970 crop. But wheat demand and prices suddenly soared again and Lang was roundly criticised even by SaskPool and Saskatchewan farmers.

Runciman was less critical. "Politically, it cost Lang dearly. But the summerfallow acreage boost one year brought a big crop the next so it had little effect on total output in the three-or-four period."

While UGG's ongoing strategy was to build its elevator system to handle grain quickly at least cost to the farmer, grain companies were still entangled in over-regulation and Runciman warned his members in 1972 that the low margins and 50 percent stocks-in-store wouldn't support a modern operation at each elevator point. It took $230,000 of borrowed capital to build a new 150,000-bushel-capacity elevator. Just to pay back the costs and 8 1/2 percent interest required 750,000 bushels a year handling over 20 years.

"Change is imperative," he said. UGG would continue its orderly expansion, moving into major points where it could get large handling. Competition would ensure good service to all farmers there, no matter to whom they delivered.

Runciman didn't reveal to UGG delegates another drama taking place that would reshape the industry. Searle Grain Company had earlier joined Federal Grain Company under Federal's banner to become Canada's biggest private elevator company. But while every company required massive investments to keep up their systems, over-regulation prevented them from getting their money back. Federal's owners were losing hope. They decided they could better invest capital elsewhere.

Federal chief George Sellers had approached Runciman, saying he despaired of a further role for his company in grain, and asked, "Would UGG like to buy Federal?"

"We were negotiating seriously," Runciman said later. "Former Searle head Cy Leach joined the talks. Then came the announcement. New Wheat Board Minister Otto Lang was setting up a Grains Group as a federal bureaucracy to run the prairie grain business.

"Both Federal and ourselves said, 'Wait a minute!'

The new Grains Group's aims would seem to give government firm control of the industry. None of us knew where that would lead. We put the thing in abeyance.

"Grain politics got into that deal in more ways than one. I spoke to Jean-Luc Pepin about it once. He answered, 'You know, Mr. Runciman, that looks to me as though you are trying to set up a monopoly.'

"Yes, there was dissent in the political arena as to whether Grain Growers and Federal Grain should be allowed to come together. It took a year and a half for the Grains Group's role to come through. When it did, George Sellers went to the three wheat pools and made a deal with them in January, 1972. The Pools carved up the huge Federal grain system.

"We at UGG read about it in the paper. We were not involved. We didn't consciously decide not to buy Federal. Had we got it, the deal would have made UGG Canada's largest grain company, bigger than SaskPool. Whether any less of a monopoly was created when the Pools got Federal is another question," he said.

"Because of the industry's over-regulation, the purchase was really to increase the Pools' market share. That was the only way to do it. The Pools bought a chunk of market share based on shipping. But Federal had all sorts of crocks of elevators. If we had got it, we would have had to dispose of hundreds of them. Could we have carried the cost? Our manager Bill Winslow wondered."

Runciman had a bird's-eye view of another grain company sale which gave him a further insight into the foibles of human nature. "National Grain President George Heffelfinger approached me in 1974. We had talked a few times about UGG taking over National. We went for lunch to the Old Spaghetti Factory restaurant in the Old Market Square area of Winnipeg to talk. George was looking for approaches.

"Then, one day my phone rang. It was George. He said, 'Mac, this business of talking about the sale has got to stop. There has been too much loose talk. I'm getting things on the street. We've got to cut it out.'

"I had never mentioned it to anyone. He had asked me not to. So his words surprised me. The next day it was announced that Cargill, the largest of the world's grain traders, had bought National Grain with its 195 elevators. I guess the word got going in Minneapolis that National was for sale and George got some flak."

Runciman chuckled for years at one sidelight. "The Farmers' Union rose up in indignation at this purchase by Cargill and condemned the deal for bringing a multinational company into Canada. In fact, about a month later, Cargill held a big reception in Winnipeg for grain industry people, to mark 50 years in the grain business in Western Canada. It had been here buying and selling grain all those years. Buying National was an extension of that. Farmers' Union either didn't know or refused to recognize it."

9

GROWERS' CALL TO ARMS -
THE ROSETOWN NEAR-RIOT -
THE SOVIET'S US
GRAIN ROBBERY

Rage Was The Mood

When that little group of anxious and angry Saskatchewan farmers led by Wally Nelson arrived in Mac Runciman's Winnipeg office back in 1970 trying to find why their grain wasn't selling, he wasn't surprised. "The lack of grain movement and income had brought desperation. Over-regulation caused much of the problem. Government policies told farmers and the trade, 'We'll tie your hands behind your back and say, Go get him, tiger!'"

The system had broken down. "Wheat growers were in Winnipeg in an honest quest to see what was wrong. It was Ed Partridge all over again - another turn of the wheel."

Rapeseed growers, cattlemen, hog producers and others had commodity groups to fight for their political interests. But wheat growers had none. Runciman believed they had no choice but to set up their own commodity group to battle for change. He urged them on.

Anger, even rage, was now their mood. "This was our wheat. We had to find a way to get it back into the market," recalled Nelson later. "We had to do like the others."

They formed the Palliser Wheat Growers' Association with Nelson as president and began a dizzying pace. They set up an office in Regina, made member Bob Ferguson managing director and a precocious young university graduate named Dennis Harrison executive director. Harrison had experience in labour-union tactics which would be useful as the group moved into the brutal field of politics. Regina farmer Bill Scott was made assistant manager.

At meetings across the province, interest snowballed. "Growers stand in line to sign up," said a wide-eyed Nelson. Memberships rolled in, up to 1000 a week and reached 5000 within a month. Their office put out a paper to keep members informed and to leave no doubt they were not a bunch of orangutans simply out to raise hell. Their purpose was deadly serious. Apathy was gone.

Director Art Thompson of Pense delivered the message over and over, "Wheat growers are the silent majority no longer. We're taking our place beside other commodity groups to protect our interests."

They set up committees and were soon travelling to Winnipeg to probe into issues and organizing member tours to Vancouver Port to see for themselves how their grain was handled. They called meetings and brought in speakers to give insights and answer questions.

The issue went to Canada's heart. Politicians had listened to the Wheat Pools and other left-wing groups in devising wheat policies, and these growers were convinced this was the cause of the crisis. They sent federal officials and every prairie MP a simple written message. "We wheat farmers are now organized. Every other commodity group...is consulted on matters affecting its livelihood before action is taken. We want to have a hand in every decision that affects us. We aim to speak with a unified voice."

Hundreds of farmers fought their way through a blizzard to attend the founding convention in Regina's Hotel Saskatchewan in January, 1971. Nelson told the overflow crowd of a year of breathtaking action.

"Creeping protectionism is the problem," he said, labelling it "a dangerous insidious trend....Our US competitors send people around the world, order books in their pockets, to sell their grain. Where there is no demand, they try to create it by educating and persuading people. Selling farm products is big business to them. They go about it in a businesslike way.

"But we have a different attitude. We focus on problems that occur because we didn't solve the problem of selling. Some attitudes are unbelievable. The Wheat Pool president told us if Canada were to work harder to sell wheat it would drive the price down.

"Can you imagine the president of General Motors...not trying to sell more cars because it might drive their price down?" asked an amazed Nelson.

The new group had already chalked up some successes, helping change the Canada Grains Act to permit protein grading, and playing a key role in forming the Wheat Board's Marketing Review Committee in 1970. It was now studying grain storing, examining the old handling system and seeking out new markets and new uses for wheat. And it was getting out more information to farmers.

In fact, the little band was beginning to bring their farmers' viewpoint into play in possibly the most important issue on the world stage - how to win the war on hunger. But this was barely a start.

The Great Rosetown Wheat Forum - Opposition Firestorm

Farm politics can be a fiercely combative game in Canada, a blood sport with no quarter asked or given. Nelson knew his little group was heading into a battle zone, that it would be fiercely resented and resisted. Some farm leaders knew those Palliser reformers would be striking into the very heart of grain politics, determined to free up farmers and give them a say in the way their grain was sold.

Within weeks the new group tasted that fierce attack. They scheduled what became known as "the Great Rosetown Wheat Forum" for July 29, 1970, in Rosetown, Saskatchewan, to inform growers of the grave issues they faced. Ten prominent industry people were to speak including UGG's Mac Runciman, SaskPool President Ted Turner, Richardson Grain's buyer and exporter Dodds Hughes and Wheat Board Commissioner Charles Gibbings as well as some Palliser farmers and others. The audience was to ask questions.

In a masterstroke, Palliser's Dennis Harrison had persuaded CKKR Radio to air the program live to a prairie network and on tape to several other stations. The wide audience of farmers could phone in questions and comments. What followed was one of the most remarkable events in prairie history.

An open, freewheeling discussion by informed people on wheat marketing was against everything the left-wing National Farmers Union believed to be sacred. An explosive meeting was inevitable. *Calgary Herald* reporter John Schmidt was there and he described what happened.

"There was standing room only and hundreds more were listening outside on car radios," he wrote. A Palliser member named Sparling was introducing the panel when it happened. "The (Farmers) Union, along with student provocateurs from the Saskatchewan Liberation Front 'packed' the community hall from rows five to 15 and took over the meeting.

"Alfred Moore of Dinsmore, Sask., grabbed a floor mike on a point of privilege. Sparling demurred, said this would delay the broadcast schedule. Moore was big and blond and dressed in a green shirt and he replied this was a farmer's meeting, farmers had been invited and farmers would run it democratically in a manner decided by the majority. Sparling was shouted down in an atmosphere which became electric when hollering, shouting of slogans and clapping broke out.

"'We don't want to be talked down to by experts,' said Moore. 'We intend to elect our own moderator' and he was greeted by pounding and a standing ovation....Nervously, Sparling called for order and courteous treatment of the panel guests. He was told in no uncertain terms his guests would be handled as the meeting saw fit and since the broadcast was not originating in the CKKR studios, it was the people's meeting.

"...Don Robertson of Liberty, Sask., came to the platform amid a storm of applause and took over...Sparling avoided potential violence by proceeding as he did. He had seen that the meeting had been packed with opposition which was able to intimidate everybody in sight. They weren't there to listen but just to hoot and holler and shout slogans.[1]

---

[1] The author can vouch for this description, for he was one of the panel of ten speakers. It was the only farm meeting he attended in a long reporting career where a feeling of genuine fear gripped those attending, where mob rule had taken over and civility abolished. Fortunately no physical violence occurred but it could have.

"Sparling had been taken by surprise by a coup which was precise, well-organized and a week in preparation."

For three hours the mob hurled obscenities at speakers, and the Palliser people worked desperately to prevent a riot breaking out. Harrison, with his political science training and his experience in labour unions, played a key role in keeping the lid on what was now a tinderbox.[2]

Schmidt's report went on, "After the formal broadcast, the meeting voted in sympathy with NFU policy that the Canadian Wheat Board retain its full powers and that the marketing of feed grains be restored to it and orderly marketing maintained.

"Palliser directors agreed afterwards, 'The forum could have been an embarrassing debacle to them had not the NFU and the 'liberation front' been so blatantly Maoist in their attempts to liberate the wheat growers from agri-business....It was NFU belief the capitalist system was so rotten it didn't want to live within it and set out to change it - overthrowing it first and then rebuilding it, of course. Those who thought differently were 'enemies of the people' and 'vassals of capitalist exploiters,' and the ones on the platform were 'booed and hissed.'"

Schmidt said many years later, "I have never encountered anything quite like it except the hog meetings in Ontario...in the 1950s when Charlie McInnis, President of the Ontario Hog Producers Association tried to 'liberate' hog producers from the truckers....

"The mood of NFU was to take on the world and even its friends. It even attacked its best friend, the Canadian Grain Commission, heckling chairman Frank Hamilton...."

Palliser's arrival on the farm scene inevitably won mixed greetings from other farm organizations and the media as well. The UGG-owned national farm paper *Country Guide*[3] called Palliser's formation "encouraging and long-overdue." The *Winnipeg Free Press Weekly* and some other papers welcomed the wheat growers to the scene.

---

[2] Harrison later drowned tragically in a fishing accident, snuffing out a promising career.

[3] The author of this book was then editor of *Country Guide*.

But the SaskPool-owned *Western Producer* was sceptical at best. Its editor sized up the new group in his April 16, 1970 edition, suggesting it would be "more market oriented than traditional western farm organizations" and admitted its members "reflected a widespread concern about the future of Canada's wheat markets." He even hesitantly welcomed the group's involvement. But he betrayed his underlying concern, cautioning, "the care with which they assemble and assess the very large and complex problems of an international market, and the degree to which they recognize the limitations of alternative plans for marketing wheat" would determine their success.

That admonition left no doubt - a fierce response would greet any effort to rock the boat. The editor added, "If the new voice only adds to the sounds of discord coming from western agriculture, they will unhappily do little more than contribute to the paralysis of influence...arising from the failure of farmers to present a united front."

Yes, any honeymoon for Palliser would be short-lived. The Pool was committed to monopoly Wheat Board selling and utterly opposed to giving individual growers a say in selling their own grain, or in fact, any part in a search for initiatives that might do that. The die was cast. The Palliser-SaskPool relationship would be a rocky and smouldering one.

When the *Producer* continued to criticize the change-oriented Palliser people, they answered back in a late 1971 newsletter. "Everyone now agrees West Coast terminal capacity must be increased," they wrote, "with the possible exception of the esteemed editor of the *Producer*."

When these growers were attacked by SaskPool, the Farmers Union and others as being "instant experts two-and-a-half miles from home," their simple response was, "We will run into criticism, but the critics should be aware, the only sure way to destroy Palliser is to eliminate the need for it."[4]

---

[4] In one tongue-in-cheek response to the *Western Producer*, Palliser's Don Jaques headed a Newsletter column...

GOODNESS GRACIOUS!

Jaques went on to reveal a fine sense of humour, writing...

"In a passionate editorial Oct. 7, the *Western Producer*, a paper singu-

Canada's Nightmare - A Strike A Month? - The Soviet's US Grain Robbery

Big world harvests kept surpluses high in those dark days for Canada's growers, but US food exports bounded to a record $7.2 billion in calendar 1970, 20 percent over 1969. They were being massively subsidized by the US government, but $6.2 billion of them were commercial sales. US exports climbed further to $7.5 billion the next year.

Canada's wheat exports trailed badly because of the transport breakdown and because the country lacked the money to compete in the subsidy giveaway. Ottawa urged the US to desist, but sagging prices soon forced it to step in with grower price supports.

Then the media began to focus on an ominous development - world farmers seemed unable to keep pace with the world's spiralling population. Per capita food output seemed to be falling. World leaders asked anxiously, "Can famine be staved off? Or must tens of millions of people die?"

---

larly sensitive to criticism of West Coast terminals, used its inimitable invective against Palliser again.

"Not one to allow realism to ruin rhetoric, the editor (accuses Palliser of) 'sweeping allegations...frantic attempts...pitifully inaccurate... lacking in substance...wildly irresponsible....' etc.

"Wow!

"Like a hired gunman defending his boss on the late show, the *Producer* writes, 'There is still time...to deny it, or produce evidence....'

Quipped Jaques...

"It's like he said, 'You got 'til sundown to get outa town, podner.'

Jaques went on...

"The *Producer* continued, 'It is a great pity that an organization with as much potential usefulness to producers should condone such tactics.'"

Chuckled the Palliser spokesman...

"It's nice to know somebody cares."

But he concluded...

"Fun though it has been, Palliser has decided to discontinue exchanges with the editor of the *Western Producer*. We welcome public discussion of these ideas, but let's keep it on a factual basis, and let's not pretend everything is rosy - that improvements will be made without prompting by the farmers, if and when the 'experts' decide they are needed."

Hungry countries lacked cash to pay for their food needs, but evidence appeared that the long-term market outlook might even be promising. A war on hunger lay ahead and emerging wisdom said that as cash-short nations developed their economies, they would be able to buy food and bring variety to their diets.

Canadian farmers made history in 1971, slashing wheat acreage and shifting to other crops. They grew 570 million bushels of barley (surpassing the 510 million bushels of wheat) and the Wheat Board made record barley sales. Runciman called it a major watershed and predicted growers were unlikely to return to straight wheat. And he was right. That shift to barley was only a start. The industry was moving into a time of upheaval. Ahead were the most spectacular and chaotic times Canada's grain industry, and perhaps the world's, had ever known.

Soviet buyers returned in May, 1971, and their massive purchases astounded growers and the industry, pushing Canada's total 1970-71 sales to a record and eating into the huge carryover. Then those buyers returned in February, 1972, for another huge purchase. It should have set off euphoria for prairie farmers. But it was the start of a nightmare. The handling/transportation system couldn't move all that grain.

Strikes, work stoppages, winter snowslides and derailments forced the Board to defer delivery of 1.5 million long tons of wheat into 1973. It wasn't a new story. When the Chinese and Soviets had bought heavily in 1966, labour troubles erupted, defeating a golden opportunity to set new records.

But now the Cold War between communist countries and the free world was making US-Soviet relations difficult at best. The US had devalued its dollar to cheapen its exports, and in doing so had unwittingly set the stage for what became known as the Great Grain Robbery.

With Canada's chaotic system unable to deliver its commitments, the desperate and shrewd Soviets sent buyers in early July, 1972, to quietly buy US grain from the trading companies. The secretive traders confirmed that the US export subsidy would apply on each deal. US grain officials missed the big picture. Within a month, the Soviets had bought 17.5 million tonnes of grain and 1 million tonnes of soybeans at bargain prices, all subsidized by the US Treasury.

When the enormity of those purchases became clear in late August, US Exchange prices soared. But the Great Grain Robbery was over.

The Wheat Board's Thunder Bay asking price for top grade wheat doubled from $1.79 1/2 a bushel at the start of the 1972-73 crop year to $3.56 1/4 at the close. But for prairie farmers, the next two years became a horror of lost opportunities. As world prices climbed, U.S. grain exports soared but Canada's too often floundered. The problem went beyond rail car shortages and obsolete elevators. Labour-management disputes escalated into strikes and stoppages.

It was an old story. "We faced three grain handlers' strikes in my time," Mac Runciman said later. "One at Thunder Bay, two at Vancouver. Each was history repeating itself. The Wheat Board announces big shipments. Then the longshoremen or grain handlers or railway men or some other union announces a strike. They shut down the elevators and get what they want. Then you go on shipping grain.

He recalled one of those Vancouver strikes. "It was August. The situation was bad. We had a record-breaking heat wave. The principals of the grain companies were in Vancouver.

"I was lying in bed about 1.00 a.m., couldn't sleep. I got up and went for a walk. At 2.15 a.m., I came around a corner and I bumped into SaskPool President Charlie Gibbings. He was out doing the same thing. He couldn't see any solutions, couldn't sleep, felt it would relax him to go out for a walk.

"It was a funny feeling to realize, here is another guy in the same quandary as you are yourself. It was almost reassuring to see he was reacting in exactly the same way.

"In school history lessons, we all learned of the robber barons on the spice and silk trade routes from India to Europe. These strikes were a modern-day repeat. They didn't add anything to building the industry or getting more money back to farmers. They weren't constructive. I found them a waste of time. They gave me high blood pressure. My memory of them is just a blur.

"Disruption by a dozen labour unions seemed unending," he said. "They stopped the farmers' income and damaged Canada's reputation as a dependable supplier of quality grain. It got so bad Japanese buyers half-jokingly asked, 'Why doesn't Canada call a strike month so we could delay our ships and evade the port tie-ups?' They brought grain movement to a halt so frequently it was tragic."

Prairie farmers were the hapless victims and it became one of the most aggravating issues Runciman faced. He wrote in his 1967 annual report that a seaway employees' strike began June 21 and ended July 15. That was followed on July 18 by a strike of elevator employees which stopped movement out of the Lakehead.

Costs of these latest strikes were stunning. By March, 1974, the Wheat Board said its inability to deliver when prices were soaring had cost 50 million bushels in sales. Interruptions on the railways, at port terminals, on Great Lakes ships and by government grain inspectors continued in 1974-75. Transportation bottlenecks compounded the problem. The Wheat Board calculated later that shipments were hit on 143 out of 220 working days, or 65 percent of the working time. Prices hit a high of $6.07 1/8 a bushel in late 1974.

Design The Grain For The Market! - Butz Sends US Exports Soaring

When the Canada Grains Council's four overseas missions returned as the decade of the 19 70's began, with the devastating story of failure in world feed grains markets, it at least revealed a made-to-order challenge for the new Wheat Growers group. Wally Nelson acted, naming Rouleau farmer and seed grower and former Social Credit political activist Daryl Rumble to chair a feed wheat committee.

Rumble notified growers that Canada had lost several hard spring wheat sales during July because "we have no soft wheat to supply package orders." He planned a Feed Wheat Symposium for Regina in October, 1971, to focus on this beckoning market, and he urged growers to come to this "first real chance to learn about the new Pitic 62 and other feed wheats." He predicted Ontario alone could be a market for 100 million bushels of this new wheat, and suggested prairie growers could have a market for all they could grow on 30 million acres within 10 years.

One hundred and seventy five growers crowded into the Regina Inn for the event. But again, the chicken-and-egg syndrome haunting their industry took centre stage. Wheat Board market development director Dr. Harold Bjarnson said the only licensed feed wheat, Pitic 62, wasn't good enough - the Board couldn't bother developing markets for it. Canada Grain Commission chief inspector M. Ainslie said not enough of the new wheats were grown to bother setting up special grades for them.

But there was no complacency in the audience. Winnipeg Grain Exchange president J.E. McWilliam got down to allocating blame, saying the industry needed fewer academics and more hard-nosed salesmen. The Grains Council's Dr. Don Dever referred obliquely to what he considered the Wheat Board's unimaginative selling methods. He said experience taught him that if you want to sell something in a foreign country, you need people located there permanently, not travelling salesmen going occasionally.

Wally Nelson intensified the political slant, urging Ottawa to give over-delivery privileges to farmers with Pitic 62 in their bulging bins so they could get cash flow. University of Manitoba's Plant Science head Dr. Bob McGinnis offered hope, saying Regina-area farmers were having good success with Pitic 62 and better varieties would soon be licensed.

This confusion didn't surprise the growers who now realized they had to become a ginger group using political action to fight for change. They wrote an agenda for action: get the name "feed wheat" removed from their grain to make it more acceptable to foreign buyers; send a market study mission abroad; remove prairie boundary restrictions to allow free movement of feed grain; and get the Wheat Board to put feed wheat on the futures market.

Nelson added, "We also have to go and sell in that world feed grain market."

But soon another event grabbed media headlines, one that would shake the world. US President Richard Nixon recognized that when an American farmer grew a bushel of grain and sent it to market, he made jobs and prosperity in every corner of the country. He hailed the surging vitality of US agriculture, and in a brilliant stroke, named a hard-nosed economist, Earl Butz, as his new Secretary of Agriculture.

Butz was no bureaucrat intent on clinging to a comfortable status quo. He was energetic, imaginative, forceful and unrelenting. He knew US agriculture had been smothered for decades by restrictions that stifled decision-making, limited growth and lulled processors, traders and foreign customers into relying on government-owned food inventories.

But he knew its enormous untapped power. He saw that the world's people must be fed and he believed that if US farmers were freed up to respond, they could be the most efficient on earth. Nixon threw his full support behind Butz and he set out to change the system.

The timing was perfect. Prices hit a high of $6.07 1/8 a bushel in late 1974 and this market turnaround smoothed Butz's path.

He began scrapping archaic US farm policies, giving farmers incentives to plant every acre. He ended parity prices and the old practice of shrinking output to hold prices above world levels. If market prices fell below target levels he would use deficiency payments that didn't distort markets. And he set US agriculture on a spectacular run. Its exports soared 60 percent to a record $12.9 billion in fiscal 1973.

Butz beamed, "The future has already arrived for US farmers." He drew up a new farm bill in 1974 allowing farmers to move into all-out production. He aimed to push US food exports to $20 billion per year within three or four years, suggesting the target might be reached in one. US agriculture was no longer a sick sister, and Butz called this only a start.

The US was the pacesetter and one US official saw nothing mysterious about it - It was just aggressive marketing. It was giving an object lesson in how to sell food effectively. Farmers, the trade and government were going arm-in-arm to promote and sell in world markets.

In one program, 70 private agricultural trade groups with full government support worked day-in, day-out with more than 100 foreign trade associations. The Americans cost-shared programs with overseas importers, processors, retailers, government officials and consumers to promote food products. And they weren't just trying to sell products they had - they sought out products buyers in more than 70 countries wanted, then tried to satisfy those wants.

In August, 1975, Butz announced "For the third consecutive year, there will be no set-aside of acres for feed grain and wheat." This was in line with his policy of full production.

When Butz later left government and went back to Purdue University as Dean Emeritus of Agriculture, he came to Canada and delivered a memorable address to the 1977 Palliser convention. The world's number one problem, he said, was to boost production to feed 80 percent more people by the year 2000. "We've got to develop a new attitude to the whole food business, both national and international...to keep some profit in it, so investment is attracted back, so research goes forward, so young people go back into it."

He described US food policy as "the most positive policy we've had in years...*a policy of plenty*, based on market orientation, market expansion, and minimal governmental interference. We transferred management of our industry from Washington back to the farm because nobody in Washington can do the job the farmers can do themselves. And we tripled exports."

He spelled it out. "The federal government has no business in the commodity business in my country. It's time we blew the whistle on big absent government, that pervasive deadening hand of bureaucracy - it destroys incentive."

He also saw an insidious attack against the old-fashioned work ethic in the US and Canada being waged by those who support the need for ever-growing bureaucracies. "Government is destroying individual initiative," he warned.

10

WALL-TO-WALL SHIPS - NO SALESMEN IN ASIA - TWENTY YEARS BEHIND - TWO OPPOSING PHILOSOPHIES

Wall-To-Wall Ships - Iowa-Style Terminals - The Famous (or Infamous) Unit Train

Those huge 1971 Soviet grain purchases that pushed Canada's sales to record levels should have unleashed euphoria among farmers, for they would slash surpluses piled on farms and in elevators, perhaps even set off that long-awaited war on hunger.

Yet apprehension was the mood. Weeks earlier, the *Vancouver Sun* set alarm bells ringing with a story that screamed in deep headlines, "Wall to Wall Ships," and focused on the city's vital grain export harbour. It labelled the congestion of ships "February Fever," saying it happened every year exports reached any volume. The port had become a grain bottleneck.

Alarmed Palliser growers had to ask, Could the system really move grain to meet big sales? A few of them headed west in February, 1971, to see for themselves. They were dumbfounded to find English Bay was, in fact, jammed with ships. It was another devastating sign of the system's breakdown. When the Soviets returned in 1972 intent on record purchases but found Canada unable to deliver the grain, they turned to the U.S. and pulled off their "Grain Robbery."

The frustration of Canadian growers was heightened by a close-at-hand example of how an efficient delivery system should work. An Iowa farmers' co-operative with

350 country elevators was then trying a Grain Trains pilot project, in which a train carried 385,000 bushels of corn (110 jumbo hopper cars each holding 3500 bushels which had been cleaned in giant inland terminals) from Des Moines to a Gulf of Mexico export terminal. Turnaround time was only seven days. That successful trial continued from late October through Christmas.

Here was the answer, thought the Palliser men - do like those Iowa farmers, clean the grain at home before shipping it. They felt they had identified one more costly flaw in Canada's system.

But in fact, the issue went deeper. Yes, if prairie grain arrived clean at export terminals, it could be loaded onto ships more quickly. But a growing car shortage left railways unable to deliver enough grain on time. This was a year-round problem, but it caught headlines in winter months when sub-zero temperatures and snowslides stalled trains and made the shortage acute.

"The railways couldn't act to get better rolling stock because they couldn't get paid for it," explained Runciman. "And no move was being made to address this." Those Vancouver terminals were often waiting for grain to clean. When the grain did arrive, ships waited while it was being cleaned. If grain could be delivered year-round in quantity, it could be cleaned and ready for the ships' arrival.

Another system weakness was the labour unions' stranglehold on the railroads, the terminals and the waterfront.

But now the Palliser farmers focused on the need to get grain cleaned and through the port during that "February Fever" season. Manitoban grower Gordon Graham raised the alarm back home, calling it "tragic that we need every dollar we can get, but buyers are turned away while grain piles up on our farms." He added, "We can't leave our lifelines in someone else's hands if our industry is to survive. We need an integrated policy."

Canada's grain companies lacked inland terminals that could clean grain. But the growers found five government-owned terminals sitting largely unused in the prairies. "Why can't these be used as grain assembly and cleaning plants where grain trains could be put together?" they asked. Palliser Director Art Thompson, who farmed at Pense, hauled a load of wheat to the Moose Jaw terminal on July 28th, 1971. It was weighed, graded and docked and he got settlement from Federal Grain Co.

The idea caught fire with growers. Led by Wally Nelson, 55 of them headed for Winnipeg on November 15, 1971. They met with officials of the Wheat Board and the Canadian Grain Commission, and railway and grain company people, urging structural changes in the system. They were constantly warned about the tangle of regulations choking the system and making restructuring nearly impossible. They answered that Palliser didn't aim to completely revamp the system - just supplement it. But they were determined.

Meeting with Mac Runciman and Manitoba Pool's Fred Hamilton, they raised the idea of unit trains. Over a decade earlier, when Runciman was an Abernethy farmer and a UGG director, company Board members had decided to find out about some of those U.S. ideas including unit trains.

"North and South Dakota, Montana and parts of Minnesota were comparable to our prairies," he said. "I went to Minneapolis along with staff members John Wachal, E.V. "Dusty" Titheridge and Frank Allison. Our goal was to visit the Grain Terminal Association (GTA) - a co-op similar in structure to UGG - which operated country elevators in the four states.

"GTA president M.W. Thatcher was a real old Hubert Humphrey politician. We had a good chat...visited a number of their shipping points on our way home. One of these had 2.2 million bushels of concrete elevator space with circular tanks like those we began building many years later.

"We asked the man in charge, 'Who makes the management decisions around here?' He left no doubt he was the boss when he barked out his answer, 'I do.' Along with a helper, he ran that big elevator, with the farm supplies and all. We were impressed."

Now, chatting with those Palliser farmers in Winnipeg, Runciman knew the US was at least 20 years ahead of Canada in moving to the bigger elevators. He told them if they wanted to see a system that could deliver grain more rapidly than Canada's "Just look south!"

"No wonder our farmers used to go down to Wolf Point, Montana, to watch a train of hopper cars loaded out of the concrete elevators with breathtaking speed," he said. "Then they would return home and see a 35,000-

bushel country elevator dribbling grain into a boxcar with a coopered door."

Runciman was in absolute sympathy with the unit train idea. He and Fred Hamilton agreed it was time to improve the system. Grain was moving reasonably well. But they knew it was a formidable challenge. The system was almost entirely in government hands. And most farmers didn't want to lose their own small country elevators in favour of big inland terminals. They opposed many of the steps needed.

"Yes, farmers say it's fine to rationalize the system," said Runciman. "Then they add, 'But don't rationalize my elevator.'"

Clarence Taylor was a crusty Regina grower who was on that Winnipeg trip. He had been seething for years at the industry's obsessive bureaucracy. Like many farmers, he was an independent-minded cuss who could be a loner on one issue, the first to join a crusade on another. He believed fiercely that over-regulation denied him his freedom to get his grain to market.

Taylor didn't miss a word in those intense discussions. But on the second day he missed his lunch. He was hungry and frustrated. He joined neighbouring farmer Daryl Rumble and Federal Grain's new manager Walter Flesher on their way to dinner. As they ate, Flesher showed a brochure of Federal's new Neptune bulk-loading terminal at Vancouver. It was handling coal, and now potash for the Potash Corporation of Saskatchewan which had launched a unit train months earlier.

Flesher figured the terminal could handle grain as well. Taylor's eyes lit up. He put the issue squarely. "Can you move a unit grain train from the Saskatoon government elevator to Vancouver?"

Flesher was only three weeks into his job and didn't realize changes in this hidebound system couldn't happen fast. He replied, "I can unload a unit train any time this week."

Taylor couldn't believe his luck. After an excited and sleepless night, he was up at dawn as usual, waiting impatiently for office hours to start. Grain Commissioner Forrest Hetland was also a grain farmer. Taylor got him on the phone. Hetland said there was enough cleaned grain at Saskatoon for a unit train and plans were being made. Taylor twisted his arm, got agreement to move quickly, then headed for the Wheat Board offices.

He had to almost barge in on Chief Commissioner Gerry Vogel, who passed him off to his transportation head Norm Hope. A stormy meeting erupted. An angry Taylor stalked out of the office, then was persuaded to return. A hesitant and worried Hope agreed to go along with this idea that seemed to be against everything the Board stood for.

Meanwhile, Flesher had brought a bundle of his Neptune Bulk Terminal brochures to an early morning meeting with the Palliser group. "When supplies ran out, it just about caused a riot," remembers Taylor. Flesher had now put his assistant, Dennis Stephens, on the project and it was coming together famously. CN's transportation head Doug Fletcher had promised to spot a unit train in Saskatoon.

Taylor had the wind in his sails, but before boarding the bus back to Regina, he phoned Flesher again. Flesher said they might not load this week, but very soon. Two weeks later, on the morning of Friday, December 3, 1971, in Saskatoon, they started loading 279,000 bushels of No. 1 Northern into 96 covered hopper cars like those used for potash. The full train headed west at 4.30 p.m., arrived in Vancouver at midnight Sunday, consigned to China on the Greek freighter *Mari Chandris* which arrived on schedule. Taylor had paid for his plane ticket to Vancouver and was there to see history made.

On Monday, December 6 at 9.00 a.m., unloading began. Within an hour, the labour union called a strike. "The grain was going through bulk facilities, denying them work," Taylor said later.

In an hour, the strike was called off. Unloading proceeded as if it was potash - each of the 96 cars was dumped into the hopper pit. The wheat moved on an endless belt, by-passing the shed, going directly to the ship. It was all on board by 4.30 p.m. The ship was one-third full. It was only three weeks after Taylor's dinner with Flesher and Rumble in Winnipeg.

This unit train idea had the potential to revolutionize terminal grain handling and vastly increase West Coast handling capacity. And it offered other benefits. Farmers would no longer give up the dockage. Paper work would be less. The rapid grain throughput would save storage costs and spoilage. It was a breakthrough.

This ginger group had crashed the system, putting together a grain train as the Iowa growers were doing. It was a landmark event for Federal Grain Company too - a way to generate more business for its Neptune Terminals. The firm had pulled out all stops, even filming the entire project. Four weeks later, that film was shown at the Palliser annual meeting to resounding applause. Palliser made plans to show it across the West.

Within a month, those plans were shot down. The Wheat Pools announced their purchase of Federal Grain. In an ominous signal of the future, the film was locked away beyond the reach of Palliser or the farm public, dampening any thought of quick revolutionary change in the handling/marketing of prairie grain. That unit train had been a victory. But a small one indeed in the war that lay ahead.

More History - Weyburn Inland Terminal

Only weeks after the unit train success, 25 Palliser members flew to Vancouver at their own expense for a more detailed look. They met with exporting firms, the National Harbours Board, railways, the Canadian Grain Commission, the Wheat Board, the Longshoremen's Union, the terminal operators and anyone else they could find involved with grain. Assistant Port Manager Bill Duncan took them on a cruise of the harbour area. They toured the SaskPool terminal, Neptune Terminals and Vancouver wharves. And they kept hearing, "This is off the record but...."

Those off-the-record talks offered alleged insights into the system's breakdown - that Canada had oversold what could be handled there; that Vancouver facilities were "Mickey Mouse;" that our inability to get more grain through was costing us sales; and now, that the Japanese had called for tenders but the Board couldn't even bid.

A distressed Wally Nelson exploded that, despite near-record prices in those early weeks of 1972, "we can't meet demand and this will further erode our reputation in serving customers through West coast ports." He asked, "How can the Wheat Board justify five inland terminals with ample cleaning facilities and unit train accommodation lying idle in the prairies?"

Because forward wheat sales at the old low prices wouldn't be caught up until well into 1973, even with full use of all facilities, farmers would miss higher-priced sales. Nelson drove home his point. "With winter coming, we don't have enough reserves in Vancouver to carry us through. Pacific terminals' capacity is 28 million bushels, yet just over 6 million bushels of saleable wheat are (there) and 6 million of other grains as of October 25."

He warned, "We have the grain, we have the trucks and we have the terminals. We had better put them to work while we still have the customers."

The angered growers were certain - prairie *inland terminals* were needed. Nelson urged the Wheat Board, "Supply the five inland terminals with grain by trucks so we can ship cleaned, graded grain to build up coastal stock."

In a sense, the growers were now attacking the grain companies, urging them to go the US inland terminals route. Runciman agreed with the concept. But he cautioned it wasn't that simple. In his 1974 annual report he wrote "In the United States, a network of inland terminals...with 400,000 to 2 million bushels storage capacity each is being built on main lines. These can load 50-to-100-car trains at 20,000 to 30,000 bushels an hour, get grain from satellite country elevators, clean it to grade and forward it to export or domestic terminals."

This was clearly a superior system. But it couldn't be built in Canada because, "US elevators buy and sell all grain for their own account....They can get freight savings on shipments of more than a single car.

"Canada's heavily regulated system is different. We can't build inland terminals because our controls prevent any progress on rail line abandonment. Our low tariffs for handling, storage and moving grain won't allow us to compensate farmers for hauling longer distances."

Until this is changed, he said, grain companies can't make massive investments in them. "If UGG were to build them now we would divert money from new high-throughput elevators and from renovating older plants.

"So inland terminals are not part of medium-term plans. Grain companies can't make massive investments in them until the rail system and the rates are changed. But farming is becoming a high-pressure, sophisticated business. Guys making money at it are good managers.

Inland terminals will come. Timing is the question."

He encouraged the wheat growers to build a terminal themselves, then farmers would make their own decisions, trucking grain to them or somewhere else. And growers did, in fact, proceed to raise money for their own terminal. They built it at Weyburn, Saskatchewan.

"Thank goodness growers bought the story that growers like Art Mainil and Clarence Taylor were telling," Runciman said later. "That terminal is a monument to the change of attitude. I knew Big Earl Robertson from Balcarres. He voted with his truck, hauling his grain conscientiously to the Weyburn terminal 115 miles away.

"Yes, that terminal nearly went under. But they got the right manager and made it a booming success. That was where men like these felt they could work. They built it in spite of all opposition."

Runciman reported in 1975 that UGG had studied building a $2.7 million inland terminal handling 8 million bushels annually. But he still saw no evidence railroads would offer freight incentives for multi-car shipments so the figures didn't add up, although two other companies had begun them. "Without drastic changes in the rail system and rates, UGG will build a few inland terminals on mainlines, continue to phase out non-competitive elevators and improve ones between these extremes which can adjust to changing times."

When Ottawa named Judge Emmett Hall to chair a Commission of Enquiry into how the grain handling and rail system got into such a sad state, it further delayed reforms to the system. Fearful Hall might recommend more controls, the UGG Board advised him to reject the claim that competition is wasteful and leads to higher costs. "A farmer must be free to take his grain to the elevator of his choice, small or large, conventional or inland terminal, on a branch line or a mainline," it said. "If the tariff tells him the costs, he can see the value of the service and make his choice. That way, farmers decide the system they want. Others cannot and should not structure the system for him."

"Branch line abandonment is coming," said Runciman. But he cautioned, "That alone could simply worsen the situation. Other changes are needed."

He said later, "SaskPool fought the inland terminals concept tooth and nail, yet today they're building them.

The Pool just seems to run along about 20 years behind the times - trying to maintain the status quo, rather than looking for the next step."

Mission To Asia - No Salesmen - Ivan McMillan's Nightmare

Stories were catching media headlines that the world feed grains market was growing fast, yet Canada's marketing tangle prevented prairie growers from responding. The Palliser growers now got funding from the Alberta Department of Agriculture and from Ottawa to send grain, oilseed and livestock producers on a Feed Grains Mission to Southeast Asia. For the first time, Western growers would be out looking for markets.

Director Allan Coulter led a momentous month-long trip in late 1973. The group visited Japan, South Korea, Hong Kong, the Philippines, Singapore, and Malaysia and met potential customers. On their return they could hardly contain their frustration - nor their enthusiasm.

"We kept bumping into grain salesmen from the U.S. and Australia but none from Canada," reported Moose Jaw grain farmer Gordon Brooks. "Buyers there had never seen our salesmen, wondered why we were so quiet, what products we had? Could they buy from us?

"They wanted a soft utility wheat. The US had it, Australia had it. But we didn't seem to have it."

Mission members found demand was on the rise for high-protein foods including milling and utility wheats, oilseeds and meat. "All countries want our feed grains," reported Coulter, "especially the new utility wheats. They literally snatched the samples out of our hands. The potential to sell these grains is there if we can deliver them and if the quality and price are right."

But Canada's competitive position had deteriorated. Lack of market development work as well as pricing and quality problems were hurting. Other countries' export subsidies were interfering too. Canada faced an uphill struggle against a well-entrenched US.

Coulter reported that grading wheat for protein (a Palliser achievement) was helping win back customers. "But in the first five minutes of our first Tokyo interview we were told our deplorable record at Vancouver is a big stumbling block. And we heard this again and again."

Mission members found some unexpected allies as well. "The Japanese said they had protested strongly to the Canadian government when it proposed to place flax, rye and rapeseed under the Wheat Board," said Coulter. "They had warned that if rapeseed went under the Board, buyers could switch to palm oil."

That historic mission did set the stage for change. On their return, Coulter and Brooks met with Runciman and were offered UGG's full support. "Mac was totally behind us," said Brooks.

"When we told the Wheat Board about feed wheat prospects, it seemed to scoff, saying 'You can't mix low-protein wheat with our good wheat.' It was stuck in its old ways. It couldn't adjust to new markets." But then it responded, appointing an able professional named Cam Brown to head a feed wheats pilot project. Brown had outgrown the Manitoba Department of Agriculture bureaucracy as well as a position at the University of Manitoba. He soon left no doubt of his new mission, sounding the message that Canada must move beyond its narrow bread wheat focus and get into feed wheats too.

"In one small step forward," Brooks said, "the Wheat Board let us grow some feed wheat to be kept separate from Board wheat, and to be shipped separately in carload lots. It went to buyers like Hayhoe Mills in Ontario and others, and they liked it."

But the Palliser men wanted a bold response, so they drafted a plan calling for the industry to set up market information and development offices in many Pacific Rim nations; to initiate feed grains and rapeseed testing programs for poultry and hogs in Japan; to urge Canadian scientists to develop quality feed barley tailored to Pacific Rim markets; to develop rapeseed with low erucic acid and higher oil content; and to produce semi-hard and soft wheats (for noodle-, cake-, and cookie- and biscuit-making) and alfalfa with higher protein content.

One of those on that Feed Grains Mission was Ivan McMillan, a man destined to play an important role in the years ahead. You couldn't have more traditional values than McMillan. He liked to grow his crops on his farm at Craik, halfway between Regina and Saskatoon, and devote his remaining energies to his children and grandchildren, his community and his church. To him, wheat meant bread. Growing it had almost a Biblical significance. It was a near-sacred calling as well as a family business. Prairie farmers were blessed with some of the most productive land on earth and he believed it should be used for the good of mankind.

McMillan's nature was to be thoughtful and deliberate. When Nelson and the others became alarmed about their industry, he joined them. His visits to Winnipeg and Vancouver were eye-openers. On that South East Asia mission, he was shocked to hear customers complain about Canada's unreliability. Back home, he was soon speaking out with a deep passion.

"With over 400 million underfed people in the world," he told one meeting, "it's little short of criminal for us producers not to go all-out. The real challenge is how to produce enough food to stave off famine. We must grow 1.5 billion bushels of grain annually if we want to hold our share of world output and trade."

McMillan had no doubt farmers could grow such a crop. "But maybe we can't move that much to market," he cautioned. "The grain industry...is a bureaucratic nightmare. Our handling and marketing system is inward-looking, inefficient, antiquated! We have no choice but to gear down production....Each sector blames the other."

He posed the ultimate question, "Why have we Canadians been operating at half-throttle for years?"

To McMillan and others caught up in those frenzied days, there was no longer a mystery. "We farmers put up with nonsense," he growled. "Something is wrong when we allowed this mess to develop."

But the tangle of government regulations and divisions within the farm community blocked needed changes. Palliser and other industry leaders had to find a way to end that bottleneck.

McMillan was soon elected Palliser President and he brought remarkable talents to the job. He was without pretensions. His straightforward approach won the respect of most people he met. When Cargill Grain put on its big 50th anniversary reception and dinner in Winnipeg, the company's head, Whitney MacMillan, who was possibly the world grain industry's most powerful man, came up from Minneapolis. Ivan McMillan was also there, as was Pioneer Grain head Bruce MacMillan. The three "McMillans" had a chat.

Later, the Cargill head observed to Runciman, "It sure has been a reunion of the MacMillan clan tonight." He added, "I didn't know any MacMillan was as smart as your Ivan is. He really has a lot on the ball."

But an increasingly frustrated Ivan McMillan was now sharpening his attack on those who blocked change. At a 1975 Canada-Japan Trade Council Symposium in Edmonton, he exploded, "Canada must be an enigma to our global customers. We are an exporting nation. Our living standard depends on our ability to maintain and expand overseas markets...yet we seem unable to do what is needed to support export marketing - like timely delivery, modernization of transportation and port facilities, and settling labour strife."

The chorus of voices for change was growing. Colonel Bob Houston of that Canada-Japan Trade Council spoke at the Palliser Convention that same year, warning that Canada risked dropping to a third-rate trading nation unless it improved its export performance. He blamed uncoordinated market development, a poor national transportation system and inadequate port facilities. An outdated confrontation style of labour-management relations also hurt. So did conflicting federal/provincial relations. "Unless these improve," he cautioned, "customers will go elsewhere."

Ideas for change now poured in. Palliser members travelled to grower conventions in the US each year and brought speakers from across Canada and the world to their own meetings to examine every issue. The media reported the conflict. The rising cry for action put new pressures on politicians.

Ivan McMillan and his board members Allan Coulter and Glen McEwen flew to a World Wheat seminar in Washington, DC, in late 1976. Keynote speaker US Assistant Secretary of Agriculture Richard Bell told how his country had captured 85 percent of the increased demand in the last five years, (Canada's exports had actually declined.) Bell said the US was the world's most reliable grain supplier with the best grains marketing system.

On his return, McMillan reported wryly, "I listened with great interest."

Rail Movement Crisis - The Crow Battle - Two Opposing Philosophies

Festering at the core of this policy deadlock was the Crow freight rate issue which couldn't go away because it went to the heart of the West's role in Confederation. When Mac Runciman labelled the grain system a failure in 1967, he called those rates a major cause, urging Ottawa to replace them so the railways could abandon inefficient lines, the system could be upgraded and farmers could boost food output.

Six years later, he said, "Our rail system is little changed from the horse-hauling days of the 1930s (because of those Crow rates)...storage and handling charges have been closely regulated since 1912....Much of our elevator system is over 40 years old...and is hopelessly expensive to operate and needs upgrading."

It was no secret why railroads wouldn't act. "If the railway abandons a line, it loses elevators. And since it can't claim losses for moving that grain on the main line, its losses increase, its earnings fall further and the number of boxcars declines."

In fact, the railways "hadn't built any six-foot-door general purpose boxcars - the only kind suitable for carrying grain - since the 1950s. Boxcar numbers had been cut in half...in the 10 years to 1973." The result was inevitable - big grain movements couldn't be made even if big sales were possible.

A Canada Grains Council study revealed the awful truth. Off some protected low-volume branch lines, gathering costs were dollars a bushel, not cents a bushel. "Identifying that cost doesn't solve the problem," admitted Runciman. "But it points it up."

A grain company could save up to $3 a ton on 10,000 tons of grain when a rail line was closed - a lot of money. "But if you are a farmer on the end of a line that is cut off and this doubles your distance to market, you will have a grievance," he said, noting "it's a delicate line between the company's best interests and those of the farmers who might be hurt. It gets into politics where a small minority can pretend to speak for the majority."

UGG was at the centre of that Crow dispute from the start. "When Tom Crerar (UGG's second president) led the farmers' Progressive Party with its balance of power in Ottawa in the early 1920s," recalled Runciman, "he insisted, 'The Crow rates must be retained. The Canadian government has a commitment to help pay for that grain movement.'"

Fifty years later Runciman was cautioning farmers against those who said, "Raise grain freight rates to compensate railroads fully for any losses." Prairie growers, like others, face the risk of low prices. But unlike our US competitors, we lack a big domestic market to take most of our grain, he said.

"And we...have no inland waterways. We rely totally on railroads to move grain. We pay the rail costs and take export price. Yet we are further from ocean shipping than growers in other exporting nations. Our grain going west must move over the Rockies, that going east must go through the Great Lakes which are frozen four months of the year, or through Churchill which is frozen nine months.

"That's why, when the rates and branch lines issues were raised in 1950 and again in 1960, UGG directors fought to retain the Crow benefit." The public had to understand that the grain growers' well-being affected the nation's well-being. "Yes, UGG is absolutely committed to change. But not at the cost of destroying prairie farmers and the West....No farmer must pay more than the present rate now or in future," he said.

UGG's remedy was clear. Let users in Canada pay the increased costs for domestic grain. And let Ottawa pay part of the cost for export grain. And he urged Ottawa to say how much money it would put in to compensate railways for claimed grain-hauling losses before large-scale branch line abandonment began.

But the ongoing damage from Crow was heavy. "Crow hurts food processors as well and undermines the rapeseed industry," Runciman said in 1976. "Raw rapeseed moves at the Crow rate. Western crushers have tried for years to move processed rapeseed under the Crow like other grain products. But their pleas are ignored. It pays full rate." He warned, "If Western Canada wants to have a food processing industry, and not be just a supplier of raw materials, then processed products must move at Crow to eastern Canadian and foreign customers."

For a short time, it seemed as if change was near. Ivan McMillan attacked those unrealistic rates for doing untold harm, leaving farmers with "inadequate railway rolling stock and motive power, poor maintenance on branch lines, and other problems....If we want a viable agriculture, the rates must be related to real costs."

And on a Saskatchewan visit, Prime Minister Trudeau bluntly told growers they were making life harder for themselves by resisting higher freight rates - because those low rates meant grain was being shipped out rather than grain-fed cattle or grain products.

McMillan had good Liberal connections and he assured growers that if branch line abandonment came, Mr. Trudeau and Wheat Board Minister Lang had promised the *statutory rate benefits* would be preserved - in fact, enshrined in legislation.

But opposition to change exploded. Saskatchewan's NDP Agriculture Minister Gordon McMurchy warned, "If there is to be wholesale abandonment of branch lines...there will be no SuperGrid (road) system (to replace them.)"

McMillan called that threat an inexcusable insult to growers, saying "To impose a political philosophy on the grain handling and transportation system is a backward step." He praised the Ottawa-appointed Snavely Commission which had determined the costs of rail movement, and added, "We've got to know the actual costs of different ways of moving grain if the Hall Commission is to determine future rail needs. All producers will benefit if these commissions are given every assistance."

But the opportunity for a leap forward was lost, and McMillan asked in exasperation, "Why are SaskPool, the National Farmers Union, the Saskatchewan government, even church groups, voicing unconditional opposition to grain terminals and rail line abandonment? And why then have they taken it upon themselves to discredit commissions like Snaveley's and Hall's even before they make recommendations? Why do they adamantly insist that Crow rates should not even be discussed?"

McMillan now understood why the prairies was gripped in policy deadlock. "We have two diametrically opposed philosophies. Some groups are passionately committed to supply management, which brings marketing boards, government controls and a tangle of bureaucratic regulations. Other groups, like Palliser, want producer freedom which leads to a market-oriented approach and an expanding industry."

Former Palliser president Wally Nelson said the government and the people were living in a fool's paradise, that the most serious threats to our grains industry were inflation and supply management. He said inflation is caused by the simple greed of some governments, politicians and labour unions, and that some government bureaucracies, "simply won't be accountable. And some Canadians believe we deserve more than we earn. As a result our goods are becoming too expensive in export markets and we could be left hopelessly overpriced.

"Supply management is even more serious," he charged, calling it "an attitude of some governments, politicians, bureaucrats, and farm organizations...which bring inward-looking programs, a loss of incentive and productivity, hindering our ability to help boost the world food supply."

He summed it up, "Farm produce must be grown, handled and moved to markets at costs low enough to keep us competitive...we will move 850 million bushels of grains and oilseeds from country elevators this year, compared to 1,020 million bushels in 1971-72. We must upgrade the...system if we are to move 1.5 billion bushels by 1985."

Wheat Board Monopoly Costs Growers, Taxpayers $600 Million Per Year

The truth of those charges was documented only too clearly a few years later. By the early 1990s, the awesome canola success story (it had grown to rival wheat in dollar value) showed beyond doubt that the great myth that the Wheat Board could have no rival in selling grains, was simply that - a myth. And it had perched precariously for half a century on the dubious idea that a government monopoly could outwit the market and the trade any day - that bureaucrats could sell grain at higher prices than growers or traders or other marketers could get, and put more money in growers' pockets.

True believers steeped in the Social Gospel simply shut their eyes to that lesson. To question the myth was to face the wrath of a powerful elite - the wheat pools, Liberal and socialist governments and other left-leaning groups.

This sacred myth was dealt another devastating blow

in a report by Alberta-born Dr. Colin Carter of the University of California, Berkeley, and Dr. Al Loyns of the University of Manitoba, two economists with impressive credentials. Carter had held a three-year Kellogg Foundation fellowship in international food systems from 1986-89 and had authored a study on US agricultural policy. He wrote a 1993 report on the Continental Barley Market for Agriculture Canada which urged deregulation of the feed and malting barley markets. He had co-authored a book on China's grain markets, and others.

Dr. Loyns had been Research Director at the high-profile Ottawa-based Food Prices Review Board chaired by Dr. Beryl Plumtre which had found that farmer marketing boards often did more harm than good. He had been a senior Ottawa bureaucrat, had worked on Canada/US trade disputes and done many market studies. He was also a grain and oilseeds farmer.

Armed with Alberta government funding, Carter and Loyns set out to examine the Wheat Board record. They weren't surprised when they found no evidence to support claims it had great marketing power and could get price premiums. A similar bureaucracy - the Australian Wheat Board - had earlier claimed it got a $20 per metric tonne premium over what farmers or the trade could get. Later analysis found that the premium was only 12-to-31 cents.

In fact, Carter and Loyns found no evidence the Board returned farmers a higher farm-gate price than US growers got from the trade. They concluded that many Wheat Board claims were deceitful, and in their 1996 report, they asked how could the Board get higher prices when world buyers demand the best prices, not the highest quality? And even if it could, these wouldn't offset its higher costs.

Claims that Board operating costs were under five cents a bushel were massively wrong. According to Loyns and Carter, they were "perhaps ten times higher." In fact, 1995 handling fees were $8 to $13 per tonne higher than in the US.

Neither could the researchers find evidence to support claims of Board market power in barley and oats. And claims that the US was not an important barley and oats market were dead wrong.

Their shocking conclusion was that monopoly selling was costing growers and the country perhaps $600 million dollars per year in lost revenues and added costs - most of it coming out of farmers' pockets. In effect, they debunked a long-time myth by saying, "Look, the Emperor has no clothes!"

Why is single desk selling so costly? They found the Board was the main buyer of wheat and barley for export, or for non-feed uses at home. But the political appointees running it got job security to age 70. Lacking a bottom line performance review, and with its operations fully guaranteed by government, the Board needn't improve handling systems to respond to markets. With few incentives to slash inefficiency, costs kept rising, cutting into returns.

And the researchers found diehard monopoly supporters ignored one of the biggest costs - the absence of farm-gate buying competition. In fact, the Board gave farmers little price information, leaving them with false price signals. Growers and the industry couldn't see how decisions were made or how the system operated, so they couldn't manage risk properly nor even their finances. Production and marketing costs were high. And because so much No. 1 wheat was sold for No. 3 prices, returns were eroded.

This would change in a free market, they concluded. But in fact, the Board virtually controlled grain production, regulating the system and defending government policy. And its "high quality only" wheat policy didn't meet world demand - half the country's exports grade No. 1, yet only 15-to-20 percent of buyers would pay for that quality, leaving massive waste. A focus on medium-quality exports would have boosted earnings.

Carter and Loyns found the grain and livestock industries were trapped by the Board's non-market rules from farm gate to final customer. When the Board bought wheat and barley for export and for domestic non-feed uses, it affected every farmer.

And the costs to farmers of monopoly selling could be up to $20 per tonne for wheat. Taxpayer costs could be another $5-to-$6 per tonne. Hidden costs for barley growers were over $20 per tonne and costs to taxpayers about $9, bringing *total costs to about $600 million dollars per year* on about 24 million metric tonnes.

"Despite all the posturing by CWB officials and farm organizations..(that growers would get lower prices if private firms sold their grain)," the authors found the Board "has no real power to influence policies of competing nations." And Board supporters often contradict themselves, saying the Board brings big price benefits because it can charge some customers more than others (price discrimination,) then telling foreign governments it's purely a marketing body that doesn't discriminate.

In fact, they found the private trade could provide so-called single-desk selling benefits like market power and risk management and develop niche markets just as efficiently. And they unearthed a largely hidden 1992 study of the Board by Deloitte and Touche that found a lack of leadership, strategic planning and accountability.

The authors noted that when Federal Agriculture Minister Charles Mayer yanked oats from Board control in 1989, growers responded by planting more. Exports soared over 2000 percent, from 43,000 tonnes in 1985-86 to 934,000 in 1993-94. The US market took all that growth. And prices, relative to the US, rose and stabilized.

When Mayer then removed barley destined for US markets, from Board control on August 1, 1993, in an open market trial, the trial ended in 40 days because of a government change, a court challenge and a legal judgement. But in those 40 days, barley exports surged to over half a million tonnes. Yet the Board had never sold more than 240,821 tonnes of feed barley to the US in a year.

Carter and Loyns pointed to an earlier Board study that said the Pacific North West was a barley surplus area. But Carter had found that to be dead wrong in a study for Agriculture Canada - it was a deficit area. He showed that Canada is a price taker anyway, that the Board couldn't influence price.

He concluded: open the border to the private trade - in effect, deregulate the market and growers will benefit.

The root of Western Canada's problem, is the lack of farm-gate buying competition, concluded the authors, because over 60 percent of Board wheat sales go to the top 10 bulk markets which demand the lowest prices.

But not surprisingly, the media largely ignored this devastating report, and the apostles of government grain selling continued their righteous protests that monopoly selling was the only way.

11

WHY HATE THE EXCHANGE? - THE SHIFT TO NON-BOARD - THE ISSUE IS FREEDOM

Why Hate The Richest Man In Winnipeg?
Flair for Communications - My Gawd,
We've Lost Oats!

Back in 1961 when Mac Runciman was named UGG president, the huge China and Russian sales were about to send a momentous signal - an imminent war on hunger could transform the world of grain. And Canada's huge prairie breadbasket was positioned to play a leading role in the most important battle facing mankind.

Yet the Social Gospel infection with its market-hating ideology had permeated Canada's political thinking. Many farm leaders had their eyes shut tightly, ignoring those ringing market signals, clamouring for more government controls, secure in their truth that markets were evil, that big bureaucracies were the only way to go.

Private grain companies which understood the role of markets had been sidelined by the Social-Gospel invective against them. Farmer-owned UGG had shown from the start it could not be so easily intimidated. Yet Mac Runciman heartily disliked those bitter political struggles aimed at breaking through the regulations choking the industry. The farm policy field seemed a never-never world to him.

Most of the conflict went back to the beginning. "Tom Crerar and his board thought the Pool idea offered some help to the predicament facing all farmers in the early 1920s," Runciman recalled. "UGG put up money to help growers organize those Pools. And the Pools first used the Grain Growers' elevators to handle their grain.

"Then Aaron Sapiro arrived with his high-blown dream of a Canadian pool and a world wheat pool dictating prices to buyers. These stirred the dreams of many farmers, but they didn't make sense and couldn't possibly work."

Yet the social gospellers' hatred of capitalism, and their unending attack on entrepreneurs, was deeply embedded in the public's mind-set. "One theme running through western agriculture from the beginning said the Winnipeg Grain Exchange was a den of iniquity, the market was unstable, price fluctuations always ripped off farmers," remembered Runciman. That perplexed him.

"Why would we hate people around the Exchange, even if some were wealthy? I never saw the Exchange as a symbol of purity. But I never saw it as a den of thieves either. It was a segment of business. People there did their jobs as they saw fit. The Stamp Commission found charges against it to be false.

"If people on the Exchange got out of line, I figured the forces of democracy would push them back. My views were influenced by little milestones along the way."

One milestone centred on high-profile Scottish-born grain trader James Stewart who had a home on Wellington Crescent and was once deemed to be the richest man in Winnipeg. Stewart had "a wartime record of service to the British and Canadian governments that had established his reputation for market shrewdness," wrote C.F. Wilson in his book, *A Century of Canadian Grain*. He had top executive posts at the Maple Leaf Milling Company, the Alberta Pacific Grain Company and Federal Grain Limited.

He had "the reputation of being the shrewdest and most able grain man in Canada," wrote another author, C.W. Anderson, in *GRAIN - The Entrepreneurs*. And, he related, Stewart went on to "successively greater heights in a career unparalleled in the Canadian grain industry." He served on the Board of Grain Supervisors. And when Ottawa created the first Canadian Wheat Board in 1919 in response to the United Kingdom's Royal Commission on Wheat Supplies and to a US move to operate its own grain corporation, Stewart was named its chairman.

But after his dizzying rise, wrote Anderson, "his fall from the pinnacle of wealth and power in 1930 was even more precipitous."

Explained Runciman: "Stewart was a speculator on the Exchange - a gambler. But the Exchange was not set up as a gambling den. Twice he was on top. He died in poverty."

Gambling like this was a misuse of the Exchange, helping explain why people disliked it. And the problem went further, said Runciman. "Farmers occasionally loved to have a bit of a gamble there too. But if grandpa went broke, the family and the community rallied around, said it wasn't grandpa's fault and blamed the Exchange."

Inevitably in those turbulent times, grain issues were at the heart of decision-making in Ottawa. New Prime Minister R.B. Bennett had appointed his friend and former business associate John McFarland[1] to manage the Pools' bankrupt Central Selling Agency in November, 1930. He had also agreed to guarantee the pool operations for the 1930 crop. But prices slid relentlessly, hitting 38 cents per bushel on December 16, 1932.

McFarland began buying future contracts to support prices. Bennett backed him. In effect, Ottawa was doing for growers precisely what farmers thought the gamblers and manipulators had done against them for so many years by selling short. This pushed Canadian prices higher. But now Argentina had lower prices than Canada, and increased its market share. Canada's carryover increased, Argentina's didn't.

A dispute over McFarland's activities broke out. Stanford University Food Research Institute had examined the issue and Paul Earl, studying Stanford's findings, found "Canada's share of world carryover stock rose...because of the inflated price."

He concluded, "Farmers allowed their moral objections to the marketplace to cloud their perceptions of how markets function and of the actual effects of McFarland's operations." It was one more lesson that markets act rationally. But Pool supporters steadfastly ignored it, never wavering in their distrust of the market.

Now, in 1961, as Runciman took over as UGG president, the political struggle was intensifying. The company faced increasing business competition, and the stream of scientific findings to help farmers grow and market their crops and livestock was becoming a deluge. The farmers'

---

[1] As related by Paul Earl in his 1992 PhD thesis.

world would be shaken to its roots and the company's role was to lead. Runciman would have to devise an imaginative program to communicate with UGG's members and the public.

John Clark was a Saskatchewan-born and raised university graduate in agricultural science who went on to earn a Masters degree in plant science. But he had a flair for communications. He started his career in Toronto with farm machinery maker Massey Ferguson, then shifted to a job at the Ontario Agricultural College at Guelph. He was quietly building his skills and his reputation. But his heart was in his native West.

Clark wrote to the new UGG president enquiring about employment. Runciman hired him and found him a God-send. He was a chatty but quiet-spoken, almost self-effacing young man with an unquenchable curiosity and limitless energy. He could spend his days at farm or business meetings, his lunches and dinners and banquets talking with anyone who had information or ideas. Then he could sit up most of the night with whoever would relax and open their minds and let the stories and ideas run.

He was soon on every mailing list he could find that sent out news of farm and agricultural developments. He was a voracious reader and his desk was piled high with papers and magazines and books. He feasted on the stories of renowned authors like Hemingway, studying their techniques for getting human interest into written material.

Clark developed an uncanny ability at phrase-making and speech-writing, and thought nothing of working through the night turning his findings into copy for speeches, news releases and for his publications. He launched a paper he called *The Grain Grower* in 1962, cramming it with the latest findings on how to grow and harvest crops and look after livestock and equipment and manage farms. He offered it for sale to UGG members and government extension workers and agribusiness people and others. It caught on.

He created a tabloid he named *Grainews* directed right at farmers. Circulation grew. He hired staff, added a "Cattlemen" section, enlisted farmers and marketing men and university people and housewives and others to write columns. He dubbed it "The paper for farmers, written by farmers." It took advertising and became one of the most talked-about and influential Western papers.

The endless years of trying to squeeze every farmer into the straightjacket of compulsory government marketing had brought catastrophes and failures aplenty. These *Grainews* farmer-journalists soon created a cottage industry mocking the incessant blundering moves of the bureaucrats and got westerners laughing and sometimes crying as never before. One of them was Albertan Lyle Walker whom Clark dubbed, "In addition to being a farmer, machinist, yarner and bureaucrat-tilter...the best farm writer in the country."

Oats is a tiny western crop, dwarfed by wheat and canola and barley and just about anything else. When Wheat Board Minister Charlie Mayer yanked oats out from Wheat Board control in 1989 and told farmers to use their own ingenuity to sell their crop, compulsory marketing fanatics (orderly marketing is the euphemism they use) saw it as a crushing setback and sent up howls of rage.

But Mayer's move offered a glimmer of hope to farmers who wanted to use their own initiative. Lyle Walker penned a memorable column in the March 6, 1989 issue of *Grainews*. Tongue-firmly-in-cheek, wielding the weapons of humour and irony brilliantly, he wrote the imagined cry of anguish of those who rank compulsory grain marketing right up there with Godliness and cleanliness. He titled it, 'MY GAWD, WE'VE LOST OATS!" [2]

---

[2] Here are highlights of Walker's column, "MY GAWD, WE'VE LOST OATS!"

"Of all the calamities, reversals, setbacks, ever to hit good old Canadian agriculture, it would be difficult to imagine anything worse. Those searing droughts of '85, '86 and '88 pale by comparison. Hailstorms are mere details. Russian aphids are nothing. A late September blizzard can decimate a hundred thousand farmers, lay waste to these prairies, reduce a million acres of 50-bushel wheat to pitiful little piles of mouse-eaten low-grade feed, harvested in the spring. But orderly marketing will carry us through.

"We can lose $2 on every bushel, three whole, entire wheat crops, sold, committed, frittered away in advance, in a hurry, a panic on a rising market. A piddling bookkeeping item is all it is, nothing more, a *bagatelle*, as the French would say. Three years later, we can repeat the process.

"We can surrender, donate our durum, hundreds of millions of bushels, watch half the value disappear in those musky, dusty cobwebs of official secrecy, hidden pricing arrangement, (for the good of the industry,) deep, dark, oily pools. We can dump a major pearling barley marketinto the Pacific, lose it forever, because of a strike by 175 labourers. La-

Clark was now editor/publisher and he carried a heart-wrenching story of a family that lost its father when his arm caught and was torn off in the power takeoff. The story had hit a sore spot in rural communities. Readers responded with similar stories. Clark seized on the idea and kicked off a farm safety campaign, offering readers

---

bour is a federal matter, a political matter, an Ottawa matter, same as barley, but labour is more important in the polling booth. Politics provides big advantages for grain growers.

"And then we sell our malting barley, by compulsion. Fifty cents, a dollar, $1.15. When we discover that the brewers pay more, we can sue, in the courts, and we are told that we are *not entitled* to any accounting....

"All of these things we can stand with no trouble at all because we're believers, followers, adherents, advocates, defenders, converts, patrons. And sometimes fools.

"But now we've lost oats. One half of one per cent of the power and the glory and the influence and the monopoly. I'm telling you, its a dark dark day for the forces of right and justice, a sad time for Eastern feeders, and a terrible shock for those of us who know in our very hearts that the great Canadian system is without a peer. Anywhere in the world.

"We cannot survive for any length of time without the power, the guidance, the aid and assistance and financial expertise of official government-appointed, government-monitored bureaucracy. This vast nation, ocean to ocean, functions wholly and solely upon government control for the good of all. Every loyal Canadian has to do his part, make his fair, full and equitable contributions, sacrifices.

"And maybe there have been times over the past half century, when our Wheat Board has inadvertently lost sales or blown markets or dropped a few billion dollars in some isolated unfortunate deal, but what harm has been done....Can this possibly be any reason for weakening the dynasty, breaking the monopoly, splitting off vital segments of support, acceptance, compliance, submission?

"When we are paid rock-bottom prices, in the aftermath of some isolated incident, we all get exactly the same, we all have the privilege, the honour, the patriotic pride of sharing bureaucratic misfortune....We are reduced to the lowest common denominator, which is the foundation, the basic premise of total, inescapable, uncontested government control.

"Over a period of 48 years, orderly marketing has assured us the lowest possible price and given us just that, in almost every case. Canadian wheat is renowned the world over for its quality, its uniformity, its colour, and its vanishing value.

"How can we stand idly by while thousands of bushels of oats fall into the hands of greedy, profit-taking private entrepreneurs, cereal makers, and grain traders....Let us not forget that in 1947, western coarse grains were placed under Wheat Board control to provide our eastern Canadian feedlot industry with an assured unlimited supply of cheap feed."

red heart-shaped safety decals with the words, "Please Be Careful, We love You, Your Family." He was deluged with requests for over 100,000 of them.

He expanded and brightened the UGG annual report, making it almost a handbook of key farm policy developments and issues and background think-pieces informing farmers on their increasingly complex business needs. He featured *lavish colour photos* of the farmers' often-spectacular world - the shimmering gold of a ripened wheat crop, the brilliant yellow of canola in bloom or the restful azure of flax in bloom. He showed the wildflowers that brighten the spring and summer days of every prairie farmer, or the colourful but dreaded weeds that farmers battle, offering simple but all-important hints on how to control them. He pictured the gaudy meadowlarks and cardinals and plovers and hawks that farmers could see in spring migration or nesting on their farms. And he displayed the majestic Clydesdales and Percherons and Quarterhorses, and the Hereford and Angus and Charolais cattle raised and cherished by so many farmers.

Clark's little group became almost a nerve centre for the ferment gripping the prairies. He worked with any farm groups that shared UGG's view, and his own, of the need to free up farmers and the industry from the over-regulation that shackled them. He and his publications played key roles in such projects as the rapeseed vote and the ongoing battle for more farmer freedom.

Political Pricing Embarrasses Trudeau -
A Tiny Step Forward

Because feed grains had fallen under the Wheat Board monopoly along with bread wheat, growers had to deliver them to the Board which would price and sell it for them.[3] This blew up into a noisy controversy in the early 1970s.

"Ottawa is becoming embarrassed by this policy," Runciman told his members then, "because its agency the

---

[3] Those rules also lumped durum wheat sales in with red spring wheat rather than into a separate durum pool, and this further blunted any aggressive sales initiatives. And they lumped malting barley sales in with other barley sales.

Wheat Board is dictating the price one group of farmers must pay for another group's product."

Ottawa wanted off the hook and asked farm groups to decide. A 1972 Canadian Federation of Agriculture (CFA) meeting hit deadlock. Eastern users didn't want to pay the cost of hauling grain from the West to their farms and feedlots. They demanded the same non-Board prices as prairie feed mills and livestock producers got. Prairie live-stock groups protested, saying, No! That would discrimi-nate against them.

The minority Trudeau government, which had few western members, hinted it might get right out of domes-tic feed grain selling and let growers sell their feed grain anywhere in the country. "Before its plan was even an-nounced," Runciman recalled later, "special interest groups pushed demagoguery to unprecedented levels, playing on people's prejudices, crying out, 'The orderly marketing system will be destroyed' or 'Eastern Canada will bleed the West.'"

Federal NDP'ers favoured Ottawa's plan to get out of selling these feed grains. Manitoba and Saskatchewan NDP governments opposed it. Ottawa's Tory opposition probably supported it, but laid low. Two farm groups en-tered the fray, but "ignored the reality of the grain busi-ness and talked politics," said Runciman. He told his 1973 annual meeting, "Disputes about the way non-Board feed grains are sold dominated farm policy in the past fiscal year." He said the issue had become entirely political and concerned with votes, not grain and meat. UGG had taken no public part in it since the failed CFA meeting had shown agreement was impossible.

But he didn't hide UGG's views. Its directors had long argued for sweeping change, saying, "Leave farmers the option to sell to the CWB, but let them sell non-Board grain to anyone in Canada if they want. Grain could move across provincial borders and Prairie elevators could then buy it for feed mills and feedlots, increasing the competi-tion."

The UGG Board urged Ottawa to provide an income security plan as well, perhaps based on net cash income, so in times of surplus, farmers wouldn't be driven by cash shortages to sell non-Board. And it wanted feed freight assistance gradually ended to remove the artificial ad-vantage given eastern livestock producers.

The alternative was complete government control, which it called unthinkable. Government already interfered too much, and farm-to-farm sales couldn't be policed anyway.

The Pools and others had fought doggedly to retain Board monopoly powers, arguing that their loss would destroy the Board. But a more adventurous Trudeau government did respond, freeing up domestic feed grain marketing as UGG had urged, allowing growers to sell their own wheat, oats and barley off-Board, as they did with rapeseed, rye and flax, and opening new opportunities to farmers and grain companies alike. Runciman urged further action like higher initial payments for Board grains to encourage farmers not to flood the off-Board market.

The Booming 1970s - New Marketing Thrust

But now another sea change was transforming grain markets. Runciman noted in his 1973 annual report that malting barley had reached $3.30 a bushel, spring wheat $5.83, durum $9.02. Vancouver rapeseed was $8.19 in July, flax topped $11 in August.

Yes, the market had turned. Astonished growers were moving into the most prosperous times ever. Those 1971 and 1972 Soviet sales had been only the beginning. Grain and oilseed exports hit a record 823.8 million bushels in the 1972-73 crop year and prices held. By late 1974, world crops had fallen short five years in a row. Growers in Canada and other countries were savouring good prices. Prairie farmers took off a record 1973 crop and with the stranglehold of regulations being beaten back, had more freedom to grow all the grain they wanted. And elevator companies could begin to remedy low returns by charging tariffs of up to 10 1/2 cents a bushel.

Grain companies now became aggressive marketers. UGG created its own export arm, and in a bold 1972 move, created a cash crop marketing arm to help farmers market special crops. It was becoming a force in domestic and world markets, extending the farmer's reach, facing the risks and opportunities of marketing his grain wherever buyers could be found.

Its first full year of this selling in 1974 went well and it doubled sales to 82 million bushels in 1975. But it also learned the pitfalls when it bought rapeseed in late 1975 before prices fell sharply. Hedging was impossible, sales were slow and the interest cost of carrying it hit 50 cents a bushel.

In another deal it bought malting barley from the Wheat Board which it couldn't hedge because no futures market existed. Within days, the Board slashed prices 75-to-90 cents per bushel. Runciman cautioned his members, "Remember, farmers and UGG benefitted from inventory value gains three years ago when prices were rising. Some risks are unavoidable." UGG was in for the long haul.

Prices fell steeply on another occasion when it was buying flax. "Manitoba Pool for one, went right off the market," said Runciman. "It just quit buying. We said, 'We're staying on.' We kept buying from farmer customers. The price kept dropping to about $1.50.

"Wheat Board selling had always kept those price signals out of the market. Farmers never heard them. Now we said, 'Let that price tell us and our customers the true situation.' It might tell growers not to grow more flax, or to grow more. This showed us and everyone else why we were there - and it wasn't to stop buying flax when we might lose some money.

"If the farmer wanted to send us his grain and take the prevailing price, we were there to get it to market and take our chances on making a profit." It was all part of an education process for UGG and for growers.

The prairie economy rested heavily on livestock and UGG now focused on this long-festering issue. It had a sizeable feed company, United Feeds Ltd., but with grain politics so all-engrossing, those livestock often got overlooked by the politicians. Runciman sounded an alarm in 1972, warning that inflation and energy shortages were pushing up costs, eroding incomes of livestock and poultry men. They were cutting back. When Ottawa removed the tariff on US beef entering Canada and placed an export embargo on fed beef to the US, Runciman labelled them "misguided moves" to give consumers cheaper beef - an attack on the industry that reduced the cattlemen's incentive.

"It's an inescapable law," he declared. "Producers must have high prices before consumers can have low prices. A beef man will use his skills and buy inputs to produce more beef if he gets an incentive. That will lower beef prices. But he must get that incentive to lower his costs....Western Canada is our major feed grain source. All farmers would benefit from a bigger livestock industry. But high feed grain prices are chasing too many feed cattle and hogs from the prairies."

He charged, "Ottawa and the provinces haven't done enough to build the West's beef and hog populations. Yet prairie growers can truck grain to their own or to nearby feedlots easier than shipping it across the country or beyond for someone else to feed.

"When world grain stocks begin to replenish, they will need those cattle and hog men to buy their grain," he warned, urging them to support the livestock industry.

Historic Big Shift To Non-Board Grain

With the market turnaround, Canada's exports almost doubled in the 10 years to 1977-78 reaching 21.65 million tonnes. Growers took off a good 1976 crop and prices and exports held strong in spring and early summer. UGG's profits hit $5.3 million, the third best ever. Farmers were moving to intensive cropping to cut their costs, and the company's fertilizer, chemicals and twine sales hit records in 1976. Negative crushing margins brought a deficit to the new United Oilseed Products rapeseed crushing plant at Lloydminster, Alberta (which UGG had built in partnership with B.C. Packers and Mitsubishi Canada, Ltd.).

But the company earmarked $20.8 million to upgrade its Vancouver terminal, and to meet the West's desperate need for "inland terminals" it was building a modern 370,000-bushel, high-throughput elevator at Dawson Creek, BC. Future elevators would have even greater capacity.

It also aimed to reduce its number of manager units dramatically and to "invade" 15 new locations, rejecting the old Social Gospel myth that competition is bad. "Increased competition at these invasion points would benefit every farmer," said Runciman.

World surpluses returned and wheat and feed grain prices tumbled near year-end 1977 to the lowest in five years. An old ghost reappeared in 1978 when the handling system was pushed to its limits triggering rail bottlenecks and forcing the Wheat Board to defer sales and choking off record exports. When UGG had to turn down good rapeseed sales, Runciman muttered it was "intolerable that farmers now have to tailor production and sales to rail or elevator capacity." He demanded remedies.

To protect farmers against net cash flow drops, Ottawa passed its Western Grain Stabilization Program in 1976, to be financed jointly by government and farmers. But further bad news came when Ottawa zigzagged again on its Domestic Feed Grain Policy, returning within-Canada sales to the Wheat Board.

But this 1976 price drop and the return to surplus proved to be a historic one. Instead of turning to Ottawa to bail them out, many cash-starved growers focused on the Wheat Board's stultifying regulations which seemed immune to change. The crusading Rapeseed Association and then the Palliser Wheat Growers' had already shone a beacon of light, shown that, yes, growers could find markets if they mustered the selling effort. And they were growing rapeseed and flax and rye and canary seed and mustard and some feed grains outside Board regulations. Yes, here was their chance.

Wheat growers began a massive shift to these special crops. Acreage soared from 866,500 in 1978 to nearly 1.1 million in 1979, reaching nearly 15 percent of Manitoba's cultivated acreage. It rose in Alberta and Saskatchewan too. The historic big shift to non-Board grain was on. It was a glimpse of the future.

Grain companies were in full support. "We are the leading supplier of western feed grains and by-products to some of the most important outlets in eastern Canada," beamed Runciman in 1977. International grain firms were also expanding into Canada, signalling tougher competition ahead.

When do-gooders at a United Nations conference tried to negotiate an internationally financed grain stockpile, Runciman called the idea price-depressing. He also rejected calls for maximum and minimum prices because "Canada had taken a licking on this in the past." He called an attempt by US and Canadian senators to fix a $5 per bushel wheat price, a "politically-motivated scheme to control farmers, not prices," pointedly adding, "neither group, particularly Canadian senators, have any responsibility in this field."

He saw the industry at a crossroads in 1980 when the Hall Commission urged a permanent rail network be protected from line abandonment and asked Ottawa to allow farmers, elevator companies and railways to get on with long-term planning. The UGG Board rejected any master plan.

Runciman, who foresaw increasing markets for rye, oilseeds and open-market feed grains and specialty crops, warned that failure to make the open market work would be catastrophic, forcing a move "to a completely centralized system with companies being the grain handling wing of the Wheat Board like in the Australian system, and the Wheat Board doing all the marketing."

UGG's Vancouver terminal was modernized in the late 1970s, and the new Richardson's/Pioneer Terminal and the Pools' new storage space came on stream. New Wheat Board hopper cars were speeding more grain through the system. And UGG had joined a consortium with the three Pools, Cargill and Pioneer to build a high-capacity grain terminal at Prince Rupert, BC, and to acquire and run the government terminal there.

Vigorous export expansion required some market stability and now the International Wheat Agreement was extended to June 30, 1981, as an information source and a means of consultation.

The price squeeze on farmers led to a battle cry in the US of "100 percent parity" and this had spread to Canada, raising the question, Do we need small and medium sized farms? UGG directors rejected the goal of cheap food for society and of producing food with the fewest farmers.

"We must preserve the dominant role of medium-size commercial farms," said Runciman. "Family farms have priorities like independence, better family living conditions and working with nature that can't be measured in dollars."

The issue was how best to preserve them. "Parity doesn't guarantee a profit for all producers," he said. In fact, it could be self-defeating. If prices were locked in to assure profits, bigger farmers would buy more land, leading to the rapid demise of small- and medium-sized farms.

Belt-tightening wasn't enough either. Farmers had to grow more bushels per acre and that required markets. He urged, "Get the British and Japanese eating as much beef as Canadians do and you will create a massive new market for Canadian farmers." He asked Ottawa to push harder through GATT to lower tariffs which devastate food exports, hurting farmers and consumers too.

He was certain - the issue was freedom. "Some farmers don't realize it just stifles initiative and progress when they turn over power and responsibility to government...its restrictions rob farmers of both freedom and security. Fortunately most farmers haven't fallen for the myth that government can create prosperity."

12

THE SOCIAL GOSPEL'S DEEP ROOTS

Runciman A Senator? No, Hazen Argue!

After his years of farming and 20 years as UGG president, Runciman could look back from a remarkable vantage point. But an event "so extraordinary you almost felt it was unreal" occurred a few months before UGG's 1980 annual meeting. It offered an unusual glimpse into his nature and his place in Canada. He said nothing about it at the time.

Canada's grain exports had hit record levels in 1980 keeping farmers' incomes ahead of inflation. The UGG Board reported strong profits and paid $6.6 million in patronage dividends, boosting working capital by $12 million.

Runciman described his "extraordinary" experience to friends later. Prime Minister Trudeau had gone to the polls early in 1980 in the wake of his National Energy Policy which was despised in the West as a raid on Alberta's and the West's energy resources. His careless "Why should I sell your wheat?" remark to prairie farmers still lingered in everyone's memory as well. His Liberals won the election. But they were almost shut out in the West. Lloyd Axworthy was their only prairie member.

The Prime Minister lacked a suitable member to name Wheat Board Minister. Runciman will never forget what happened next.

"Mr. Trudeau's Principal Secretary Jim Coutts used to phone me occasionally. One evening he called from the PM's office and asked a question that almost floored me. 'Would I become Minister responsible for the Wheat Board?'

"I answered, 'Jim, how on earth can that be done? I am not even a Member of Parliament, let alone ministerial.'

"Coutts saw no problem at all. 'We will appoint you a Senator, then name you minister.'"

Runciman would not have it. "I turned it down. I couldn't take it under those circumstances at all. The next day Marj and I sat and watched on TV with awe as Hazen Argue was sworn in as Wheat Board Minister."

Argue's appointment led to a distasteful development for Runciman. Argue was a Saskatchewan farmer who had been elected to the House of Commons for Assiniboia in 1945 as a CCF'er. He was then the youngest member. He was a fiery emotional orator and was seen by some as a sort of prodigy.

Following the 1958 Diefenbaker sweep, Argue became House leader of the eight-member CCF caucus and was elected national CCF leader in 1960. But when the CCF and the Canadian Labour Congress formed the New Democratic Party in 1961, T.C. Douglas defeated him for the leadership. Six months later Argue resigned, was reelected to the Commons as a Liberal in 1962, defeated in 1963 and named to the Senate in 1966.

But Argue was really an ardent socialist. He believed implicitly in big government. He had little understanding of the market place or of its role in a modern society. His political philosophy could scarcely have been more at odds with Runciman's and that of UGG.

Within months, Argue was responding to his socialist roots and his left-wing advisors and urging that rapeseed be brought under the Wheat Board. Mac Runciman had already fought a vigorous battle in a vote to keep rapeseed on the open market. Now, with Argue trying to roll back the clock, he had to roll up his sleeves and speak out again.

The Left-Wing Co-ops - A Righteous Way of Life

At Runciman's 1981 retirement, he had been at the centre of Canada's farm policy-making for over two decades and was perhaps the West's most sought after speaker on grain and agricultural matters at meetings across the West and beyond. And he was serving as director of several prestigious Canadian companies.

Sixteen years later, as this book is being written, he looked back and identified perhaps the most important issue he faced - one he had found at the heart of Canada's grain politics and its political life.

Yes, the pioneers who founded UGG in 1906 had won the freedom to sell their grain to the highest bidder. But in the late l950s when he was elected a UGG director, grain was piled up again and prices had slumped. The massive Chinese and Russian purchases brought a brief reprieve soon after he was named president in 1961. But a new element had come into the explosive mix of farm politics.

"The extreme wing of the co-operative movement seemed to have swallowed the Social Gospel," he recalled. "These people thought human evil was a result of the capitalist system, that if they could get rid of profits they would change human nature. They had this *holy crusade against profits*. And they kept obstructing farm policy.

"Their slogan, 'Service, not profit,' really said 'Profit is a corrupting motive - money is the root of all evil. If no one pursues the almighty dollar, everyone will be perfect.'

"With their utopian Social Gospel, these co-ops seemed to be trying to instill a righteous way of life - to say that to be a true co-operative in the West meant to be left-wing. They didn't look back on history and see that human nature hasn't changed.

"Ed Partridge (UGG's first president) was of that element. He believed if you could just change human nature so people would do what they should be doing, you could make a perfect society. His book, *War and Poverty*, is a collector's item worth about a hundred bucks. The big print is what he is saying. The small print is pages of quotes from left-wing writers.

"That tough old Swan River Valley pioneer John Kennedy, who worked so hard to set up the company, joined with Crerar to straighten out the Partridge situation in the first year.

"I never thought the future of western agriculture lay in political philosophy," Runciman remembered. "It lay in finding practical procedures to allow the industry to grow. I tried to see what was going to happen down the road - where must we try to go?"

At one meeting he quoted the words of early UGG president Tom Crerar, "What people want is more freedom...freedom to buy and sell when they please, freedom to order their daily lives as they wish so long as they do not overstep the boundaries of the rights of others...and freedom from special privileges in any of its forms."

Said Runciman, "Those words precisely sum up what I have tried to stand for."

But that Social Gospel had taken deep root, setting the stage for an ideological struggle that would grip the grain industry, the West and go to Canada's heart. It continued through Runciman's presidency and beyond, with UGG on one side, the Pools and the left-wing co-ops too often on the other. It was a microcosm of the left-right struggle in Canada itself.

But the resulting swing to big government had created another grain monopoly - one that held growers in its grip perhaps even more tightly than the railway/grain companies' monopoly that had triggered UGG's formation. Runciman found SaskPool's obsession with left-wing ideas and politics never seemed to end. "It always seemed to be in an eternal struggle at the Board table to maintain the status quo. It has been a very successful elevator company. But not a central selling agency as the Pools were conceived in the Sapiro principle."

Other farm groups were caught up in this. "Saskatchewan Farmers' Union was supposed to be dealing with its members' practical problems. But no one doubted where its support went in elections. It had an ideological agenda. It was really a left-wing political party."

That obsession had politicians caught up in bureaucracy-building and spending. The tangle of controls led to the "parallel between conditions that drove Partridge to Winnipeg in 1905 to seek freedom for farmers, and those in the crisis of the late 1960s when grain was piled up and the farmers' cash flow virtually stopped."

It was then that the UGG Board faced up to the awful truth - the regulation-plagued transportation and handling system had failed. Runciman constantly urged farmers, "Never ask government to do something you can do for yourself."

Here was the industry's central problem - farm groups were hopelessly divided, unable to agree on a path to the future. UGG walked the tricky line of remaining with the co-ops and other farm groups. It joined the Co-operative Union of Canada hesitantly, then was out again.

The Pools even led an ongoing attack for a few years trying to discredit UGG as a co-op, "because it hadn't bought that Social Gospel," recalled Runciman.

"UGG was solidly established on the old Rochdale Co-operative principles, but it never bought into utopianism," he said. It stayed in the Canadian Federation of Agriculture for years, supporting it financially and hoping to influence its decisions.

"But much of what came out as CFA policy didn't make sense. Conventional wisdom was often just the political jargon of farm organizations. It conflicted with what I believed for UGG. I couldn't be comfortable with it. I used to get ulcers at annual meeting time in January. Seeking common ground with the Pools was often the most distressing part of policy-making."

Runciman finally concluded that the co-operative movement had become the NDP movement, the left-wing politics of Western Canada, making the grain system so hidebound noone could invest in it. Puzzled why people would be obsessed with that socialist ideology, he told one farm group, "Some people think they are quarrelling about the economic system when they are really quarrelling about human nature. And it will take a long time to find an organization that is immune to human nature."

Mac Runciman put on his elder statesman's hat at UGG's 1981 annual meeting, and noted how politicians too often come along to a gullible public, pumped up with dreams of spending taxpayers' money on big projects designed to win the votes of this group or that. He told how the UGG board had responded to one grandiose scheme.

"Politicians had approached UGG and other co-operatives in the late 1970's with an eye-popping proposal. Join Ottawa in a $100 million investment in a co-operative resources holding company, they urged. It will explore and develop Canadian oil resources, trigger economic development.

"Most co-ops succumbed to the lure of this grand dream,[1]" said Runciman. But UGG's directors had resisted. And this was right in line with UGG traditions.

"Look back to 1906 when those tough pioneers

---

[1] Federated Co-ops put in $20 million, SaskPool $12 million, Alberta Wheat Pool $8 million, Manitoba Pool $2.5 million, the Co-operators $10 million, Credit Union of Saskatchewan $4-to-$5 million, Co-op Atlantic $1 million.

founded our company as the first farmers' co-operative grain firm. These men stood alone against the establishment. And succeeding UGG boards have often rejected popular causes."

Runciman had no doubt. Present board members were made from the same mould. They had been neither impressed by this plea to leap into the energy business with all its promise of quick payoffs, nor intimidated into joining the crowd.

He gave four reasons for rejecting the proposal:
* UGG's focus and expertise was grain and allied businesses
* More "Canadianization" of the oil business may be a worthy goal but government financial aid to one group and not to others was unfair, and besides, UGG needed any available capital itself
* UGG preferred not to go into business with government
* the get-rich glamour of the oil business was fading with North America's move to world oil prices, and the breakdown of OPEC price-fixing. And besides, the US seemed to offer more oil exploration prospects than Canada.

"Finally," said Runciman, "UGG had a different set of values. It would tend to its own business of providing prairie farmers with the best possible services.

"We saw co-operatives as a way of doing business - of selling the farmers' grain and buying supplies and developing farm policy proposals. But not a platform to expound philosophy."

That pragmatism had been instilled in Runciman from the start. "When I was a kid of eight or nine in Scotland, my dad was secretary of a local farmers co-op. When supplies came in, I would get on shank's mare and go and notify people to come and pick them up. My idea of co-operativism was helping other people."

When the Rapeseed Association was set up in the mid-1960s with Runciman as president, it brought growers, handlers, processors, scientists and marketing men together to plan and build their industry. These men had kept rapeseed largely outside the ideological fights and the red tape that entrapped the older grains and it freed them to write a spectacular success story. By 1994, the Cinderella crop, canola, rivalled even wheat in value, showing the way to a historic change of direction.

Runciman's ability to bring people together to address

common problems was recognized again when he was named president of the new Canada Grains Council. He treasures a letter from Hon. Jean-Luc Pepin who was appointed Wheat Board Minister in 1968 and who "provided great support to us." When Pepin was later transferred to External Affairs, he wrote Runciman, "You and a few others such as Bill Parker (Manitoba Wheat Pool President) welcomed the French-speaking Quebecer interested in understanding the West and the wheat economy and you guided him with great kindness."

During Runciman's 20 years as UGG president, he and his boards joined with growers' commodity groups like flax, barley, rapeseed and cattlemen to work for freedom from the thoughtless and destructive bureaucracy. At times his entire energies seemed to be directed to freeing up growers and the industry to use that fertile prairie land to feed the world.

The social gospellers' failure to understand the need for a vigorous market-oriented livestock industry cost farmers and the West and Canada heavily, and Runciman turned to that issue in his final address to his delegates. Rising interest rates and high feed costs were then squeezing livestock farmers. Beef consumption was slumping. Prairie cattlemen were closing feedlots and selling their herds. Inevitably the cry went up, "Get governments to set up compulsory beef cattle marketing boards."

Said Runciman, "It's the nature of the times. When a free-market commodity gets in trouble, a marketing board is proposed."

His experience had left him in no doubt, "Too many people think monopoly selling is the answer to every question. The Senate Agriculture Committee on the Beef Industry had rushed in with four options, all with heavy government control.

"UGG directors offered a different solution, one in line with long-time UGG policy. Offer a voluntary board to those who want protection, but allow others to measure their skills against open market risks and opportunities."

Runciman added wryly, "If a marketing board wants to create an elite society of cattlemen, then model it after the present egg, broiler and turkey marketing boards. But if the aim is to stabilize cattlemen's incomes, try a plan like Prairie Grain Stabilization."

He then turned to the long-simmering Crow freight rate issue which undermined grain exports and blocked food processing., He said what's needed is simple - a transportation policy which guarantees the Prairie's comparative advantage in livestock and processing. "Some farm groups and bureaucrats are trying to turn the clock back. They want domestic feed grains taken off the open market and put back solely under the Wheat Board. The UGG Board disagrees totally."

His advice: "Hold onto the present Domestic Feed Grains Policy - a dual system which allows farmers to sell to the CWB or the open market, or both."

Runciman's years of fighting farm political battles brought him hesitantly to a harsh judgement. "Western agriculture has been poorly served by politics over the years...politicians are not going to get something for Saskatchewan (with its stagnant population shouting out the message that it had a weak political base) that Quebec or Ontario doesn't want you to have....By the time you tempered things that Quebec and Ontario wanted, modified them a bit to suit British Columbia, the prairies usually lost out."

He added, "I'll give Quebecers credit. They were never shy of asking, and they presented their stuff well. They seldom came out on the short end of the stick"

Runciman saw UGG as more than a grain company. "It is part of a farmers' movement doing the things farmers want done. Marketing grain and eliminating the handicaps in grading, pricing and transportation, and getting farm supplies to farmers - these promoted the social, economic and policy needs of farm people and improved their lot the fastest."

By the 1970s the regulations strangling the industry had begun to yield. Grain companies began a massive streamlining, slashing the number of manager units by 36 percent from 3,240 to 2,075 in the 10 years to 1982. And breakthroughs in science and technology were transforming farmers' cropping and livestock practises and adding to industry pressures. It was a time of progress.

POSTSCRIPT

A Renaissance Of Agriculture

With deregulation inching ahead in the 1980's, new UGG President Lorne Hehn's speeches focused on the growing strength of the vibrant grains and oilseeds industry. Prairie wheat made up three quarters of Canada's farm exports and was 20 percent of world wheat exports. It boosted Canada's trade balance and created an avalanche of jobs.

But, he cautioned, market economics enabled this industry to develop, and it could still be devastated by weather, disease, weeds and insects as well as price changes, interest rates, government policy and inflation. His point was simple - growers would fail if they weren't free to respond to markets.

When Hehn resigned in late 1990 to become Canadian Wheat Board Chief Commissioner, the powerhouse grain industry was grossing $10-to-$12 billion a year. It had $80-to-$100 billion of assets and $10-to-$20 billion of debt. Farmers were spending $5 billion a year on supplies, machinery and interest, and on credit, labour, utilities, taxes and insurance. Servicing them was becoming an enormous - but a fiercely competitive - business.

Europe's farmers had feasted on huge subsidies, more than doubling wheat output to 79 million tonnes in the 1980s and pushing exports from 9 percent to 20 percent of the world market. When the US hit back in 1985 with its Export Enhancement Program subsidies further depressing prices, the trade war was on. Ottawa had no choice but to pay growers massive subsidies.

UGG's new President Ted Allen was a young company director with one of those oversized farm and irrigated cash crop enterprises not uncommon in southern Alberta. Farmers were now seizing on a blinding array of new technology to grow big crops and compete and win on world markets. And best of all, governments were finally turning away from stultifying control programs, favouring insurance programs to support farmers' money needs. The long struggle to end the Crow Benefit payment which had imprisoned the prairies seemed about to pay off, heralding a streamlined transportation system. And the new General Agreement on Tariffs and Trade (GATT) pointed to more open markets and a more level world playing field.

Although Allen and his board saw nothing but growth ahead, they cautioned that prairie growers still had to haul their grain and livestock further than those in competing countries. Allen laid out UGG's blueprint for action. "Business must adapt too, building and managing a world-class system for the future," he said. UGG was shutting down obsolete old elevators and building high throughput ones with 8,000 tonnes storage capacity, an 8-minutes-per-car loading rate and able to handle 80,000 tonnes annually to serve its new markets. On-site specialists offered customers advice and products to help them grow and market crops.

"Our extended service centre - our supermarket," Allen called it.

But he faced one mountainous challenge. All elevator co-ops had built up big debts of deferred patronage dividends owed members. These were millstones around their necks. Where would they get capital to build more supermarkets?

A stunning request reached UGG shareholders in June, 1992. Would they approve selling shares to the public on the equity market? This would take the first of the farmers' co-operatives away from a once-sacred principle - place three non-farmers on the board. "Farmers will keep control," Allen promised.

Delegates voted yes, pitching UGG into a historic restructuring. It issued public equity in 1993 and 1994, raising money for a huge investment program to enable it to excel as a low-cost mover of grain, and offering farmers the full benefit of their own efficiency, hard work and innovation.

The industry was truly in breathtaking change. Two years later, SaskPool asked its members the same question, and made its share-offering in 1996.

Meanwhile, prairie growers had made 1994 a watershed year - diversifying massively into peas and lentils and harvesting a record-breaking canola crop. Thanks to strong canola prices, a crop other than wheat - and one they could sell outside Wheat Board regulations - promised to be their top income source for the first time.

But red tape still hampered growth. A frustrated Allen told

delegates at his 1994 meeting, "We informed the Grain Trans-portation Agency in July that we had confirmed sales in China, Japan and Mexico, but it answered in September that we would get less than 60 percent of our car needs." The company couldn't ship the crop to export terminals, grow-ers paid high carrying costs, handlers lost sales and Cana-da's reputation was trashed again.

Overregulation also caused "the 19-day car turna-round average that hasn't improved in 85 years...(and) prevents market signals getting through freely," said Allen. "And farmers, grain companies and others can't react to signals they don't get."

Ted Allen who was just as outraged as Runciman had ever been, explained that the system blurred market signals and eroded competitiveness. "Railways can't aban-don branch lines, so low-cost lines subsidize less efficient ones....Grain could be *trucked* for 10 cents a tonne/mile....but it cost $3.43 per tonne/mile to move grain off one 25-mile piece of Saskatchewan track."

In fact, "High-throughput elevators should have been built years earlier. But even these won't fully drive down costs because the handling system averages costs and hides inefficiencies."

But irresistible forces were at work. Governments were running out of money and the public demanded bal-anced budgets. The UGG Board pleaded for action. "The grain industry has come of age," declared Allen. "If politi-cians will free it up, growers and their companies and pri-vate companies could work together, returning Canada to pre-eminence like in the early days when Winnipeg was seen as the world's wheat leader."

Allen called for deregulation, not special benefits, and urged Ottawa to allow those with vision to adjust to new challenges. "We subsidize a colossal distortion in grain pricing with the Crow Benefit. Then we try to offset (it) with provincial programs to support livestock. We create (an office) to help diversify the prairie economy, then dis-courage it with the Western Grain Transportation Act, and we complain about high taxes and the deficit. We have created a vast web of countervailing government programs because we refuse to address the basic issue."

He called the subsidized freight rate which "encour-ages us to export raw commodities....the biggest single im-pediment to livestock and secondary industry in Western

Canada." He said, "We can't build a competitive livestock industry and encourage secondary processing...if we retain it. The dismal failure of centralized planning around the world...should have showed us (that) the only way to achieve efficiency is through the market.

"Let Canada return to world leadership. Pay the Crow benefit to farmers, not railways, and free up grain to be a vibrant industry." He urged Ottawa to reform the grading system and the Wheat Board too, to open the door to truck competition, and to use US rail and water systems to cut costs and improve service. And he said it should dismantle the Grain Transportation Agency and allow railroads to abandon uneconomic branch lines.

Those prophetic words foretold a stunning policy breakthrough. With soaring debt threatening Canada's bankruptcy in late 1994, Ottawa legislated an end to that most sacred of all farm bills - and undoubtedly the most costly and punishing to the country - the 'Holy Crow,' while partly compensating farmers with short-term payments.

Astonishingly, hardly a murmur of protest was heard. The left-wing forces which had filled the air with cries of doom for decades to block Crow change seemed to vanish into thin air. Common sense had prevailed.

Canada was finally raising its eyes to glimpse the opportunities ahead. UGG had issued shares to raise funds and moved into its alliance with giant Archer-Daniels-Midland. SaskPool had also gone public and launched a giant investment program beyond Saskatchewan and the Prairies, aiming to become a world company. Sensing a new freedom to do business, U.S.-based world grain and food processing giant ConAgra launched a huge grain terminal investment program in the prairies. Cargill, too, was investing heavily in grain and livestock facilities. And long-time private grain companies like Paterson Grain, James Richardson International and Parrish and Heimbecker were again investing.

Yes, the breakthrough had come with a vengeance. Allen predicted "a renaissance of world agriculture." And Canadians would be at the forefront, building on their land base, climate and farm business acumen.

Can We Learn From Our Mistakes?

What conclusion can be drawn from this story of nearly a century of mismanagement and missed opportunity with one of the world's great resource areas? Does it really matter...

*that we Canadians listened seriously when pastor Salem Bland preached in the early 1900s, "The distinctive task of the age is the abolition of capitalism."

*that we swallowed the Social Gospel idea (labelled a false doctrine by historian W.L. Morton) that capitalism was evil and big government the answer and took it to our society's heart?

*that we cheered the Bolshevik Revolution and turned the marketing of our huge and vital grain crop into an exercise in politics and demagoguery rather than a hard-nosed business of identifying markets and serving them well?

*that we were unable to fully use one of the world's great breadbaskets to help in the war on hunger, let alone in creating wealth and jobs for our children and grandchildren?

*That, as Mac Runciman said in the early 1970s, "Our grain handling system has fallen 20 years behind that of the US" and it would take us decades to begin to catch up?

*That perhaps Canada's most resource-rich province, Saskatchewan, has had a population of about 1 million for 60 years - that it has hardly gained in all that time?

Does this matter to us?

Or let me ask that question in another way. Can we Canadians learn from our mistakes and finally turn to the future, to free up prairie growers to build strongly on our great resources base and to return to world leadership to the benefit of ourselves and our children and the world's people?

Canada's Grain Story: From Prairie Wilderness ... To Breadbasket

1857   The British government instructs Capt. John Palliser to explore the British prairie region to see if it has value. After three seasons of study, he reports favourably on the park belt but not the plains.

1871   Prime Minister John A. Macdonald lures B.C. into Confederation by promising a transcontinental railway within 10 years. He incorporates the CPR in 1878 and work begins.

1877   The first wheat shipment for overseas leaves Winnipeg by flatboat up the Red River.

1883   E.A. Partridge huddles in a little shack on his homestead in the District of Assiniboia, North-West Territories, at Christmas time.

1885   Riel rebellion erupts, Partridge takes up arms to help put it down.

Late 1800s W.R. Motherwell and other settlers focus on excessive dockage and perceived short weight, demand the right to deliver grain over the platform right into the rail cars.

1900   Manitoba Grain Act passed as a grain industry Magna Carta.

1901-1902 Led by W.R. Motherwell, growers form the Territorial Grain Growers' Assoc., triggering "perhaps the greatest farm organization movement the world had ever seen and setting the prairies on a course of political action which would shape the west and all of Canada."

About 1900 Some US Protestant pastors believe they have made a blinding discovery of a new universal truth - that the most severe of the world's ills were caused by the 'capitalist system.' Their "social gospel" message   is rejected in the U.S. but when they come to Canada, they are joined by Canadian pastors and set out on a holy crusade to abolish capitalism.

1903   Manitoba Grain Growers' Association formed.

1905   E.A. Partridge makes historic trip to the Winnipeg Grain and Produce Exchange, dubs it "The House with the Closed Shutters."

1906   Led by E.A. Partridge, growers form the Grain Growers' Grain Co. Ltd., the first farmer-owned and managed grain handling co-operative in western Canada. It operates as a commission firm, pays shareholders patronage dividends. Later that year, its officials - Partridge, Kennedy and Spencer - pledge personal assets to keep bank from closing out its account.

1907   T.A. Crerar named President, General Manager at the co-op's first annual meeting

1913   Alberta Farmers' Co-operative Elevator Company Limited incorporated.

1913   Grain Growers' Grain Co. leases a flour mill in Rapid City, Man., selling apples and coal to farmers, and opens a livestock branch.

1917   United Grain Growers Ltd. formed with the union of the Grain Growers' Grain Co. and the Alberta Farmers' Co-operative Elevator Co. Ltd. It operates 332 country elevators, 184 coal sheds and over 200 warehouses.

1917   Prime Minister Robert Borden, seeking strong western voices in his National Wartime Government, names UGG President Tom Crerar Minister of Agriculture. Crerar stays on as UGG president as well.

1919   Protestant pastors with their Social Gospel mission to "overthrow the capitalist system," and labour, aiming to "organize labour industrially into One Big Union to convert it to the doctrines of class war and Marxian socialism," come together at the Winnipeg Strike, in a political witch's brew.

1919   Crerar resigns from cabinet. One hundred delegates attend a Winnipeg conference called by the Canadian Council of Agriculture to examine a "New National Policy" of free trade, nationalization of the railways and "direct democracy".

1920   Eleven independent agrarian MPs form the National Progressive Party with Tom Crerar its leader (Crerar remains as UGG president.)

1920   Grain prices crash and some Progressive Party members want to take the party sharply left. Crerar, no radical, resigns the Party leadership.

1923   American lawyer Aaron Sapiro hits Canada like a meteor flaring through the sky, aiming to revoke the market system and transform society. His stupendous dream is of a Canadian and then a world wheat pool where farmers could set prices. Sceptical U.S. growers and the public had rejected his vision, scoffed at the idea of politicians and bureaucrats selling grain. But the Social Gospel has taken root in Canada and Sapiro proclaims the country centre stage in world wheat, seduces many prairie   farm leaders to his dream. The CCF political party is born, and Pastor J.S. Woodsworth would lead the way in carrying the message to Parliament.

1923   UGG contributes $5,000 to aid Saskatchewan growers' campaign to establish a Wheat Pool.

1923   New Alberta Wheat Pool bypasses Winnipeg Grain Ex-

change, sells 80 percent of its wheat directly to export customers.

1924 Saskatchewan Wheat Pool formed and the three Pools set
up a Central Sales Agency (CSA) to bypass the Winnipeg Exchange, sell direct to buyers.

1925 UGG buys controlling interest in Burrard Elevator Company which leased a terminal from the Harbours Board.

1928 Sapiro's dream of giant world wheat pool collapses.

1929 Black Tuesday hits on Oct. 29th with devastating fury.
Wheat prices plunge. The Wheat Pools are unable to
recover even initial payments on their 1930-31 pool,
and the federal and prairie provincial governments step
in to bale out their Central Sales Agency in 1930.

1931 Manitoba Premier John Bracken appoints lawyer and
University of Manitoba lecturer Esten K. Williams a
Royal Commission to investigate charges against the
Manitoba Pool. Williams finds that the Pool has built a
system of elevators that are larger and more elaborately equipped and more costly than was intended by
the elevator policy, and that resulting losses were being
covered by overdocking, short weight and undergrading.

1931 Seeking a villain to blame for their CSA bankruptcy,
the Pools accuse the line elevator companies of Exchange
"skulduggery." Sir Josiah Stamp, lured from Britain by
Prime Minister Bennett to look into the charges, finds
no evidence of unfair Exchange practises.

1943 Monopoly Canadian Wheat Board begins selling prairie wheat.

Late 1950s In travelling Canada's grain areas, UGG director
A.M. (Mac) Runciman finds lack of shipping capacity is
cause of grain pile-up on farms and in elevators. Why
this lack? Farmers have let grain marketing become an
ideological/political struggle, not a hard-nosed selling
business.

1961 Mac Runciman elected UGG President. Canadian Wheat
Board under Hon. Alvin Hamilton, makes the biggest
wheat sale in history, selling to the Chinese.

1963 Record-breaking wheat sale made to the Soviet Union.

1966 Soviet buyers return for a record-shattering $800 mil-
lion of wheat, the largest grain sale in history.

1967 Euphoric news for growers. The world media focuses on
the "population explosion" and the "War on Hunger."

1967 World demand for edible vegetable oils soars. U.S.
soybean growers had pushed exports to over $1 billion
in 1966. A few prairie leaders form a Rapeseed group
fashioned after the US Soybean Association, to build
this oil seed crop which can be sold outside the Wheat
Board's regulations. Mac Runciman is named president

and James McAnsh executive director. They set out to get growers to "mind their own business." They fight off efforts to bring rapeseed under Wheat Board control, write a glittering success story, see it rival wheat as a money-earner for farmers.

1969   Farmers' bins again bulge with record inventories. US grain is moving and puzzled Canadian growers ask, Why isn't ours moving? The days of barter have returned for farmers. Mac Runciman begins telling the story at meetings "Trapped! Like the Wild Hogs of Horseshoe Bend."

1969   Trudeau government establishes Canada Grains' Council, with Mac Runciman as chairman, to bring industry groups together to plan overall strategy. C o u n c i l raises funding for four industry teams of five people each to examine world feed grain markets. They visit 26 countries, find the markets almost beyond comprehension, are horrified to find Canada lacks an effective marketing presence.

1970   With wheat piled up on farms and their cash flow virtually stopped, a few growers led by Wally Nelson of Avonlea, Sask., begin to meet and seek solutions. They are shocked at their findings, set up the Palliser Wheat Growers Assoc. in 1971 to try to free up their politics-mired and crisis-ridden industry. They find policies based on pork- barrel politics rather than boldness and economic logic are pitting one farm group or region against another. Politics, not the market place, rules.

1970's New U.S. Secretary of Agriculture Earl Butz begins scrapping his country's archaic farm policies, gives farmers incentives to plant every acre and sets U.S. agriculture on a spectacular run. Its exports soar 60 percent to a record $12.9 billion in fiscal 1973.

1970's Debilitating impact of the Crow rates, which subsidize the shipment of raw grain but not processed grain products become apparent. It hinders pro-cessing and manufacturing in the prairies, handicaps livestock and poultry producers there.

1971   Huge Soviet grain purchases in Canada should have unleashed euphoria   among farmers, but *Vancouver Sun* headlines scream "Wall-to-Wall Ships," label the ship pile-up "February Fever," say it happens every year that exports reach any volume. The port is a grain bottleneck.

1973   On a Palliser Wheat Growers' mission to Asia, growers find "Buyers have never seen our salesmen, wonder why we are so quiet, and what products we   had? Could they buy from us?" The mission also discovers that farmers aren't growing some grains buyers want.

1973   A Canada Grains Council study describes handling/

transportation system as an industry in shackles, a massive bureaucracy unable to respond to beckoning markets.

1989   Federal Agriculture Minister Charles Mayer yanks oats from Wheat Board control and growers respond, planting more. Exports soar over 2000 percent. But this trial ended in 40 days after a government change, a court challenge and a legal judgement.

1993   In a 40-day open-market trial, AgMinister Mayer takes barley destined for US from Board control. Exports surge to over half a million tonnes - yet Board feed barley sales had never surpassed 240,821 tonnes in a year.

1995-96 In a historic restructuring, UGG sells shares on the equity market to become a public company, raise money to build modern elevators.

1995   Saskatchewan Wheat Pool stuns the industry, joining with Cargill Ltd. to build a huge export terminal in Vancouver.

1996   Ottawa finally ends the Crow Rate.

1997   Wheat Board Minister Ralph Goodale rejects dual marketing for barley growers, allows vote on whether to remove all barley sales from the Board. An amazing 37 percent vote yes. They are prepared to see barley withdrawn totally from the board.

1997   Manitoba Grower Andy McMechan emerges as a martyr/hero after being jailed for five months for selling his grain to waiting North Dakota buyers rather than turning it over to the Wheat Board.

1997   UGG fights off hostile takeover bid from Manitoba and Alberta Wheat Pools, forms alliance with agribusiness giant Archer Daniels Midland Co.

ABOUT THE AUTHOR

Don Baron was born and raised in the Ottawa Valley, graduated from Ontario Agricultural College in 1949, went into farm journalism and in 1952 joined the editorial staff of the western magazine *Country Guide*. When it became a national publication in 1955, he was named its first eastern field editor. He covered Central and Eastern Canada's farm communities and meetings for seven years before being named Country Guide editor in 1963, working out of Winnipeg.

In 1975 he was named Head, Agriculture and Resources Broadcasting, for CBC TV, working out of Toronto. His producers filmed across Canada and beyond, making some of the most controversial shows ever to come from this division. These shows garnered some of the largest viewing audiences every achieved by this CBC division and brought food and resources programming to the very centre of the network's schedule .

In 1979 Don became Executive Director of the groundbreaking farmers' commodity group, Palliser Wheat Growers Association. He served from 1983 to 1990 in the Saskatchewan government, as speech writer to Premier Grant Devine and as Chief of Staff for Hon. Joan Duncan.

He was elected President of the Agricultural Institute of Canada in 1974 and President, Canadian Farm Writers' Federation. He was a Commission of Enquiry into Vegetable Marketing in Manitoba and a member of Manitoba's Commission on Targets for Economic Development. His work has appeared in Maclean's, Toronto Star and other publications.

Don has written two earlier books. BATTLEGROUND - The Socialist Assault on Grant Devine's Canadian Dream, (coauthored with Paul Jackson) tells the story of the Devine Saskatchewan government from 1982 to 1991. BEYOND ROGUES' HARBOUR - the Epic Story of a Canadian Anglo-Saxon Family, tells of a pioneer family tracing its roots from Ireland, Scotland and England. These people (some of Don's ancestors are among them) homesteaded first in the Ottawa Valley, then in western Ontario, and then in the West when this story has its beginning.

If you wish to inquire about bulk book purchase orders or if you are interested in contacting Don for interviews or speaking engagements, he can be reached at Don Baron, 14 Wood Cr., Regina, Sask. S4S 6J7, Phone: 306-586-4578

BIBLIOGRAPHY

Anderson, Charles W., *GRAIN, The Entrepreneurs*, Watson and Dwayer Publishing Ltd., Winnipeg, 1991.

Berton, Pierre, *The Promised Land, Settling the West*, McClelland and Stewart, 1984.

Boyd, Hugh, *New Breaking*, J.M. Dent and Sons (Canada) Ltd. 1938

Candlish, Mills, Martinelli, Earl. *State of the Industry, A Special Committee Report*, Canada Grains Council, 1973.

Country Guide, All issues over many decades.

Colquette, R.D., *I Was There*, Personal Memoirs.

Colquette, R.D., *The First Fifty Years*, The Public Press Ltd. 1957

Davidson, Clive B. Wheat, *Politicians and the Great Depression: Two Memoirs*, Edited by Menzies, Peterson and Nickel, The Natural Resource Institute, U. of Man.

Davisson, Walter P., *Pooling Wheat in Canada*. The Graphic Publishers Ltd., 1927.

Earl, Paul D. *Rhetoric, Reality and Righteousness, The Ideological Debate between the Farm Organizations and the Grain Trade, 1917-1935*. PhD. Thesis, University of Manitoba, 1992

Fairbairn, Garry. *From Prairie Roots*, Western Producer Prairie Books, 1984.

Grain Growers Guide (which became Country Guide.) Selected issues.

Jackson, James A. *The Centennial History of Manitoba*, McClelland and Stewart, 1970.

Knuttila, Murray, *That Man Partridge*, Canadian Plains Research Centre, University of Regina, 1994.

Kyba, Patrick, Alvin: *A Biography of the Honourable Alvin Hamilton*, Canadian Plains Research Centre, University of Regina, 1989.

Levine, Allan G., *The Winnipeg Grain Exchange on Trial: The Case of the Grain Growers' Grain Company Reconsidered*, Canadian Plains Research Centre, University of Regina.

MacEwan, Grant, *Harvest of Bread*, Prairie Books, 1969

McAnsh, James, *The First Six Years, 1967-1973*, Rapeseed Assoc. of Canada, 1973.

Morriss, William, *The Canadian Wheat Board*.

Morton, W.L., *Manitoba, A History*. University of Toronto Press, 1957

Moorhouse, Hopkins, *Deep Furrows*, George J. McLeod Ltd. 1918

Newspaper clippings, *Winnipeg Free Press, Regina Leader Post, Saskatoon StarPhoenix, Calgary Herald* and others.

Nichols, James Hastings, Professor of Church History, University of Chicago, *History of Christianity, 1650-1950*. The Ronald Press Company, New York, 1956

Palliser Wheat Growers' Newsletter. All issues over several years, Palliser Wheat Growers Association.

Rapeseed Association of Canada, *Proceedings of the International Conference on the Science, Technology and Marketing of Rapeseed and Rapeseed Products, 1970*.

Rea, J.E., *The Wheat Board and the Western Farmer*, The Beaver, Feb.-Mar.'97

Swartz, C.O. *The Death of The Canadian Grain Salesman*, Report on Farming, 1976

The Canadian Encyclopedia, Hurtig Publishers, Edmonton

United Grain Growers Ltd. Annual Reports, All of them

United Grain Growers Archives, University of Manitoba Libraries, Department of Archives and Special Collections

Western Producer, Selected material, Western Producer, Saskatoon

Wilson, Barry. *Beyond the Harvest*, Western Producer Prairie Books, 1981

Wilson, Charles F. *A Century of Canadian Grain: Government Policy to 1951*. Western Producer Prairie Books, 1978

Wood, Louis Aubrey, *A History of Farmers' Movements in Canada*, University of Toronto Press, 1975, Reprint of 1924 edition, Ryerson Press, Toronto.

Partridge, E.A. *A War on Poverty - the one war that can end war*.

Simpson, Francis, Shoal Lake, Manitoba. Speeches. 1960 and on.

Penner, Norman. Winnipeg 1919, *The strikers' own history of the Winnipeg General Strike*, James Lewis and Samuel, Toronto, 1973.